INDUSTRIAL ECONOMIC REGULATION

If the 1980s were the decade of privatization and deregulation, it looks as though the 1990s will be the decade when regulation returns to centre stage. Privatization itself led to the creation of new regulatory bodies, and concerns about mergers, the role of transnational corporations and developments in Europe have all prompted calls for more active government.

In this volume leading researchers of industrial economic issues focus on the processes by which governments in market economies deliberately take action to influence economic activity in firms and industries. The book provides teachers, students and researchers with a coherent framework for analysing regulation and then explores key, current issues, including the relationship between information and regulation, the regulation of monopolies and the role of regulation within the European Community. Regulation has conventionally been defended as a remedy for market failure. Whilst arguing that this remains an important function, the book also argues that regulation can be a positive instrument for promoting industrial development.

Roger Sugden is Director of the Research Centre for Industrial Strategy and senior lecturer in industrial economics at the Birmingham Business School, the University of Birmingham. He has published widely in the area of industrial economics, particularly on transnational corporations. His previous publications include *Transnational Monopoly Capitalism* (with Keith Cowling, 1987), *A New Economic Policy for Britain* (edited with Keith Cowling, 1990) and *The Nature of the Transnational Firm* (edited with Christos Pitelis, 1991).

INDUSTRIAL ECONOMIC REGULATION

A framework and exploration

Edited by Roger Sugden

London and New York

First published 1993
by Routledge
11 New Fetter Lane, London EC4P 4EE

Simultaneously published in the USA and Canada
by Routledge
29 West 35th Street, New York, NY 10001

© 1993 Roger Sugden

Typeset in Scantext September by
Leaper & Gard Ltd, Bristol
Printed in Great Britain by
Mackays of Chatham PLC, Chatham, Kent

British Library Cataloguing in Publication Data

A catalogue record for this book is available from the
British Library.

ISBN 0–415–06773–1 cloth
ISBN 0–415–06774–X pbk

Library of Congress Cataloging-in-Publication Data
Industrial economic regulation : a framework and exploration/
Roger Sugden, editor.
p.   cm.
Includes bibliographical references and index.
ISBN 0–415–06773–1. – ISBN 0–415–06774–X
1. Industry and state—Great Britain. 2. Industry and state—
European Economic Community countries. I. Sugden, Roger.
HD3616.G72I485   1993
338.94—dc20   92-26233
                                                CIP

CONTENTS

v

FIGURES AND TABLES

FIGURES

TABLES

CONTRIBUTORS

Dr Martin Chick is a lecturer in Economics and Social History at the University of Edinburgh. He is editor of *Government Industries and Markets: Aspects of Government–Industry Relations in the UK, Japan, West Germany and the USA since 1945* (1990) and has written widely on nationalization and privatization. He is currently writing a book on the economic planning of the Attlee governments, 1945–51.

Keith Cowling is Professor of Economics at the University of Warwick. He is author of *Mergers and Economic Behaviour* (with others) (1980), *Monopoly Capitalism* (1982), *Transnational Monopoly Capitalism* (with Roger Sugden) (1987), *Industrial Policy after 1992: An Anglo-German Perspective* (ed. with Horst Tomann) (1990), *A New Economic Policy for Britain: Essays on the Development of Industry* (ed. with Roger Sugden) (1990) and *Current Issues in Industrial Economic Strategy* (ed. with Roger Sugden) (1992).

Dr Chris Doyle is Senior Research Officer in the Department of Applied Economics at the University of Cambridge. His research is on microeconomic issues, particularly in the field of industrial organization, privatization and telecommunications. He has published several papers on these topics and is at present coordinating two projects, one examining international telecommunications and the other focusing on telecommunications in Czechoslovakia.

C.E.H. Farrands is Principal Lecturer in International Relations, Nottingham Polytechnic. He has written numerous articles on international relations, technology policy and foreign economic policy in Europe. His most recent book is an Economist Intelligence Unit Special Report on *New Materials in European Manufacturing*. He has also contributed to a series of studies of European foreign and foreign economic policy.

Ioanna Glykou-Pitelis is Assistant Professor at the Technological Education Institute, Kavala, Greece. She has written 'On the Possibility of State Neutrality' (with C. Pitelis) in *Review of Political Economy* (1991) and *Managerial Economics* (1990).

George Harte is a lecturer in the Department of Accounting and Business Method at the University of Edinburgh. He is an Honorary Research Fellow of the Research Centre for Industrial Strategy, University of Birmingham, and an Academic Fellow of the Institute of Chartered Accountants in England and Wales. He has published papers on social auditing, ethical investment, human resource accounting and green reporting.

Dr C.N. Pitelis is the Barclays Bank Lecturer in Industrial Organization and Corporate Strategy at the Judge Institute of Management Studies, the University of Cambridge, and Fellow in Economics, Queen's College. Dr Pitelis has published *Corporate Capital: Control Ownership, Saving and Crisis* (1987), *The Nature of the Transnational Firm* (ed. with R. Sugden) (1991) and *Market and Non-Market Hierarchies* (1991).

Dr Ajit Singh is Fellow and Director of Studies in Economics at Queen's College, University of Cambridge. Since his first book, *Takeovers* (1971), Dr Singh has written extensively in this area. His present research is concerned with a comparative analysis of corporate financial structures in semi-industrial and industrial economies and this includes an analysis of the role of takeovers in the newly emerging markets.

Dr Roger Sugden is Director of the Research Centre for Industrial Strategy and Senior Lecturer in Industrial Economics at the University of Birmingham. He is the co-author of *Transnational Monopoly Capitalism* (1987) and co-editor of three books, *A New Economic Policy for Britain* (1990), *The Nature of the Transnational Firm* (1991) and with Keith Cowling *Current Issues in Industrial Economic Strategy* (1992).

Dr Jim Tomlinson is Reader in Economic History at Brunel University. His main research interests are in the history of economic policy in twentieth century Britain. He has just completed a book on *State Intervention and Industrial Efficiency: The Experience of 1939–51* (with N. Tiratsoo), and will publish a textbook on the history of industrial policy since 1900 in 1993.

Peter Totterdill is Coordinator of the Nottinghamshire Work and Technology Programme and other policy initiatives relating to the textile and clothing sector. Dr Totterdill also has his own economic development consulting practice. He is author of several articles and papers on local economic development and labour market policy, and is currently editing a book on industrial policy and the clothing industry (with L. Crewe and D. Gillingwater).

Michael Waterson is Professor of Economics at the University of Warwick. He has published a substantial number of papers in academic journals, books and elsewhere. His work has ranged widely over the field of industrial economics. His most recent book is entitled *Regulation of the firm and natural monopoly* (1988).

INTRODUCTION
On industrial economic regulation

Roger Sugden[1]

This volume focuses on industrial economic regulation; its concern is processes by which governments in market economies deliberately take action to influence economic activity in firms and industries, for example through reforming company law, promoting unified markets, enacting mergers legislation, and a variety of other measures. It includes consideration of some issues that have attracted considerable attention in the 1980s and early 1990s but it also attempts to broaden analysis and debate in ways that are likely to be increasingly relevant to current and future concerns.

The 1980s were a time when an active role for government was viewed with deep suspicion and indeed hostility in many countries, for instance in the US under Reagan, Britain under Thatcher and in the transition economies of Eastern Europe. Regulation remained an important issue yet often in a relatively narrow sense, as will be illustrated subsequently in this volume. Nobody seriously denied that governments had some role to play in influencing economic activity in firms and industries but regulation was seen in many ways as undesirable. Hostility towards government action was partly based on ideology, as Ajit Singh comments in the context of US and British mergers policy in Chapter 7, and on observed government failures, for instance in the centrally planned Soviet bloc. Moreover this negative view was perhaps supported by the often negative language of regulation, seen as 'intervention', 'interference', 'restricting' and 'constraining'. This point can be illustrated in many ways. Consider for instance the typical view that 'regulation in a general sense may be taken to mean government intervention in a market-based activity' (Waterson 1988).[2]

The negative language can be harmless when there is a consensus that governments can play a useful role in a market economy but it can become a deceptive and harmful burden on other occasions, such as during the 1980s. In periods when there is ideological hostility to governments and overwhelming faith in 'free markets', to talk of regulation as government intervening in markets can easily lead to a prejudging of its usefulness. Such a prejudgement would be obviously superficial, based on language and not substance. Nevertheless it could be significant.

In some ways antipathy towards government playing an active role has continued into the early 1990s but this attitude appears to be changing. For instance Britain has witnessed growing calls for more active government from a wide cross-section of interests. Furthermore the pace of change will probably increase rapidly in the very near future, not least as the emerging East European countries react to the problems of allegedly pure market systems, see for example Lloyd's (1992) comments on Russia.[3] Hence industrial economic regulation in a broad sense is an important issue, for both now and the future; it matters to economists, policy-makers and people involved with firms and industries, despite and in part because of recent history.

In focusing on industrial economic regulation there are two specific aims in this volume. First, to provide researchers, teachers and students with a coherent framework for organising their thinking. Second, to explore some interesting issues within this framework.

The framework is essentially provided by the structure of the volume, which divides analysis into five parts that logically and sequentially focus on the key areas for consideration.

Part I concentrates on governments' power to regulate; do governments have the basic ability to influence industrial activity? The extent of governments' power is often ignored in economists' policy discussions yet it is clearly a vital consideration, for instance because it can affect the design of regulatory processes, for example if different forms of regulatory bodies vary in their susceptibility to capture.

Part II looks at the rationale for regulation; assuming governments have the power to regulate, what is the economic basis for their action? In practice, whether or not there is regulation and what form it takes encompasses more than economic issues, not least political factors. For instance, although governments often perform policy U-turns they can become locked into ideological approaches which constrain their politically feasible options; such a constraint was arguably part of the Thatcher legacy to British Conservatives. Nevertheless, a sound understanding of the economic rationale is central, and perhaps the core issue, in analysing regulation.

Given that governments are to take action deliberately to influence economic activity, it is important to ask whether or not regulators – and others in the regulatory system – have information of sufficient quality to perform their tasks. The information problem is the focus of Part III. It arises in three respects: in identifying areas where regulation may be needed; as an aspect of regulation *per se*; and in considering whether regulation has addressed targeted areas and only those areas.

Part IV concentrates on instruments of regulation: given that governments are to influence economic activity and bearing in mind the need for good quality information, what form should regulation take? In many ways this question impinges on all of the other Parts. However, it warrants a particular focus if only because to some extent it brings other issues together and in one sense is a culmination. From this viewpoint it would not have been wrong to finish the volume with a discussion of instruments.

As it is, Part V concludes the volume by looking at government collaboration; given that governments attempt to influence industrial activity, what about situations where they can co-operate? This is also a logical end-point because in a number of ways the study of governments acting together sensibly comes after examination of governments acting in isolation.

This division into parts is designed to enable analysis to build upon itself, to cover all relevant areas and yet concentrate attention on areas which can easily be neglected, for example information and government collaboration. The division needs to be treated cautiously because the parts are obviously related and indeed overlap. For example the choice of regulatory instrument depends upon one's objectives, a function of economic rationale. The need for caution is a characteristic of all analytical frameworks of this kind, which is only to say that they should not be pushed too far. Nevertheless our divisions make sense. For example economic rationale refers to the general basis for regulation and instruments to specific methods of regulation. To illustrate, Part II includes the analysis of potential efficiency problems resulting from monopoly power whereas Part IV includes the examination of merger regulation as an instrument to curb monopoly power. This reflects a systematic ordering and hence treatment of issues: potential efficiency problems lead to a consideration of monopoly power which hence leads to a consideration of mergers.

Thus the distinction between parts makes sense but is not without a blurring at the margins. Such blurring should not cause discomfort. Providing the framework ensures a focus on the rationale for, and hence the instruments of, regulation, for example, it will have served its purpose. Whether or not a particular study fits neatly into the analysis of either the rationale or the instruments is irrelevant. Indeed even within the confines of this volume some of the material in chapters from one part should strictly be in chapters in another part; as a matter of editorial policy it seemed inappropriate to be too strict on this point, if only to indicate how the wider literature on regulation can be placed within the framework even though individual studies cross the various divisions. Insofar as researchers, teachers and students use the framework for analysing the regulation of firms and industries, the important point is to position individual studies from the wider literature in the part where they are most comfortable but to read these studies with all parts in mind.

The second and more important specific aim of this volume is to explore some interesting issues in industrial economic regulation. Here the basic ideas are: to develop understanding about issues requiring detailed attention; and to encourage research on these issues in the context of an appreciation of current knowledge, in other words to give researchers an anchor point and stimulus for their future work. The intention is to provide stimulating foundations by discussing a range of issues from a range of angles. In each part of the volume the idea is neither to identify and discuss all issues nor to cover all angles. Thus, for instance, no part is attempting to provide teachers and students with all of the appropriate reading on any one area.

Our exploration of particular issues begins with a contribution by Jim Tomlinson. He explains and assesses a body of literature which raises queries about public agencies' ability to pursue public objectives. Looking at public choice theory and the 'new economics' of regulation, Tomlinson criticizes a tendency to see government action as either all based on the pursuit of private interests or all based on altruism. It is suggested that governments have some ability to influence industrial activity and accordingly, in a limited sense, the discussion of regulation in subsequent parts is justified as worthwhile. (The chapter abstracts concluding this Introduction give more depth on the contents of each chapter.)

Tomlinson's chapter is followed by two contributions on economic rationale. Michael Waterson authoritatively brings together two subjects that separately and jointly have long occupied economists: allocative inefficiency as the foundation for government action, and problems associated with monopoly power. His introductory examination takes the reader through various issues, both theoretical and empirical. Building in part from Chapter 1's concern with capture, Waterson advocates a selective approach to regulation. Chapter 3 turns attention to government strategies for fostering industrial development. Compared to allocative inefficiency and monopoly power, for example, this issue has been given relatively little attention by industrial economists from an Anglo-American tradition. Nevertheless it has been gaining greater prominence in the last few years, a trend which is likely to continue. Challenging the desirability of 'free market economies', Keith Cowling and Roger Sugden propose that the scope for regulatory activity be extended beyond its typical confines in many countries.

In so doing they assess Britain's recent policy of privatization, one of the issues also discussed by Martin Chick in Chapter 4. This is the first of two contributions on information. It takes an historical perspective – focusing in particular on the nationalization of utility and basic sector industries by the 1945–51 Attlee Government in Britain – and thus provides an important contrast to the analysis conducted elsewhere in the volume. In part this is designed to illustrate the general need to explore issues from different angles. Moreover a benefit of this historical perspective is that it positions specific issues in a wider context; Chick illustrates the design of regulatory systems as a process in which the information problem plays one role amongst several.

The fifth chapter, by George Harte, also encourages problems being addressed using different types of analysis. This refers to a general need, covering Information and other parts of our framework. Unlike other contributions, this chapter is written by an accountant. Thus we are attempting to encourage a genuinely interdisciplinary approach.[4] Furthermore it is unique in this volume in the way that it concentrates on a particular industry. This is designed to reflect and promote the idea that for industrial economic regulation in general, case studies can provide significant analytical developments: firstly, it is arguably true that the regulation of specific firms and industries can only be understood by actually considering those firms and industries; secondly, analysing actual cases may lead to more general points being inferred and/or appreciated. Harte explores the role of accounting information in economic regulation and focuses in particular on the provision of bus services in Scotland. He suggests, for instance, that although we might expect regulation to imply the need for and use of good quality accounting information, it appears that little such information is currently used in regulating that industry.

The next two contributions move the centre of attention to regulatory instruments and perhaps to more comfortable ground for many economists. Earlier analysis in this volume examines problems of monopoly power as a rationale for regulation. From a largely technical angle, Chapter 6 builds on this issue. It outlines and examines ways in which a natural monopoly or dominant firm can be regulated. Chris Doyle's theoretical discussion characterizes, explains and comments upon various models in the context of brief notes relating to particular cases. He concentrates on issues that have been very prominent for many countries in the 1980s and 1990s. A concern with monopoly is also maintained in Chapter 7, where another subject which has previously attracted a great deal of attention is given authoritative consideration; Ajit Singh looks at ways of regulating mergers. He explicitly raises queries relevant to the direction of future research and policy, particularly in Britain, the US and the European Community. The contribution calls for a new, radical approach to merger regulation that goes beyond traditional concerns.

Future policy in the European Community is given further, detailed attention in Part V, which focuses on government collaboration. The considerable recent and ongoing changes in European economies suggest an industrial policy environment where the direction of future initiatives is in many ways open. Debate over possible options is therefore very important and hence the two studies in this part are especially timely. In Chapter 8 Chris Farrands and Peter Totterdill explore the extent to which regulations should be formulated at the local, national and European Community levels. Their concern is the fostering of industrial development and hence the chapter pursues another theme seen earlier in the volume. An approach to take Europe into the next century is prescribed. One of the suggestions is for a regulatory framework which is not seen as direct intervention, but as a sophisticated means of combining public and private interests while keeping a competitive environment. Finally, Chapter 9 maintains the topical European concern by concentrating on the activities of and policies towards transnational corporations, and on the possibility of North–South convergence, all in a Community context. Ioanna Glykou-Pitelis and Christos Pitelis conclude the volume by proposing a theoretical basis for discussing the relationship between transnationals, the European Community and Community policies, and by putting forward a strategy for convergence. They advocate policies deliberately designed to yield Pareto improvements favouring the worse off.

ON INDUSTRIAL ECONOMIC REGULATION

NOTES

1 The author would like to thank David Bailey and Marc Cowling for comments and suggestions.
2 The view is typical insofar as it is in line with a vast literature. Compare the language used in the opening sentence of this Chapter. More generally, the intention is not to become bogged down in a definition of regulation. The opening sentence presents a broad view whereas some might prefer a narrower approach; this volume's framework and exploration can comfortably accommodate different views.
3 He suggests that ' "Don't take the market too seriously: none of us in the west do" is the (rather confusing) message now being insinuated into the policy debate' in Russia.
4 Some might argue that economic history is not economics and hence that Chapter 4 also indicates the need for an interdisciplinary approach!

REFERENCES

Lloyd, John (1992) 'So far so good – but so fragile', *Financial Times*, 6 April.
Waterson, Michael (1988) *Regulation of the Firm and Natural Monopoly*, Oxford: Blackwell.

CHAPTER ABSTRACTS

Introduction: on industrial economic regulation
Roger Sugden

This is a comparatively brief introduction to the volume. It sees industrial economic regulation as concerned with processes by which governments in market economies deliberately take action to influence economic activity in firms and industries. This is argued to be an important topic for both now and the future.

Two aims of the volume are identified. First, to provide researchers, teachers and students with a coherent framework for organizing their thinking. In explaining and commenting upon the proposed framework, limitations are mentioned and its purpose clarified. Second and more important, to explore some interesting issues within the framework, more specifically to develop understanding about issues requiring detailed attention and to encourage research on these issues in the context of an appreciation of current knowledge. In considering these points, the Introduction also briefly discusses subsequent contributions to the volume.

1 Is successful regulation possible? Some theoretical issues
Jim Tomlinson

Advocates of regulation tend to believe implicitly that the state has the capacity to regulate. However Jim Tomlinson points out that over the last thirty or so years a substantial literature has questioned whether or not public agencies can pursue public objectives. His chapter provides a critical explanation and assessment of this challenging literature.

Most of Chapter 1 concentrates on public choice theory, which actually covers far more than regulatory issues, and the so-called 'new economics' of regulation, seen to some extent as a subset of public choice theory. Both areas are introduced, some of their common elements are discussed and then each one is explored in further detail. Both are alleged to deploy doubtful epistemological arguments to claim a scientific method and to evade criticism of their fundamental assumptions, particularly the assumption that utility-maximising individuals are the starting point for analysing all forms of political and economic activity. Moreover this rational maximization is itself queried. Tomlinson highlights a tendency to see things in black and white, to argue that government action is either all based on self-seeking or all based on altruism; in contrast he sees shades of grey.

Turning to the more detailed examination of each area, the chapter first of all outlines the 'new economics' of regulation research programmes. It then notes, for example, that the new economics does not doubt the efficiency of public agencies, unlike the view commonly seen in British political debate. In fact public agencies are seen as efficient mechanisms for attaining the objectives of the private interests they serve. The chapter goes on to question the focus on the outcomes of regulatory activity rather than on the means to achieve these outcomes. Thus Tomlinson suggests that the new economics is pushing at an open door in contending that public agencies are unable to achieve some utopian sense of the public good; the real issue is whether notions of the public good are partial determinants of the outcome of regulation. The chapter also suggests that even the work of Posner and Stigler – two leading proponents of the extreme capture thesis – effectively implies that some regulation can avoid private domination. As for the more detailed examination of public choice theory, this includes a consideration of bureaucracy, more specifically of how we should understand the behaviour of bureaucrats involved in regulation.

2 Allocative inefficiency and monopoly as a basis for regulation
Michael Waterson

Many economists see problems of allocative inefficiency as the foundation for government action. Thus a consideration of this area is an obvious starting point for analysing the economic rationale for regulation. Moreover, amongst industrial economists attention has traditionally focused on problems associated with monopoly power. Accordingly it is important to study the issue of monopoly power leading to allocative inefficiency as a basis for regulation. Michael Waterson's chapter is an introductory examination of this issue.

He begins with a non-technical discussion of what is meant by allocative inefficiency; identifying issues which can obstruct the seemingly simple strategy of pursuing a competitive economy, second-best arguments are explored and thus the appropriateness of piecemeal approaches is doubted. The chapter then concentrates on monopoly. Using diagrams, it looks first at the case of constant returns to scale and then at the more complicated increasing returns. This leads into discussions of off-setting welfare gains and losses, natural monopoly, entry and contestability. Having questioned the practical relevance of contestability, the section concludes that monopoly welfare loss is likely to be reduced, but not eliminated, by potential and actual competition.

Waterson's final substantive section looks at factors influencing the desired extent of regulation. Bearing in mind empirical estimates, some suggesting that deadweight loss may be a very small proportion of national income, and building from Chapter 1's concern with regulatory capture, he uses examples to contemplate whether or not regulation is worthwhile. Because regulation is not costless, a selective approach is advocated. Moreover it is suggested, for instance, that natural monopoly provides a rationale for regulation but not a sufficient condition.

3 A strategy for industrial development as a basis for regulation
Keith Cowling and Roger Sugden

Chapter 3 analyses the rationale for regulation within a framework of government strategies for fostering industrial development, an area which has received increasing attention in industrial economics in recent years. In so doing, the chapter advocates that the scope for regulatory activity be extended beyond its typical confines in many countries.

Keith Cowling and Roger Sugden identify and examine concentrated decision-making power within firms as a fundamental source of difficulties in 'free market economies'. Focusing on a firm's strategic decisions, it is argued that these are typically made by, and in the interests of, a subset of those involved with a firm. This leads into a discussion of, for instance, price collusion, deindustrialization, the international division of labour and short-termism.

Tackling the difficulties head-on, it is argued that a firm can only serve the interests of a community as a whole if a firm's strategic decisions are made by all of the community's people. This need for democratic control is then explored. It is emphasized that community control neither requires central planning nor entails the regulation of a 'free market economy', but that it does entail planning and it does require a regulated market system that can be fairly accurately described as a 'democratic market economy'.

Using this rationale for regulatory activity, Britain's recent privatization and consequent regulation of firms and industries is then assessed. From an examination of its alleged aims, recent policy is characterized as ill-conceived and inappropriate, as a lost opportunity which favoured planning by the elite and thereby missed a valuable chance to establish the sort of planning institutions which are central to economic success.

4 Nationalization and the background to recent regulatory issues
Martin Chick

Martin Chick's contribution focuses on the need for appropriate information. It does so using an historical perspective and hence it adds a contrasting dimension to the analysis seen in other chapters. One of the benefits of this historical perspective is that it presents a relatively full account of particular events, positioning specific issues in a wider context. Thus Chick illustrates the design of regulatory systems as a process in which information plays a part, though obviously only a part.

His particular concern is the nationalization of utility and basic sector industries by the 1945–51 Attlee Government in Britain, although his explanations build from a consideration of events earlier in the century and attention is also given to later issues, including the privatization programmes of recent Conservative governments.

The chapter identifies two central questions regarding the structure and organization of the industries that Attlee nationalized. First, why did the transfer of ownership take place alongside an extension of monopoly? Second, why were the industries organized on a centralized basis? It is suggested that the interest in these questions stems from recent principal–agent analyses. More specifically, the interest is because the state (principal) created industries (agents) where information was asymmetrically distributed strongly in favour of the agent, something which arguably affected the outcome and process of recent privatizations, for example. In answering the questions, Chick notes, for instance, that centralized structures were partly desired as a means to extend supply and to have relatively low uniform prices, even though it was perceived that centralization would blur some efficiency data. He argues that suppression of information on local costs and efficiency put increased weight on the capabilities and functions of managers, who were left to devise a means of operating their massive monopolies without many indications of how this might best be done. The chapter also observes, for example, that although Treasury concern led to closer monitoring of the industries, some argued in the 1960s that more and indeed broader information was needed.

5 Regulators' need for quality information and the provision of bus services in Scotland
George Harte

Chapter 5 is similar to its predecessor insofar as it focuses on information and, when compared to other chapters, illustrates that contrasting dimensions should be brought to the analysis of regulation. It is unlike other contributions to this volume in two respects. First, it is written by an accountant (in a manner accessible to non-accountants). The particular interest in this is that insofar as an understanding of the economics of regulation requires an analysis of information, it is vital to have input from accountants simply because various aspects of preparing and analysing information are the very subject of accountancy. Secondly, the chapter is different in the way that it concentrates on a particular industry, although it identifies and explores issues beyond that industry.

George Harte outlines the role of accounting information in economic regulation, referring to the reasons for and methods of regulation. He notes that this role has not been widely researched but he draws interesting parallels with two relatively well-studied areas, namely: management accounting in organisations and the portrayal of economic reality in corporate reports. He suggests, for instance, that accounting can contribute to setting the agenda for regulation and that if it adopts a narrow perspective those dependent on an industry may suffer. It is concluded that neither neoclassical economists concerned with regulation nor those criticizing the mainstream are likely to be satisfied with the input of traditional accounting reports; for instance issues such as traffic congestion, the performance of 'old' versus 'green' buses, and the design of buses to facilitate access for the disadvantaged will not be reflected in traditional accounts.

Following a brief outline of the course of bus regulation in Scotland since the 1930s, Harte makes various comments based on interviews with staff at a Traffic Commissioner's office and with management of a large bus company. Questions are raised over the quality and quantity of information that the Commissioners have had at their disposal. He also assesses the contribution of accounting information by examining bus company financial statements and annual reports. A narrowing of concerns since the 1985 partial deregulation is discussed. Harte suggests, for example, that although we might expect regulation to imply the need for and use of good quality accounting information, it appears that little accounting information is currently used in regulating Scottish bus services.

6 Regulating firms with monopoly power
Chris Doyle

Chapter 6 outlines and examines ways in which a natural monopoly or dominant firm can be regulated. Thus it focuses on issues that have been very prominent for many countries in the 1980s and 1990s, when state ownership of firms and industries has in many cases been replaced by private ownership combined with relatively arm's length regulation.

Chris Doyle begins his theoretical and largely technical analysis with a discussion of regulation by instruction from an omniscient and omnipotent regulator. This is seen as a bench mark case where public ownership and regulated private ownership are indistinguishable. Two-part tariffs and, in particular, Ramsey prices are explored. He then considers situations where a regulator (principal) sets rules and the regulated (agent) chooses a response, so-called decentralized regulatory environments. Initially assuming that the regulator has complete information, Doyle examines rate-of-return regulation and price-capping, looking in detail at RPI − X in revenue weighted and revenue yield forms. As elsewhere in the chapter, various models are characterized, explained and commented upon in the context of brief notes about particular cases, especially in Britain.

Asymmetric information is then introduced, recognizing that in practice regulated firms' managers know more about demand and cost conditions than regulators. Doyle looks firstly at direct mechanisms, where regulators design rules based upon information that they request from firms. In doing so he makes comparisons with the Ramsey pricing bench mark. This and other comparisons are pursued when attention turns to indirect mechanisms, where regulators design rules based upon publicly available observables.

By way of conclusion, the chapter briefly raises various other issues, for example asymmetric regulation, yardstick regulation and regulation of quality.

7 Regulation of mergers: a new agenda
Ajit Singh

One of the subjects that has long concerned industrial economists is regulation of mergers. Ajit Singh provides a lucid overview of important contemporary issues in this area. In so doing, he weighs both theoretical and empirical evidence, and explicitly raises questions relevant to the direction of both future research and future policy, particularly in Britain, the US and the European Community.

Chapter 7 focuses on the regulation of mergers as an instrument to tackle various welfare issues, not only to curb the abuse of monopoly power but also to address such issues as short-termism. It begins with a consideration of Oliver Williamson's trade-off model for assessing the impact of mergers. With respect to the impact on monopoly power, for instance, Singh questions whether or not mergers regulation influences industrial concentration. Nevertheless it is concluded that many industrial economists have argued for relatively strict controls.

Singh then points to important historical differences in the regulatory philosophy concerning mergers in the US and Britain, but also to major changes in both countries in the 1980s bringing about a degree of convergence. This leads into a relatively long discussion of markets for corporate control; belief in the merits of such markets are seen to have partially stimulated the convergence.

The case for a laissez-faire policy towards mergers is outlined and thus the case against the anti-takeover legislation instituted by many US states in reaction to the 1980s merger wave is mentioned. However, Singh also looks at arguments against the laissez-faire approach. He concludes that the alleged benefits of markets for corporate control are greatly over-stated: the operations of the markets not only do not enhance efficiency, but the results of the takeover process may be perverse in a number of ways. Hence he calls for a new, radical approach to merger regulation, going beyond traditional concerns and questioning, for instance, whether it is desirable that the right to dispose of whole corporations should be the sole prerogative – as is presently the case under Anglo-Saxon corporate law – of absentee shareholders.

8 A rationale for an appropriate level of regulation in the European Community
Chris Farrands and Peter Totterdill

Bearing in mind the considerable recent and ongoing changes in Europe, Chapter 8 is especially topical because it explores the extent to which regulations designed to foster industrial development should be formulated and implemented at the local, national and Community levels. Building from an examination of regulatory practice in the European Community in the 1990s, Chris Farrands and Peter Totterdill prescribe an approach to take Europe into the twenty-first century.

It is suggested that there is a powerful case for a broad regulatory climate determined at the Community level, and that responsibility at least for making overall rules about regulation procedures should be managed by European Community institutions. However, it is also suggested that the Community should not be responsible for the specific choice of regulations in all cases; rather, much of the regulatory process must be managed at lower levels.

The authors explore different approaches. Drawing on the example of Britain, they argue that traditional strands of post-war regulation have typically been centralized and technocratic, and thus insufficiently responsive or dynamic to address Europe's future needs. It is suggested that the European economy needs a regulatory framework which is not seen as direct intervention, but as a sophisticated means of combining public and private interests while keeping a competitive environment. They examine the New Industrial Districts, characterized by agglomerations of small firms with a high degree of interdependence and co-operation, and explore the benefits of a so-called strategic-discursive mode of regulation. In advocating a significant role for local regulatory activity, they emphasize for example that this does not mean local elites simply mediating in the distribution of central resources (in contrast to the current operation of England's Training and Enterprise Councils). For their approach to work, Farrands and Totterdill also point out that national governments must probably lose power and certainly authority. Power would not be lost to Brussels, but to local and regional partnerships.

9 European integration, transnational corporations and North–South convergence
Ioanna Glykou-Pitelis and Christos Pitelis

The European Community focus seen in the preceding contribution is maintained in Chapter 9, wherein Ioanna Glykou-Pitelis and Christos Pitelis examine particular aspects of government collaboration at the supranational level.

In a European context, they concentrate on the activities of and policies towards transnational corporations, and on the possibility of

North–South convergence. In doing so, the authors present an analysis founded upon a relatively detailed theoretical consideration of national and transnational firms, nation states and international organizations, and of the relationships between these actors. Having summarized and assessed mainstream and radical left perspectives, they propose a theoretical basis for discussing the relationship between transnationals, the European Community and Community policies. It is argued that international organizations are institutional devices for exploiting the international division of labour and team work; that the organizations are complementary to markets, firms (including transnationals) and nation states; and that they are arenas where different interests enact sometimes unequal conflicts and/or where policies emerge reflecting such conflicts.

The chapter examines the role and effects of transnationals in the European Community in general and the North–South divide in particular. Past Community policies are outlined and evaluated. The disadvantages of fostering large firms, the association between transnationals and deindustrialization, and the meaning of the term 'European' transnational are all considered. The 'divide' is explored and explained, focusing on such factors as comparative advantage, imperfect competition and 'strategic trade' policies.

The authors then propose a European strategy for convergence. Building on their earlier analysis, they advocate Community policies deliberately designed to yield Pareto improvements favouring the worse off, for example to increase the welfare of countries in the South without reducing the welfare of the countries in the North. To achieve this the chapter suggests, for example, measures to increase the competition faced by European transnationals from weaker Community members. It is argued that this would increase both the bargaining power of the South *vis-à-vis* existing European transnationals and the incentives the latter face to improve their competitive advantages. Moreover, it is claimed that these increased incentives are likely to benefit existing transnationals in the long run. However, the authors also indicate that whilst appropriate strategies can be identified and designed, their implementation would raise problems.

Part I
GOVERNMENT POWER

1

IS SUCCESSFUL REGULATION POSSIBLE?

Some theoretical issues[1]

Jim Tomlinson

Advocates of the regulation of private industry are predisposed to believe that public agencies can achieve their regulatory aims, that the state has the capacity to be successful. Such an attitude can no longer be treated as axiomatic. In the last thirty or so years there has arisen a substantial literature which challenges the very possibility of public agencies delivering public purposes. The very idea of the achievement of the 'public interest' as a realizable objective has been systematically derided and attacked in this literature.

As always with academic discourse, it is very difficult to judge how significant this body of writing has been in influencing public policy. However, it would seem plausible to argue that it has been an important element in engendering that 'fear of government' (e.g. Thompson 1990, chapter 2) which has so infected the politics of many of the advanced capitalist countries in recent years. Be that as it may, advocates of regulation need to respond to the challenge of this literature, as it strikes at the foundations of their position, as indeed it strikes at the foundation of any form of public intervention in the economy. This chapter focuses on the theoretical assumptions of this literature.

THE NEW THEORY OF REGULATION

The attack on the possibility of successful regulation has come from two related but separable sources. On the one hand there is the literature concerned specifically with regulation, but also very much relevant is the public choice literature, though its concerns have been much wider than simply the issue of regulation.

Regulation of private industry has been a long-standing issue in American policy, unlike in Britain where, until the recent privatizations, nationalization was the dominant form of public intervention in industry.[2] This regulation, going back to the creation of the Interstate Commerce Commission in 1887, had normally been treated as an attempt to impose the public interest on industries where the forces of competition did not operate. Government stepped in to do what the normal operations of the private market were prevented from doing in a few exceptional cases.

This 'market failure' view of the benignity of regulation came under attack from a range of sources from the mid-1960s. A pioneer in this was the neo-Marxist historian Gabriel Kolko (1963, 1965) who reassessed pre-1914 American policy, and argued that the regulatory agencies of that era were 'captured' by capitalist interests who used them to subvert their purported public purposes.[3]

At almost exactly the same time as the appearance of Kolko's work, regulation came under scrutiny and attack from the opposite end of the political spectrum, in the work of Stigler. The *Journal of Law and Economics*, with a sceptical attitude to regulation began publishing in 1958, but a key article in the development of the new regulation literature was published in that Journal in 1962 by Stigler and Friedland.[4] The key question of this article was – does regulation make any difference to the behaviour of the industry regulated? This was examined for the case of electricity. The conclusion was that regulation had no discernible effects on the industry's behaviour. The reasons were twofold, they argued. The industry does not, in the long run, have the monopoly power which is commonly assumed, but in any event the regulatory body does not have the ability to force the utility to operate at a specified combination of output, price, and cost – the utility can always evade the regulation's intent. This scepticism about the effects of regulation (see also Stigler 1965) did not of itself involve a fundamental challenge to the regulatory ideal, but in 1971 he broadened the scope of the attack.[5] The central thesis of the paper was that 'as a rule, regulation is acquired by the industry and is designed and operated primarily for its benefit' (Stigler 1975a: 115). This view was explicitly counterposed to the view that regulation was aimed at benefitting the public at large, or that regulation is irrational and inexplicable. In essence Stigler's was a neo-classical economist's version of the capture thesis. Whatever the origins and rhetoric of regulation, its effects will be to advance the interests of the industry regulated.

The capture theory of regulation can and has been arrived at from a variety of angles. Stigler would have had no difficulty in agreeing with Kolko's argument that:

4

the intervention of the Federal government not only failed to damage the interests of the railroads, but was positively welcomed by them since the railroads never really had the power over the economy, and their own industry, often ascribed to them. Indeed the railroads, not the farmers and shippers, were the most important single advocates of federal regulation from 1877 to 1916.

(Kolko 1965: 3)

However Stigler's approach, in the American political and academic context, was to be much more significant. Most of the subsequent literature has built up on his approach.

Central to that approach was the idea that regulation is a good like a consumer good, with a demand and a supply function. Politicians supply regulation primarily in exchange for votes, industries demand it because of its capacity to coerce consumers or other producers. But once this approach was put forward it raised the question why should the supply of regulation only respond to the demand of producers. Peltzman (1976) argued that Stigler's approach to the political process was insufficiently general, that consumers too had votes with which to 'buy' regulation, and that therefore regulation would respond to the politicians attempt to maximize votes from a variety of sources. So regulation would rarely be a case of simple capture by the industry, but on the other hand its outcomes would never reflect the public interest, but the interests of those crucial to the vote-maximizing aims of politicians.

Also very important in the generalization of this new approach was Posner. Like Peltzman he moved the debate away from a simple 'capture by producers' approach to emphasizing regulation as the product of coalitions between the regulated industry and some of its consumers, the former obtaining some monopoly profits from regulation, the latter obtaining lower prices, all at the expense of unorganized, mostly uninfluential consumer groups (Posner 1971; also Posner 1974). Posner's particular contribution was to apply this approach to the analysis of the law, and generally to press the argument for the superiority of common law procedures for dealing with issues more often addressed by regulatory bodies (Posner 1977).

On the foundations of Stigler's and Peltzman's work has developed a whole 'new economics' of regulation which is represented in journals such as the *Journal of Law and Economics*, the *Bell Journal*, and the *International Review of Law and Economics*. Some of the complexities and difficulties of this school are returned to below, but enough has been said to bring out the generality of the approach, and its foundations in a profound mistrust of the state grounded in neo-classical economics' maxims about human behaviour. This linkage logically takes us on to public choice.

PUBLIC CHOICE

Public choice can be defined as 'the economic study of non-market decision making, or simply the application of economics to political science' (Mueller 1989: 1). Economics here means, of course, neo-classical economics, in other words the assumption that in politics as in all activities people are motivated by individual maximizing.[6] Public choice aims to apply this approach to the specific actors of politics especially to voters, politicians and bureaucrats. 'To simplify the matter, the voter is thought of as a customer and the politician as a businessman/entrepreneur' (Mueller 1989: 1). Such a view of the political process has no single origin point, and can be found in Adam Smith (a point returned to below) and in modern times in such writings as Schumpeter (1954) and Downs (1957). The literature in the field is vast, though pride of place must still go to the journal *Public Choice*, organ of the Virginia School and inspired by the work of Buchanan and Tullock. A summary of much of this is in Rowley (1987). The field covered is much greater than industrial regulation as traditionally conceived, and covers everything from voting procedures to public expenditure determination. But like the new economics of regulation, its cutting edge is a profound scepticism about the capacities of government to deliver anything sensibly considered the public interest, given the realities of self-seeking behaviour in politics.

One area of public choice analysis close to the concerns of regulation is the analysis of bureaucracy. In his pioneering book on this in 1971, Niskanen argued that bureaucrats were to be understood as 'budget-maximizers', because most of the benefits (pecuniary and non-pecuniary) they sought to obtain are correlated with bureaux and budget size. Coupled to this was the argument that those legislators charged with overseeing bureaux would tend to gain from larger bureaux because of the vote-generating possibilities of bureaux spending. Regulatory bodies, like other bureaux, would then expand excessively.

Later work by Niskanen complicated this picture but without altering the fundamental thrust:

the most important hypothesis derived from this theory is that government budgets are too large, that is, they will be larger than that preferred by the median legislator, and in a representative government, larger than that preferred by the median voter.

(Niskanen 1975: 638)

Thus the new economics of regulation and public choice theory are closely related – indeed to a degree the former is a subset of the latter.[7] In looking at them in more detail it is therefore appropriate to discuss some of the common elements before looking at each separately.

Back to basics: epistemology

Like many social scientists both the new economics of regulation school and public choice theorists attempt to defend their arguments by deploying epistemological policemen. As for many neo-classical economists, the people usually chosen for this role are Popper and Friedman. Whilst Popper and Friedman are plainly far apart in philosophical sophistication, they tend to be deployed in a similar manner in this kind of literature. This is simply summed up by Posner when he argues that, following Friedman (1953), 'the true test of a theory is its utility in predicting or explaining reality' (Posner 1977: 13). The purpose of this argument is to deny the relevance of the realism of the postulates of a theory – what matters is simply its capacity in generating falsifiable hypotheses. A slightly more sophisticated version of this argument is deployed by the public choice theorist, Rowley, who cites Popper (1968) in his support. For Rowley:

the self-seeking postulate is employed in positive public choice essentially as an 'as if' proposition, which when combined with relevant auxiliary conditions, generates testable predictions concerning the political variables to exogenous change. To the extent that such predictions differ from those of alternative approaches, and conform more closely to the evidence, so the self-seeking postulate is justified, whether or not it reflects the reality of the political market behavioural calculus.

(Rowley 1987: 2)

As always with epistemological arguments, the purpose in deploying Friedman and Popper is to rule out *a priori* certain kinds of argument. Just as Popper's original aim was to rule Marxism and psychoanalysis out of court as scientific endeavours, so the anti-regulationists want to rule out any questioning of their story about the motives of agencies in the public sector. In a strict 'as if' framework motives would be irrelevant, just as the motives of the owners of the firm are irrelevant in Alchian's classic defence of the profit-maximizing model of the firm (Alchian 1950). All that would matter would be the congruence between the theories' predictions and the observed outcomes.

Friedman's version of this methodology is crude and easily rejected. It proposes a clear distinction between theory and observation which is unsustainable. It presupposes a world of experience separate from presupposition or conception which is unsustainable – observation can never be 'neutral'. The argument is also incoherent because it suggests that experience is independent of knowledge, yet at the same time what is to count as experience producing knowledge can only be specified in knowledge (Hindess 1977, chapter 4).

Popper's epistemology is plainly more sophisticated than Friedman's. He, for example, has always rejected the possibility of a strict observation language, independent of theory. But the project of Popper is still to provide clear demarcation criteria between 'scientific' and 'non-scientific' discourses. Whilst this project has become more complex and refined over the years it has not provided a means of distinguishing good from bad theories on the basis of some universal criteria (Williams 1975). However vigorously he wields his truncheon, the epistemological policeman has feet of clay.

At one level of argument all this probably matters very little. Any passing acquaintance with the writings of the new regulationists will quickly reveal that they are not consistently 'as if' theorists. Rather, they normally have a missionary-like belief in the revelation that public sector actors maximize their own interests. Thus Stigler (1975a) suggests that no case of regulation which contradicts this hypothesis will be found: 'Temporary accidents aside, such cases simply will not arise: our extensive experience with the general theory in economics gives us the confidence that this is so. Indeed there is no alternative hypothesis'. Where evidence does not support the hypothesis this does not come 'from the "failures" of the hypothesis but from the extreme crudeness of the measures of benefits and costs' (Stigler 1975a: 140).

So it is clear that some important proponents of the anti-regulation position do not believe in the defence of the position mainly by epistemological criteria. Nevertheless it is important to note that such criteria have been used, and for two purposes. One is to provide the basis for claims for scientificity – for 'positive' social science, such claims obviously requiring some demarcation criteria to establish what is non-scientific or normative. Such distinctions are in practice little adhered to by the anti-regulationists. For example as Rowley (1987: 3) remarks 'The ideology of the Virginia School in essence is one of profound preference for market over non-market decision-making which permeates almost all of the writings of its scholars'.

The second purpose of this style of epistemological defence is to try and evade criticism of the fundamental postulates of theory, above all the utility-maximizing individual as the starting point for analysis of all forms of social and political as well as economic activity. It is this fundamental postulate which needs to be discussed next.

Back to basics: rational maximizing

The anti-regulation position commonly involves a polemic against the naivety and blindness of those who accept individual rational-maximizing in production and consumption but reject such an approach to the activities of public sector bodies. This polemic involves telling a story of the history of economic thought, which as usual in such stories has its heroes and villains. Adam Smith did quite well, recognizing that much economic legislation could be analysed in terms of self interest, but failing to recognise that 'All legislation with important economic effects is the calculated achievement of interested economic classes' (Stigler 1975b: 240). But after Smith it was downhill all the way for nearly two hundred years: 'From 1776 to 1964 the chief instrument of empirical demonstration on the economic competence of the state has been the telling anecdote' (Stigler 1965: 11–12). For Stigler the particular villain in this history is Pigou, seen by many as the founder of modern welfare economics, with his alleged belief that complex market failures could be unproblematically and costlessly eradicated by state action. Stigler quotes from Pigou's (1924) *Economics of Welfare* where he argues that externalities can be corrected because it is 'possible for the state, if it so chooses, to remove the divergence in any field by "extraordinary encouragements" or "extraordinary restraints" upon investments in that field' (quoted in Stigler 1975: 113).

But this is to grossly misrepresent Pigou's position. In the same book as cited by Stigler, Pigou wrote:

> It is not sufficient to contrast the imperfect adjustments of unfettered private enterprise with the best adjustment that economists in their studies can imagine. For we cannot expect that any State authority will attain, or will even whole-heartedly

seek, that ideal. Such authorities are liable alike to ignorance, to sectional pressure and to personal corruption by private interest. A loud-voiced part of their constituents, if organised for votes, may easily outweigh the whole.

(Pigou 1924: 301)

This is a consistent feature of Pigou's arguments. In the tariff debates of the early 1900s he had argued that whilst in principle a tariff could be designed that would favour Britain, a realistic view of the political process made the likelihood of such an optimum tariff being brought into being extremely remote (Pigou 1904).

No doubt most radical reformers tend to misrepresent their pre-decessors in order to try and make their own case for reform more compelling. But this kind of rewriting of history in this instance involves a key theoretical issue. The basic grid through which previous writers are assessed has only two sections – those who ascribed fully to the view that all government action is based on self-seeking, and those who believe it is all based on altruism. 'In one setting individuals are assumed to be selfish; in another they are selfless. The analyst cannot have it both ways' (Shughart and Tollison 1985: 39).

This dichotomy, like most dichotomies, serves more as a rhetorical device than an aid to understanding. The purpose of this part of the paper is precisely to attack this dichotomy as providing the exhaustive possibilities of argument. As Sen (1982: 106) puts the point 'The rejection of egoism as description of motivation does not, therefore, imply the acceptance of some universalised morality as the basis of actual behaviour. Nor does it make human beings excessively noble'.

To postulate all actors as rational maximizers is entirely vacuous unless this is linked to some notion of what is maximized. The nature and determinants of what is maximized is in many ways the central theoretical issue in the anti-regulation literature. The problem for the anti-regulators is that whilst normally committed to notions of methodological individualism, i.e. that social action can always be reduced to the aims and desires of individuals, this is entirely unhelpful in generating a general theory of how society works. This problem is usually overcome by introducing an 'implicit structural determinism' (Hindess 1988: 93; 106–7). This means that the calculations of in-dividuals are ascribed to their place in the social or political structure – all bureaucrats calculate this way, all voters that way, all politicians another way.

This reduction of actors' calculations to their social locations raises a number of difficulties, apart from compromising the methodological individualism of the anti-regulators. It means that the predictions of the theory are subject to radical revision from changes in the definition of the calculative consequences of particular social locations, a particular problem when these consequences are rarely justified in any detail. (This point is returned to on pp. 18–20 in the more detailed discussion of public choice theories.)

The more general difficulty is one emphasized by Hindess (1988). He emphasizes the reductive and implausible account of agents' calculations that linking them directly to social locations involves. This difficulty is widely recognized in other areas where such accounts are deployed. For example, most social scientists, including most Marxists would recognize the problems of deriving workers' or capitalists' political views directly from the fact of them being either workers or capitalists, as is done in some vulgar Marxism. It is widely recognized that much more enters into the determination of political views than social location. Exactly a similar point can be made with reference to 'bureaucrats' or 'politicians' or 'voters'. Of course they will have a conception of their interests, but what this conception involves depends crucially on the means of calculation available to such actors, and can never be simply derived from being a member of these categories. To put the point in more general form, 'interests' are literally inconceivable without 'ideas' about those interests, 'ideas' which in turn have social conditions of existence. Without some discussion of those ideas and their institutional conditions of existence the rational maximizing approach remains radically inadequate.[8]

Furthermore, emphasis on the means of calculation of actors' interests undermines the case for actors to behave similarly in all arenas:

> There is therefore no reason to suppose that the techniques and ways of thinking employed by an actor will be consistent with each other. This point undermines the portfolio model's assumption of an holistic rationality. Actors may well think differently in different areas of activity, and there is no reason to suppose that they are by and large rational and consistent.
>
> (Hindess 1988: 109)

Stigler (1975: 137) argues that 'there is, in fact only one general theory of human behaviour, and that is the utility-maximizing theory'. But whilst he regards that generality as a strength of the theory, the point here is that it is a crucial weakness, because it is such a general theory only by dint of obscuring the differentiated conditions of existence of forms of calculation. This in turn would provide a plausible account of the behaviour of actors (bureaucrats, politicians, voters) without reducing their behaviour to membership of such categories.

The case against regulation

From this general perspective the research programme of the economic theory of regulation may be seen as twofold. On one hand is the demonstration of the efficiency of market mechanisms in solving almost all problems. For example there is the argument that 'natural monopolies' if unregulated will not in the long run be harmful to consumers because competitors will arise (Stigler 1975: 72): also the more general argument that much 'market failure' arises from an inadequate specification and enforcement of property rights rather than from inherent defects of the market mechanism. Thus the appropriate means for dealing with pollution for example is to make the polluter pay the costs of pollution activity, e.g. by means of a tax, rather than attempt to prevent pollution by administrative means. (See for example Posner 1977: 279–81.)

The other strand to the research programme is the demonstration of the inefficiency of regulation in dealing with the problems it purports to solve. This takes the form of exposing the non-impact of regulation, for example that regulation seems to have made no difference to the level of electricity prices (Stigler 1975, chapter 5). There is also the demonstration that regulation mainly aids the regulated industry, if often at the cost to the industry of subsidizing uneconomic activities out of the profits (Hilton 1972), and the argument that regulation agencies may face an impossible task – for example when charged with linking the costs and prices of monopolists when the necessary instruments of measurement and control do not exist (Posner 1974: 339).

The economic theory of regulation does not rest on any attack on the efficiency of public agencies in the way which is a staple of British political debate. On the contrary, public agencies are seen as efficient in achieving the objectives of the private interests they serve, although not of course the public interest. Thus Posner (1974: 339) asserts that although public agencies do not compete in product markets, 'that is only to say that the agency is like a private monopolist, and there is no convincing theoretical or empirical support for the proposition that the internal management of monopolistic firms is any laxer than that of competitive firms'. This of course is starkly in contrast with British arguments where the 'public' status of an agency is often seen as a synonym for inefficiency.

Posner is centrally concerned to stress that public agencies are not inefficient pursuers of the public good, but efficient pursuers of their own objectives. This is the vital point, for it means that the analysis of regulatory (and other state) agencies can proceed as if they are maximizers like any economic agent. Less central to the argument is the implication of the above quote that the whole of the Leibenstein-type literature on the 'internal' inefficiency of firms is to be jettisoned. No justification is offered for this, though clearly the whole 'satisficing' approach to the firm would undercut the extension of 'maximizing' assumptions from the analysis of firms to the analysis of state agencies. Stigler (1976) has explicitly attempted to refute Leibenstein's notion of inefficiency as separate from the standard notion of allocative inefficiency: for a reply see Leibenstein (1978).

The theory then suggests that the incidence of market failure is both exaggerated and misunderstood, but that in any case regulation is likely to make the situation worse rather than better. (There is a difference in emphasis here, with Stigler inclined to stress the efficacy of market mechanisms, and Posner slightly more inclined to suggest the superiority of legal over administrative means to correct market failure.) Overall regulation is both unnecessary and ineffective.

One other, less general, implication of this peculiar methodology is that it finds it difficult to cope with situations where the evidence adduced as fact is commensurate with more than one theory. For example, despite Posner's offhand dismissal (1974: 341), much of the regulation literature is compatible with an orthodox Marxist framework which makes due allowance for class struggle in determining that not all forms of regulation will simply benefit the owners of the regulated industry. For example, Marxists may well contend that under certain conditions of class struggle trade unions may be capable of imposing their political will on these agencies. Equally, as Posner has admitted, the economic theory of regulation is 'so spongy that virtually any observations can be reconciled with it' (1974: 348). Regulation appears in such a wide range of industries with such different conditions: 'It is not a coherent theory yielding unambiguous and therefore testable hypotheses' (ibid.: 349).

Perhaps the most important empirical consequence of the positivist methodology is that it tends towards reducing the attention given to the mechanisms whereby regulatory agencies come to serve private interests. This results from the focus on outcomes which can serve as a means to test theories, at the expense of the means allegedly at work to achieve these outcomes.

Such a 'black box' approach to the supply of regulatory activity is particularly notable in Stigler's pioneering (1971) article, but is to some extent modified by his 1975(a) book, especially chapter 10. Much of this refers to questions concerning the qualifications, character, etc. of regulators, an issue which is returned to below. However it would be unreasonable not to point out that as well as the general theory that regulatory agencies act like all other agents, on the basis of cost–benefit calculations, proponents of the economic theory of regulation also pray in aid of their position the economic theory of cartels.

This is not just an analytic device (i.e. argument by analogy) because regulation may be seen as having similar economic effects to private cartelization – basically to push output below and prices above competitive levels. The benefits of regulation producing cartels are therefore obvious in this framework. The costs will be more problematic. For any individual economic agent the optimum position is to see regulations applied to everyone else but themselves. Each agent therefore has an incentive to evade the impact of the regulations. This means costs will be incurred in policing functions, in keeping everyone in line. Conditions will therefore favour regulation where these costs are lowest, which will tend to be where the number of economic agents involved are small and their interests homogeneous.

One obvious problem with this, as Posner recognizes (1974: 345–6) is that if conditions favour private cartels this is likely to make regulatory cartels unnecessary from the firms' point of view. Therefore it is hardly surprising that regulation often appears in areas unsuitable for successful private cartels. More generally the theory of cartels can say nothing about the distribution of the costs of regulation between the regulatory agency and the regulated firms which is presumably a crucial component of the firms' cost–benefit calculation. We might suggest here that the economics of regulation literature tends to conflate the usefulness of the economic theory of cartels in understanding some of the effects of regulation with its much weaker ability to explain how regulation is 'supplied'.

Notwithstanding the attempts to use theories of cartels to explain the mechanisms of the supply of regulation, the fundamental focus is still on outcomes. The point is summarized by Stigler:

> The announced goals of a policy are sometimes unrelated or perversely related to its actual effects, and the truly intended

effects should be deduced from the actual effects.... This is not a tautology designed to gloss over a hard problem, but instead a hypothesis on the nature of political life.... If an economic policy has been adopted by many communities, or if it is persistently pursued by a society over a long span of time, it is fruitful to assume that the real effects were known and desired. Indeed, an explanation of a policy in terms of error or confusion is no explanation at all – anything and everything is compatible with that explanation.

(Stigler 1975a: 140)

We will leave aside for the moment the assumption built into this quote that the history of regulation is so clearly one of pursuit of private interests, noting only that Posner himself (1974: 352) has outlined the partial (in both senses) character of studies of regulation, and that there are many counter examples to the economic theory of regulation (see also McCraw 1975). The central point is whether we can deduce from outcomes of policies the 'real' intents of a policy's proponents as Stigler suggests. The answer is surely that we cannot. This may be argued in the following way. Political like other social processes are characterized by actions which are not determined in their effects by the intentions of their authors. Policy outcomes will be affected by a whole range of factors other than these intentions – one might go so far as to say that the history of economic policy, for example, is commonly a history of unintended consequences.

Against this it might be argued that the repeated character of the outcomes is not compatible with unintended consequences – there must be a learning process at work. If every time A is attempted B results, will not the pursuit of A be modified? The problem with the point is that it ignores the particular character of political argument in democratic regimes (or rather implies that such arguments are essentially fraudulent), which imposes a necessity to argue for policies as in the general interest and to use the means (state agencies) which constitutionally represent that general interest. The argument is then that the character of political discourse in democratic regimes constrains the kinds of argument that are deemed legitimate in advocating policies. The constancy of claims to be furthering the public interest in setting up regulatory bodies is not fraudulent (whatever the outcome), not a mask for ulterior motive, but a consequence of certain political arrangements, which impose a requirement to present public policies in a particular manner.

15

The argument does not have to be that proponents of public regulation are in error or confused about the outcomes of that regulation (though the evidence of its effects, contra Stigler, may be said to be confusing). Rather it is that the rhetoric of democratic politics in which the state is said to represent the public interest is not just a rhetoric which masks the working out of private interests (cf. Posner 1974: 346–7). It is not 'utterly uninformative and indeed misleading' (ibid.: 355). It does affect the objectives of agents in public bodies. This is not a question of defending a 'naive' view of the state in which public agencies represent in some Utopian sense the public good and are able to achieve that good. The economics of regulation is pushing at an open door in contesting that position. What can however be asserted is that such notions of the public good do have definite effects on the activities of public bodies, even if they do not on their own determine the outcome of these activities.

The stress on outcomes feeds into the ambiguity of much regulatory writing on the mechanisms which allegedly generate the effect of regulatory bodies pursuing private interests. On one hand, as already noted, these mechanisms are commonly given a low priority. It is only outcomes that really matter. On the other hand a complete disregarding of the mechanisms at work would leave the argument vulnerable to the riposte that if these mechanisms were changed then the outcomes could be different – the public interest could be pursued effectively.

Posner (1974: 336–7) is sensitive to this point, and attempts to refute it by saying that regulatory bodies efficiently attain the objectives they were set up to attain i.e. private ones. This argument, and the general tenor of the economics of regulation literature, is that regulatory bodies are incorrigible – we know that because we know the unanimity of the outcomes of their actions. But this is dangerous ground because even the most die-hard anti-regulator favours a legal framework for economic activity, but why should 'regulation' by law be seen as (potentially at least) pursuant of the public interest and all other form of regulation never so? This problem is recognized by Posner (1974: 349–350) when he argues that taken too far the economic theory of regulation would be 'incredible' because it would imply that society was incapable of having any institutions to offset the role of private interest groups. He argues in particular that without some notion of the judiciary as operating in the public interest it is impossible to explain the existence of a legal framework for the free market system (which he of course assumes to be unambiguously in the public interest). Thus Posner must logically attempt to show the superiority of legal processes over administrative ones in regulating economic activity. He does not deny the existence of market failure (cf. Littlechild *et al.* 1979) but argues that the failure is 'ordinarily a failure of the market and of the rules of the market prescribed by the common law' (Posner 1977: 271). Changing these rules is preferable to the establishment of administrative agencies.

Posner's argument has the great virtue of suggesting the in-principle similarity of law and regulatory agencies in exerting public control over markets, and thus reducing the choice between them to pragmatic one, dependent 'upon a weighing of their strengths and weaknesses in particular context' (ibid.: 271). However the pragmatism seems to involve noting the problems of regulation by public bodies in a variety of areas, but remaining decidedly vague on why legal enactment would be always superior (ibid.: 271–85).

This defence of the role of judiciary as exempt from the criticisms of other regulatory agencies is substantiated by specifying the conditions which make this exemption possible: 'The terminal character of many judicial appointments, the general jurisdiction of most courts, the procedural characteristics of the judicial process, and the freedom of judges from close annual supervision by appropriations committees' (Posner 1974: 351). Now without entering into an argument about whether these conditions are the crucial ones for the character of the American judiciary, the important point is the clear implication that under definite conditions regulatory bodies may in fact be corrigible, may escape the inevitable subordination to private interests.

Stigler attacks the naivety of economists who believe that regulatory bodies can be changed by preaching to the regulatory commissioners or the people who appoint them (1975a: 132). But the conclusion is not that regulatory commissions cannot be changed, rather that (talking about the Interstate Commerce Commission): 'The only way to get a different commission would be to change the political support for the Commission, and reward commissioners on a basis unrelated to their services to the carriers' (ibid.).

He also (1975a, chapter 9) devotes considerable space to analysing the characteristics of commissions and their personnel – e.g. the lack of economists, the lack of politicians, and the undue weight of oldish executives and lawyers. From this he draws the conclusion that 'the commissioners are of an age, background and prospects such that they are not likely to benefit by a major controversy with the regulated industry'. Again the clear implication of such arguments is that with different personnel regulatory bodies could be different.

The limits of public choice

As already noted, public choice theory involves almost every aspect of political and governmental behaviour, some of them initially a long way from the problems of regulation. The discussion here is limited to three areas of public choice discussion, which illustrate some of its difficulties, and why when deployed in the context of regulation its arguments need to be treated with considerable scepticism.

From its very beginnings the public choice approach has been beset by the 'paradox of voting' (Downs 1957). If this most fundamental of political acts is to be seen in a utility-maximizing light there is a paradox. On any conceivable calculation the positive benefits received by any individual voter in a large-scale democracy in return for voting will be infinestimal – their vote will make no difference at all to the outcome. Equally, acquiring knowledge about what is being voted about is irrational in a utility-maximizing light – why acquire information (incur costs) in order to inform a decision which can have no measurable benefits?

This paradox has generated an immense literature. Much of this has ascribed a value to the act of voting itself, rather than its consequences. But as Mueller (1989: 79) remarks 'This modification of the rational voter hypothesis does reconcile the act of voting with individual rationality, but does so by robbing the rational self-interest hypothesis of all its predictive power'. In other words the argument has become circular – because we know individuals are rational maximizers and they cannot obtain substantial consequential benefits from voting, they *must* get benefit from the act itself.

Mueller's own solution to the problem raises as many problems as it solves. He postulates that there is a conditioning process in society which reinforces altruistic behaviour, and which is particularly powerful for the well-off and educated, who are the ones most likely to vote in elections. This line of argument is compatible with the survey material on voting behaviour which 'strongly suggests that considerations beyond one's narrowly-defined self-interest influence a citizen's vote, once he/she is at the polling booth' (ibid.: 96) but raises its own difficulties. Apart from any lack of evidence of what these altruistic 'conditioning' devices are, the auxiliary hypothesis of widespread altruism in voting is a bizarre way of bolstering a self-interest theory of politics. If our true, rational maximizing selves cannot express themselves in the secrecy of the polling booth, where can they be expressed?

Public choice has made much of explaining the growth of public expenditure by rational-maximizing models. The basic idea here is simple – politicians aim to maximize votes by offering expenditure programmes, but subject to the constraint that taxes will reduce voter support. 'The government is likely to adopt any act of spending which, coupled with its financing, is a net addition of utility to more voters than it is a subtraction i.e. it pleases more than it irritates' (Downs 1957: 70). A central difficulty with this argument is that the politicians' capacity to garner votes depends on the voters *perception* of the benefits and costs of expenditure programmes and taxation. Most public choice arguments suggest that because the beneficiaries of most expenditure programmes are relatively concentrated, but the impact of taxation is dispersed, there will be an asymmetry which will lead to a continual rise in expenditure levels.[9] On the other hand Downs (1960) argued that in a democracy budgets would tend to be too small because voter ignorance of the often uncertain and indirect benefits of government expenditure would be contrasted with the clear and mainly direct costs of paying taxes.

The point here is not to adjudicate between these two views, but to emphasize the ambiguity of so many public choice arguments because they depend on a whole range of auxiliary hypotheses to flesh out the rational maximizing postulate to give some 'operational' meaning. These *ad hoc* hypotheses can then be used to justify any prediction which is deemed to be compatible with actual states of the world.

Public choice discussions of public expenditure are one area where some empirical work on Britain has appeared (Toye 1976; Tomlinson 1981). The evidence provided in this work suggests that the public choice approach does not help us understand the pattern of public expenditure in Britain in the post-war period, and like so much 'New Right' economic writing extrapolates madly from the highly specific conditions of the 1970s. The rise in expenditure in that decade cannot be easily explained in a public choice framework, and that rise was soon reversed, without any of the changes which public choice theorists advocated to bring such a reversal about.

Finally, the public choice discussion of bureaucracy brings us close to the specific issue of regulation – how are we to understand the be-haviour of the bureaucrats involved in regulation? Niskanen's initial work established a model in which bureaucrats were part of a bilateral monopoly. On the one side government was a single purchaser of the regulatory body's output, on the other that body was the only supplier of that output. Whilst this had problems from an economics point of view, e.g. that under conditions of double monopoly there is no equilibrium output, its basic thrust was clear and has remained unchanged in subsequent work (e.g. Niskanen 1975). Bureaucrats were to be viewed as utility maximizers whose scope for exercising that maximization was very large under modern conditions. Tullock (1987: 1042–3), for example, argues that the typical civil servant is under little pressure to do as his or her political masters want because of security of tenure and a promotion system not tied to pleasing political superiors.

This general approach to bureaucracy in particular and government in general has been subject to powerful criticisms. Margolis (1975) argues three points against the public choice approach. First he suggests that it involves too few elements in its analysis of government – basically only voters, legislators and bureaucrats. Against this he argues that at a minimum the executive and political parties and other organizations of the citizenry need to be introduced. The executive (for example, the US President) works under quite different political constraints, e.g. the voting constituency, from the legislature. Equally it is difficult to believe that political parties are not significant actors in most modern politics.

More specifically Margolis points out that bureaucrats are significantly divided – some are political appointees with quite different career patterns from career civil servants. On the other hand career civil servants generally move between a number of bureaux, rather than their fortunes being tied to the fate of one particular bureau.

Secondly Margolis points out that government is not just a provider of outputs to consumer households, as the public choice approach argues (e.g. Tullock 1982: 151). It is also involved in issues of social stability and 'nation building' which could never be the concern of private agents (Margolis 1975: 645).

Finally, he notes the 'national myopia' of most discussion of bureaucratic and government growth. Obviously much of the regulation and public choice literature has to be seen against the long history of regulation in the US economy, and its perceived failings. But this has led to a focus on the peculiarities of US political arrangements to explain a general phenomenon – the growth of bureaucracy and government almost worldwide. Thus while much of the public choice literature claims to be grounded in the first principles of neo-classical economics, it is very much the product of American regulatory history.

STATE FAILURE AND MARKET FAILURE

The arguments above have attempted to show that the general attack on regulation from the neo-classical perspectives of the anti-regulationists or public choice theorists rests on weaker foundations than those theorists would have us believe. Insofar as they apply consistent epistemological principles, these are too crude to play the policing role they aim to fulfil. Theoretically, the approaches claim much too much both in the usefulness of rational-maximizing approaches to political behaviour, and in the plausibility of these approaches in accounting for all the diversity of regulatory behaviour. At the theoretical level these neo-classical approaches do not achieve their prime purpose of demonstrating that regulation in the name of the public interest is inherently flawed.

As already suggested, much of this work starts from an over-drawn contrast between the alleged naivety of public interest theories of the state in contrast with the supposed realism of the rational-maximizing *a priori*. This has led much of the literature in this area to be characterized by a contrast between those who emphasize state failure, as opposed to those who emphasize market failure. Proponents of regulation commonly start from this latter notion as providing a rationale for such regulation (see also Part II of this volume). Is this a good theoretical place to start?

Market failure, it should be emphasized, is a concept with a broad appeal in economics literature. It could cover work, for example, in a classic liberal-Keynesian framework (e.g. Meade 1975, chapter 7), or in a much more *dirigiste* approach (Cowling 1990). So market failure is a broad church, covering very different views about the appropriate scope of government in general and regulation in particular. In the current context what is at issue is not the specific policy prescriptions it may lead to but its analytic starting points.

The modern analytic concept of market failure derived initially from welfare economics, and the specification of the conditions for a Pareto optimum. 'The best way to understand market failure is first to understand market success, the ability of a collection of idealised competitive markets to achieve an equilibrium allocation of resources which is pareto optimal' (Ledyard 1987: 326). Whilst this origin made clear the highly restrictive assumption necessary to achieve such an optimum, and therefore the ubiquity of market failure, it has shortcomings as a starting point for advocacy of regulation. First, it involves a highly specific notion of productive efficiency in which that notion is related to

21

a general theory of (capitalist) production. Production is conceptualized in terms of a combination of factors, where those factors are dis-embodied from any organization or calculative framework. This 'general theory of production' is conceptually bound to elevate markets to the role of key determinants of efficiency, because production is essentially about market-driven combinations of factors. If markets work efficiently then productive efficiency is achieved.

The broad analytic point then is that 'market failure' applied to production issues is embedded in a very particular notion of production which needs to be analysed in order to see the limits of that concept. This notion of production assumes that if all the relevant (factor and product) markets are perfect then maximum efficiency will result. Forms of organization, modes of calculation and other specific characteristics of enterprises are secondary phenomena. If market forces are fully operative then the 'fit' enterprises will survive by a Darwinian process of selection.

But this is a Panglossian world. The objection to this notion that markets have such general and compelling effects on efficiency can be criticized at different levels of generality. At the most general level the Darwinian selection aspect has been powerfully criticized by Winter (1964). He points out that such an argument requires highly restrictive conditions to be operative. For the argument to work firms must have the capacity to consistently adjust behaviour over a range of different conditions – what is 'adaptive' behaviour to market pressures in one period may be quite inappropriate in another. But if firms are to be consistently successful in this adaptive sense then (in the absence of genetic inheritance!) they must have forms of organization and calcula-tion which enable then to adapt to those new market conditions. Organizational and calculative features then *do* matter.

The implication of this argument is that whilst in a capitalist economy (defined broadly as production of commodities by means of commodities) financial reproduction is necessary for enterprise survival, differential profit levels arising from differential success in coping with market conditions do not lead to those profit levels being used as finely graded criteria of enterprise viability. Profit levels are only one of the means of assessment deployed by financing institutions in making funds available to firms. Equally takeovers and mergers are not generally of low profit firms being absorbed by high profit firms (e.g. Singh 1975; Meeks 1977).

The point is not, of course, that markets do not impact on firms or affect their efficiency. But markets cannot be seen as compelling either organizational and calculative homogeneity or optimum efficiency. The problem with the neo-classical theory of production is that it excises crucial features of the enterprise which matter for efficiency. Similarly to start with 'market failure' is precisely to start from an assumption about what markets 'should' do and then explain why they do not. The argument here is that markets never could fulfil this function, so to start from there is a theoretical false step.

The alternative starting point is to postulate the significance of organizational and calculative features of firms in responding differentially to market pressures. Countries which suffer from persistent inefficiencies in their enterprises could then by said to be suffering from 'enterprise failure' rather than 'market failure'. Regulation would then start from knowledge of the conditions of this enterprise failure. Of course this is to open up a set of issues which the general theory of production exists largely to avoid. It is to open a Pandora's Box of issues which cannot be contained within orthodox economics terms of reference. But in this case better Pandora's rather than the Black Box.

NOTES

1   I am grateful to Martin Cave and Roger Sugden for helpful comments on earlier drafts of this paper.
2   Nationalization also tended to displace that other American form of industrial policy, anti-Trust. See Mercer (1992).
3   For historians' discussion of regulation in this period, including the work of Kolko, see e.g. Keller (1990).
4   Republished in Stigler (1975a), Chapter 5.
5   Stigler (1964) and (1971), republished in Stigler (1975a), Chapters 6 and 8.
6   This approach of course goes much wider than politics into all areas of human behaviour, most obviously in the work of Becker (1976).
7   Also related is the rent-seeking approach, which, applied to regulation, argues that regulation imposes a cost on society because resources are wastefully expended on the fight to obtain the economic rents generated by regulation, hence expanding the harms done by regulation. See Rowley *et al.* (1988).
8   Note that this is a different line of criticism from that of Sen (1982, Chapter 4) who is concerned to make a clear distinction between sympathy, which underlies altruistic activity which also benefits the altruist (e.g. giving to charity makes you feel good), and commitment where no such benefit to the giver accrues.
9   This assumes a balanced budget.

REFERENCES

Alchian, A. (1950) 'Uncertainty, evolution and economic theory', *Journal of Political Economy* 58: 211–21.

Becker, G. (1976) *The Economic Approach to Human Behaviour*, Chicago: Chicago University Press.

Cowling, K. (1990) 'The strategic approach to economic and industrial policy', in K. Cowling and R. Sugden (eds) *A New Economic Policy for Britain*, Manchester: Manchester University Press.

Downs, A. (1957) *An Economic Theory of Democracy*, New York: Harper.

—— (1960) 'Why the government budget is too small in a democracy', *World Politics* 13(2): 321–43.

Friedman, M. (1953) 'The methodology of positive economics', in his *Essays in Positive Economics*, Chicago: Chicago University Press.

Hilton, G.W. (1972) 'The basic behaviour of regulatory commissions', *American Economic Review*, Papers and Proceedings LXII: 47–54.

Hindess, B. (1977) *Philosophy and Methodology in the Social Sciences*, Brighton: Harvester.

—— (1988) *Choice, Rationality and Social Choice*, London: Unwin Hyman.

Keller, M. (1990) *Regulating a New Economy*, Cambridge, Mass.: Harvard University Press.

Kolko, G. (1963) *The Triumph of Conservatism*, New York: Harper and Row.

—— (1965) *Railroads and Regulation*, Princeton: Princeton University Press.

Ledyard, J.O. (1987) 'Market failure', in *New Palgrave Dictionary of Economics*, London: Macmillan.

Leibenstein, H. (1978) 'X-inefficiency Xists – reply to an Xorcist', *American Economic Review* LXVIII: 203–11.

Littlechild, S. *et al.* (1979) *The Taming of Government*, London: Institute of Economic Affairs.

McCraw, T. (1975) 'Regulation in America, a review article', *Business History Review* XLIX: 159–83.

Margolis, J. (1975) 'Comment on Niskanen', *Journal of Law and Economics* 18(3): 645–59.

Meade, J.E. (1975) *The Intelligent Radical's Guide to Economic Policy*, London: Allen & Unwin.

Meeks, G. (1977) *Disappointing Marriage: A Study of the Gains from Merger*, Cambridge: Cambridge University Press.

Mercer, H. (1993) *Constructing a Competitive Order: The Hidden History of British Anti-Trust*, Cambridge: Cambridge University Press.

Mueller, D. (1989) *Public Choice II*, Cambridge: Cambridge University Press.

Niskanen, W.A. (1971) *Bureaucracy and Representative Government*, Chicago.

—— (1975) 'Bureaucrats and politicians', *Journal of Law and Economics* XVIII: 617–44.

Peltzman, S. (1976) 'Towards a more general theory of regulation', *Journal of Law and Economics* XIX: 211–40.

Pigou, A.C. (1904) *The Riddle of the Tariff*, London: Macmillan.

—— (1924) *The Economics of Welfare*, London: Macmillan.

Popper, K. (1968) *The Logic of Scientific Discovery* (2nd edn), London: Hutchinson.

Posner, R. (1971) 'Taxation by regulation', *Bell Journal of Economics and Management Science* 2(1): 22–49.

—— (1974) 'Theories of economic regulation', *Bell Journal of Economics and Management Science* 5(3): 335–57.

—— (1977) *Economic Analysis of Law* (2nd edn), Boston: Little Brown.

Rowley, C. (ed) (1987) *Democracy and Public Choice*, Oxford: Blackwell.

Rowley, C., Tollison, R. and Tullock, G. (1988) *The Political Economy of Rent-Seeking*, Norwell, Mass.: Kluwer.

Schumpeter, J. (1954) *Capitalism, Socialism and Democracy*, London: Allen & Unwin.

Sen, A. (1982) *Choice, Welfare and Measurement*, Oxford, Blackwell.

Shughart, A. and Tollison, R. (1985) 'The Positive economics of anti-trust policy', *International Review of Law and Economics* 5: 39–57.

Singh, A. (1975) 'Takeovers, economic national selection and the theory of the firm', *Economic Journal* 85(3): 497–515.

Stigler, G. (1965) 'The economic role of the state', *American Economic Review* LV: 1–18.

—— (1971) 'The theory of economic regulation', *Bell Journal of Economics and Management Science* 2: 3–21.

—— (1975a) *The Citizen and the State: Essays on Regulation*, Chicago: Chicago University Press.

—— (1975b) 'Smith's Travels on the Ship of State', in A.S. Skinner and T. Wilson (eds) *Essays on Adam Smith*, Oxford: Clarendon Press.

—— (1976) 'The Xistence of X-Efficiency', *American Economic Review* LXVI: 213–16.

Stigler, G. and Friedland, C. (1962) 'What can regulators regulate? the case of electricity', *Journal of Law and Economics* V: 1–19.

Thompson, G. (1990) *The Political Economy of the New Right*, Cambridge: Polity.

Tomlinson, J. (1981) 'The economies of politics and public expenditure: a critique', *Economy and Society* 10(4): 381–402.

Toye, J.F.J. (1976) 'Economic theories of politics and public finance', *Journal of Political Science* 6(4): 432–51.

Tullock, G. (1982) 'Welfare and the law', *International Review of Law and Economics* 2: 151–63.

—— (1987) 'Public choice', in the *New Palgrave Dictionary of Economics*, London: Macmillan.

Williams, K. (1975) 'Facing reality: a critique of Karl Popper's empiricism', *Economy and Society* 4(3): 309–26.

Winter, S.G. (1964) 'Economic natural selection and the theory of the firm', *Yale Economic Essays* 4(1): 225–72.

Part II

ECONOMIC RATIONALE

2

ALLOCATIVE INEFFICIENCY AND MONOPOLY AS A BASIS FOR REGULATION

Michael Waterson

This chapter begins examining the question: what is the economic basis for regulation? Within an essentially capitalist productive sector to an economy, governments often choose to intervene by constraining pricing and co-ordinatory behaviour, preventing certain activities, or even altering industrial structure. This chapter enquires whether there is an economic basis for such actions, with a particular focus on the problems created by monopoly.

The chapter starts with a broad consideration of allocative efficiency and its determinants. This is then narrowed down to home in on the relationship between monopoly behaviour and allocative inefficiency. The next section discusses the link between monopoly structure and deleterious monopoly behaviour, as evidenced by monopoly welfare losses. The fourth section examines some of the considerations to be borne in mind in deciding how to counter monopoly abuses, whilst not discussing forms of regulation, which are covered in Part IV of this book. The final section provides a very brief conclusion.

WHAT IS MEANT BY ALLOCATIVE EFFICIENCY?

The first and second theorems of welfare economics essentially say, respectively, that every competitive equilibrium is Pareto-efficient (no one can be made better off without making someone else worse off), and that every Pareto-efficient allocation can be achieved as a competitive equilibrium for some distribution of the endowments. (For a discussion of these theorems, see an intermediate microeconomics text such as Varian 1987, chapter 29.) Clearly then, if distribution of endowments is satisfactory (and this is a big question), it is best to go for a competitive economy. This is one clear way in which we can ensure that the economy operates as efficiently as possible, given total endowments and current state of technological knowledge. Then it is allocatively, and by assumption also technically, efficient.

Allocative efficiency implies the equation of relative marginal benefits of goods between consumers, and the equation of these marginal rates of substitution to ratios of prices or marginal (social) costs of production. In symbols:

$$\mathrm{mu}_x^i/\mathrm{mu}_y^i = \mathrm{mu}_x^j/\mathrm{mu}_y^j = \mathrm{mc}_x/\mathrm{mc}_y \qquad (2.1)$$

where x and y are two sample goods, i and j are two representative consumers, mu is marginal utility, and mc is marginal cost. Allocative efficiency has nothing directly to do with the initial endowments.

It is well known however, that various factors can get in the way of this seemingly simple strategy, the pursuit of competition. One of these is increasing returns to scale and, associated with this, monopoly. Monopoly can exist without scale economies, but their presence renders large number competition of the type envisaged above impossible, as we see later. Increasing returns violate one of the cornerstone assumptions of the production side of the competitive equilibrium model, convex production sets.

A second factor is externalities, mainly detrimental externalities in practice, and their effect upon the model. All agents' actions will have influence on other agents through prices (e.g. my purchase of a good will, infinitesimally, affect the price others pay). But where there is a non-priced effect, as with air pollution for example, allocative in-efficiency will result. The social cost of the activity differs from the private cost.

Thirdly, economies in practice involve not just private goods, but also goods which are to a greater or lesser extent public. Provision of a good such as street lighting or television broadcasting does not lend itself readily to pure pricing solutions. How can people be persuaded to pay up to their marginal valuation for a good which they will receive in any case?

A fourth case is imperfect information. A potential buyer's relative lack of information about a good compared with the information possessed by the seller, for example, can distort or even destroy a market, as Akerlof (1970) demonstrated in his famous 'lemons' paper on used cars.

All these factors can make for allocative inefficiency in an economy because they each destroy the link between relative marginal benefits of goods and relative marginal costs of their production. Indeed it is doubtless true that all real (as opposed to fictional) economies have many such problems. Unfortunately it is not necessarily true that a piecemeal approach to tackling these difficulties is best. The general theory of the second best (Lipsey and Lancaster 1956) implies that, given one unavoidable distortion, it is inefficient to deal with other distortions in the economy on the basis that the given distortion does not exist. This is an awkward conclusion because it yields so little guidance on appropriate action in the real world. However, it does at least suggest that competition will not solve all individual allocative inefficiency problems.

In practice, specific piecemeal intervention is widely advocated by economists and policy makers and widely implemented. This would not be contrary to the spirit of the second-best theorem if the sectors in which piecemeal intervention is practised were sufficiently separable from the remainder of the economy. Yet the gas and electricity industries, for instance, are commonly separately regulated, despite their obvious interconnection. Moreover, and somewhat confusingly, regulatory literature on 'second best pricing' is concerned with the design of optimal prices for an industry in which marginal cost pricing is infeasible, given that the industry must break even (see e.g. Sherman 1989, chapter 5). That is prices are to be set such that there need be no reliance on outside factors such as general taxation for example, rather than the prices being related to the general theory of the second best. This chapter will follow the same (dubious) practice of discussing intervention as if the industry concerned were separated from others so that piecemeal intervention is relevant and desirable.

Regulation in a general sense may be taken to mean governmental intervention in a market-based activity. It can, but need not, be with the aim of correcting allocative inefficiency. Indeed there are often implicit if not explicit distributional aims in addition, as the previous chapter has noted. Regulation takes a wide variety of forms. It is widespread and longstanding in the control of externalities, for example in reducing pollution and harms to employees. It is common in areas where consumer information is imperfect, or is deemed to be imperfect, such as taxi services and retail of alcoholic drinks. Neither of these is the main focus of this chapter, which is concentrated upon monopoly power, its creation of allocative inefficiency, and so monopoly as a basis for regulation.

31

MONOPOLY AND ALLOCATIVE INEFFICIENCY

Assuming a monopoly sets price above marginal cost, it will obviously violate condition (2.1) for allocative efficiency. Suppose there is a monopoly in the sale of product x, we would then have:

$$mu_x^i/mu_y^i = mu_x^j/mu_y^j = p_x/p_y > mc_x/mc_y \qquad (2.2)$$

(where p's are prices). Considering good y as a numeraire, each consumer would be purchasing insufficient of good x (more generally, relatively too much of good y compared with good x) by comparison with its marginal cost. The next unit of good x would cost less to produce then the benefit a consumer would obtain from its use. In the spirit of the partial analysis we are pursuing, Figure 2.1 rephrases the loss of allocative efficiency from monopoly in good x in terms of its cost and demand curves, and consumer surplus.

Here (and this is a crucial assumption) constant returns to scale and fixed factor prices are assumed. Hence, each firm's long-run average cost curve is horizontal and coincides with the marginal cost curve. The supply curve for each firm if good x were to be supplied by a perfectly competitive industry would be at the level of each firm's long-run marginal cost (LRMC), so the industry supply curve (S), being the horizontal sum of the firms' supply curves, would also be at that level. Therefore setting supply equal to demand (D), consumers pay p_c and total output is x_c. The monopolist faces the same industry demand curve D but, being the only firm, realizes that demand is downward sloping, and therefore that at any level of output marginal revenue is below price (average revenue). Thus, in setting marginal revenue equal to marginal cost to maximize profits, the monopolist chooses an output x_m which is sold at price p_m. As a result of the high price and consequent restriction in output, monopoly profits of an amount $p_m AB p_c$ are earned.

In the perfectly competitive industry, a consumer at Z on the demand curve is willing to pay up to a price p_z for the good. Under the competitive regime, the consumer only pays p_c. Hence, she experiences consumer surplus, of an amount $p_z - p_c$, the difference between the maximum she would be willing to pay and what she actually pays. The same sort of thing can be said for consumers at every point on the demand curve. Therefore, the total amount of consumer surplus obtained from consumption of the good in the competitive case is the large triangular area EFp_c – the area under the demand curve but above price. Similarly under monopoly, consumer surplus of the smaller

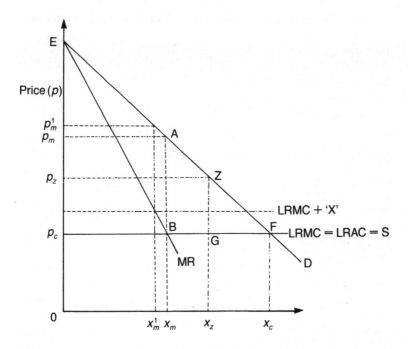

LRMC Long-run marginal cost
S Industry supply curve
D Demand
p Price
MR Marginal revenue

Figure 2.1 Monopoly and allocative efficiency

triangle EAp_m is earned. But notice that the monopolist, in making super-normal profits, has deprived consumers of more surplus than it has itself gained. The difference, the triangle ABF, is known as monopoly welfare loss. (Of course, if the demand curve is non-linear the area is only roughly triangular.)

Measuring monopoly welfare loss by reference to consumer surplus is not entirely accurate. The reason is that we have not taken into account income effects, and so changes in the demand for other goods engendered by the distortion in the market for good x. However, Willig (1976) has shown that if the income elasticity of demand for x is low, or if expenditure on the good takes a relatively small proportion of income, then consumers' surplus is a rather good approximation to the under-lying change in welfare, whatever prices are taken to measure the true valuation. We shall assume Willig's conditions to be met, and hence assume monopoly welfare loss is well measured by the triangular reduction in consumer surplus.

The concept of consumer surplus and the loss described might seem esoteric. To make it more concrete, you experience consumer surplus when you go, say, to buy a pair of trousers and expect to pay £35 but the shop has just the pair you want at £27. A consumer surplus loss arises for those people who go with £25 in their pocket to buy a pair of trousers and can find none they like at less than £27. Thus if the trousers were supplied by a monopolist at a price of £27, and the competitive price were £20, the first consumer would lose some consumer surplus as a result of trousers being in monopoly supply, but there would be no monopoly welfare loss. The second consumer, who would have experienced some consumer surplus if buying under competition, is not able to experience it under monopoly and therefore illustrates the source of monopoly welfare loss. Furthermore, in the simple situation depicted in Figure 2.1, since monopoly welfare loss is a triangle with the same height and same length base as the monopoly profit rectangle (BF = p_cB since MR has twice the slope of D), it can be evaluated at half monopoly profit, a potentially substantial sum.

The situation so far described is rather more straightforward than the case where there are increasing returns to scale. As already said, if firms' production sets are not convex due to increasing returns, then the second welfare theorem is not satisfied. An industry with increasing returns cannot have perfect competition as an equilibrium market structure. To see this, suppose there were a large number of firms in the market each selling at a price equal to (what would be a rather high) marginal cost. A firm willing to expand output could reduce its costs and so do better than break even by charging the same price as the others. As it expanded output, price would fall slightly and some firms would be forced to increase output to reduce costs themselves, or drop out. It is not necessarily true that the industry equilibrium structure would be a monopoly (we would have to specify the process of competi-tion in more detail in order to say what the eventual outcome would be). But it would be far short of perfectly competitive.

In this case monopoly welfare loss is rather a misnomer since competition is not an available option. Nevertheless, allocative effi-ciency can sensibly be discussed.

An industry in which it is most efficient for one firm to be the producer is called a natural monopoly. As just implied, this does not necessarily mean there will be only one producer in practice. Natural monopolies arise (in the single product case) where scale economies are very extensive relative to demand. Thus the simplest example (and a sufficient condition) would be an industry where average cost falls continuously, perhaps because there are important facilities used over a wide range of output levels.

In such a case, a monopoly produces benefits to allocative efficiency unavailable through competition although also, so it would seem, allocative inefficiencies as a result of prices being above marginal cost due to the absence of competition. Figure 2.2 illustrates this – the

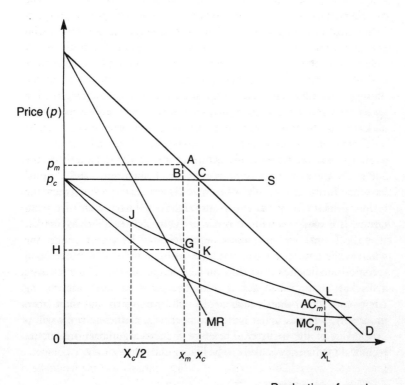

Figure 2.2 Increasing returns and efficiency

35

competitive price may be assumed to be at p_c, whilst monopoly price is higher, so reducing consumer surplus but resulting in substantial resource savings due to increasing returns, which emerge as that part p_cBGH of monopoly profits p_mAGH.

In the multiproduct case, whether an industry is a natural monopoly depends not only on economies of production of a single line, but also on cross-relationships on the cost side between products. Thus economies of scope come into play. Economies of scope exist between products where the cost of producing a package of given quantities of (two) products, is less than the costs of producing the quantities separately, algebraically, $C(x_1, y_1) < C(x_1, 0) + C(0, y_1)$. Yet economies of scope plus economies of scale do not necessarily imply a multiproduct industry is a natural monopoly. The reason is that economies of scope involve a comparison between points on the axes of a cost function drawn in output space and an interior point. Thus, rather more specifically, declining ray average costs (declining costs along an output ray) plus transray convexity along any hyperplane cut through the output point (costs rise away from the output point along the transray cut) will guarantee natural monopoly (Baumol et al. 1982). Figure 2.3 illustrates the idea. The point of this discussion is that deciding whether an industry is a natural monopoly, i.e. whether monopoly is potentially allocatively efficient, is not straightforward in practice.

There is another factor which should be raised here. It has so far been assumed that, whatever the structure of industry, the underlying cost curves are the same. But some people (e.g. Leibenstein 1966) take the view that firms are typically not technically efficient and that losses from technical inefficiency can easily outweigh losses from allocative inefficiency. It is easily seen for example in Figure 2.1 (curve LRMC + 'X') that the former will essentially be represented by a rectangular area whereas the latter is a triangular area. Also, an increase in costs due to technical inefficiency will create an addition to allocative inefficiency if a markup is applied to actual costs. Further it has been argued (e.g. Crew et al. 1971) that X-inefficiency will be prevalent in conditions of monopoly, whereas under perfect competition, inefficient firms will be driven out of the industry. Therefore if these arguments are correct, technical inefficiency is likely to be higher under monopoly.

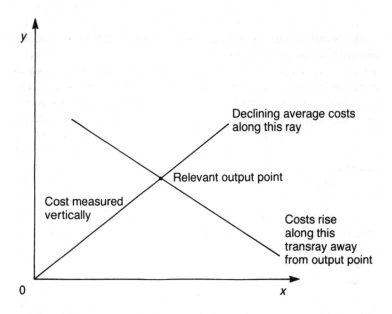

Figure 2.3 Multiproduct costs and natural monopoly

THE LINK BETWEEN MONOPOLY STRUCTURES AND MONOPOLY WELFARE LOSS

In both Figures 2.1 and 2.2 it is assumed in calculating monopoly welfare loss that the monopolist sets marginal revenue equal to marginal cost in order to choose a profit-maximizing price-output combination. This assumes the firm is unconstrained by either actual or potential competition. Actual competition naturally has some constraining influence on pricing but so equally, can potential competition have. For example, British Airways and LRC industries, the makers of Durex condoms, both have dominant positions in the UK domestic market. But each faces actual competition to some extent, and each is aware that the competitive threat could increase. Thus each is likely to be charging prices to some extent below monopoly price.

Notice that if, in Figure 2.1, price were reduced to p_z in anticipation of competitive threats, there would still be an area of monopoly loss represented by ZFG, but it would be less than half the profits then earned. It is only if competition is so constraining as to force price down to p_c, that monopoly welfare loss disappears.

The situation is rather more complex in Figure 2.2. First, as already implied, if actual competition were to appear, an inefficiency would be created. For example, if a second firm entered and took half the market, at the same time as the total market expanded to x_c, then average costs would rise from those at G to those at J. This would counterweigh the benefits due to a reduction in monopoly welfare loss as price fell to p_c. What would be more socially desirable is the *threat* of competition. If instead, competitive threats persuaded the monopolist to reduce price to p_c, average costs would fall to those at K, and the benefits of lower prices would not have to be set against any increased resource costs. The threat of competition would be likely also to reduce X-inefficiency.

In a partial equilibrium sense, taking this market as separable, it is clear that the most socially desirable situation would occur if the monopolist felt so threatened by potential entry that it expanded to output x_L, at which it would just break even charging price equal to average cost at L. Price, in this case, cannot fall to marginal cost without a subsidy from outside the industry, which our partial equilibrium approach tends to rule out. But could this degree of potential competition really occur?

Baumol *et al.* (1982) have investigated the question of social desirability in a natural monopoly market. They show that if a market is perfectly contestable, the incumbent firm is forced to price down to average cost in a one-product industry. The reason is that any price above average cost will make the firm vulnerable to 'hit and run' entry, where a rival takes the market for a short period. In a multiproduct natural monopoly, Ramsey-optimal output vectors are sufficient to prevent entry. Ramsey-optimal prices are those set at welfare maximizing levels above marginal costs, given a binding breakeven constraint. So, if a market is perfectly contestable, despite there being only one firm, monopoly welfare loss is at a minimum, given that subsidies to the industry are ruled out and production takes place in a technologically efficient manner. This then leads to the question of the conditions under which a market is perfectly contestable.

Unfortunately, a set of precise conditions is not available. What can be specified is a set of sufficient conditions, which may therefore be stricter than required. Dixit (1982) proposes the following conditions:

1   That all producers have access to the same technology.
2   That this technology may have scale economies which in turn may

arise through fixed costs but not sunk costs.

3   Incumbent firms can change prices only with a non-zero time lag.

4   Consumers must respond to price differences with a shorter time lag.

The first two of these are generally agreed to be necessary. In particular the second will rule out a large majority of all practical natural monopoly cases. Most public utilities (electricity, etc.) communication (telephone, etc.) and transport facilities (rail, etc.) have extensive sunk cost elements.

Even in those cases – airlines are often suggested as a prototypical example – where sunk costs are rather low, access to technology, in particular booking systems, has been a problem for new carriers. Thus even if the third and fourth conditions could be relaxed somewhat, the set of natural monopoly cases which are perfectly contestable may be virtually nonexistent. In addition there is no reason why, if the conditions are almost satisfied, then the industry is almost perfectly contestable – this is a matter of some debate. For example if the incumbent can respond by price cutting to breakeven levels immediately entry takes place, then entry will never be worthwhile, even if a monopoly price is set by the incumbent prior to entry. Indeed, a monopoly price by the incumbent could be maintained without entry even in some circumstances where the incumbent can respond fairly rapidly such that the entrant would not have long enough in production to recover fixed costs sunk for a short period.

Thus, to continue with the airline industry for the present, although the US industry has been deregulated, and some argue that it is contestable, it nevertheless appears still to be true that market power has an effect on pricing. For example, Brander and Zhang (1990) find that on a number of duopoly routes, although price is below collusive levels, it is definitely above the Bertrand pricing levels which would be implied by contestability theory. Borenstein (1989: 362) also finds that 'dominance of major airports by one or two carriers ... appears to result in higher fares for consumers who want to fly to or from these airports'.

More generally there is substantial US and UK evidence that market structure in terms of industry concentration and entry barriers has some effect on profitability, or at least that high concentration and high barriers are linked with higher than average profitability – for a comprehensive exposition of the issues, see e.g. Hay and Morris (1991, chapter 8). This is a hotly contested area with protagonists taking a variety of positions, but the debate suggests very strongly that the world (or the

UK) generally is not perfectly contestable. Also, we must not forget that firms currently are subject to regulation aimed at potential anticompetitive practices; in a country without such regulation there would most likely be substantially more monopoly welfare loss (Kay 1983).

FACTORS INFLUENCING THE DESIRED EXTENT OF REGULATION

One of the things which (almost) every final year student of economics knows is that Harberger's (1954) estimates of monopoly welfare loss indicated they were a very small proportion of national income (in the US). Taking this in conjunction with the view that regulators can be 'captured' by their charges (see Chapter 1) one might be tempted to say that regulation is not worthwhile. Let us consider arguments to the contrary.

First, Harberger's estimates are low by comparison with most others; a set of comparative estimates is given in Sawyer (1980). As Sawyer points out, there are two approaches apart from Harberger's, which is essentially an attempt to measure triangular areas like ABF in Figure 2.1. Bergson utilizes a general equilibrium method involving measuring changes in utility and comparing the existing monopoly situation with one involving a hypothetical constant degree of monopoly. An alternative general equilibrium approach is based upon work by Diamond and McFadden involving expenditure function calculations. Sawyer develops all three methods for UK data as well as incorporating changes to assumptions implied by criticisms of the original studies, in particular Harberger's. This leads to a wide range of values for monopoly welfare loss, from below 1 per cent of manufacturing output to very much higher figures. Sawyer concludes 'that the welfare loss of monopoly may be substantial, and cannot be lightly dismissed' (1980: 353).

Second, as a proportion of turnover the direct cost of regulation is very low. Oftel, which regulates the UK's telecommunications industry, has a budget of the order of $\frac{1}{20}$ of 1 per cent of BT's turnover, and it has many more duties than just regulating BT. Harberger's estimate was that monopoly welfare loss was about $\frac{1}{12}$ of 1 per cent of national income. Given the dominant position of BT, the potential for monopoly welfare loss within the UK's telecommunications industry is fairly clearly substantially greater than the average potential across the economy as a whole. Therefore even if Harberger's figure were taken at face value, the case for regulation would not be ruled out. It would obviously be strengthened if higher values for monopoly welfare loss were believed plausible.

However, the fact that one needs to make these arguments means that selectivity in regulation for monopoly practices is desirable. Regulation is not costless.

It is necessary to distinguish between regulation appropriate to natural monopoly and regulation appropriate to cases of monopolistic practices in industries which are not obviously monopolistic. With the latter situation, there is no particular reason to identify monopolistic behaviour with any specific industry. Therefore a practice-specific rather than industry-specific approach is appropriate. A practice-specific approach will also allow some conformity of treatment across cases, which arguably is desirable (perhaps on 'second best' grounds). The next issue is whether there are particular practices which are important or potentially prevalent enough to warrant dedicated agencies or procedures. For example, many countries believe that collusive pricing practices are a case in point; in the UK they are dealt with by the Restrictive Practices Court. Other monopolistic practices are then in the hands of another body – in the UK, the Monopolies and Mergers Commission. See Part IV of this book for more details on mergers.

With a natural monopoly, it might seem that the straightforward argument is for an industry-specific agency for each such monopoly. But even if a certain industry is a natural monopoly, this would not itself imply the need for regulation. A rather trivial example drawn from Waterson (1991) makes the point. In the Newcastle upon Tyne area there is a company which specializes in the delivery of tea and coffee on a regular order basis to the consumer's door. Such an activity is probably subject to economies of scale at its current level of operation (if more households used the service, the average cost of delivery would fall) but the activity is limited by the extent of demand for this service. It is probably a natural monopoly. But no sensible person would suggest this activity should be regulated, even though entry would not be particularly easy, because the extent of the monopoly is not great. Consumers have the obvious and, for the majority, fairly straightforward, alternative of going to a supermarket and buying similar products, which in turn constrains the firm. In other words, the presence of natural monopoly (or perhaps, a concentrated natural oligopoly) provides an argument for economic regulation since the structure implies the potential for monopoly power, but not a sufficient condition. Other factors must be taken into account.

To a considerable extent this issue is concerned with the technology of regulation. A small natural monopoly will have only a small potential level of monopoly welfare loss. But the nature of regulation may be that a small agency will prove ineffective. To be concrete, suppose a £5 billion turnover industry is regulated by a £5 million annual budget agency, which manages to benefit society by 1 per cent turnover, i.e. £50 million. A £5 million annual turnover natural monopoly might need a £50,000 annual budget agency to effect benefits of 1 per cent. But then all the benefits would be absorbed in agency costs, so the regulation would be without point.

However, it is also related to broader questions concerning the importance of the industry and the desirability of regulation. Given that we cannot necessarily expect regulators to behave entirely in line with the public interest – as Jim Tomlinson argues in Chapter 1 – it might be felt that intervention should be reserved for only the most egregious cases, where there would be a clear substantial likelihood of demonstrable adverse effects on consumers in the absence of regulation. Thus the extent of the monopoly, the extent of control the firm has over consumers, can be an important criterion for regulatory intervention.

The extent of control, or importance of the industry, is related to its size. It is not directly related to the market's price elasticity of demand, though it may well be rather more directly related to the income elasticity of demand. Where demand for the good is high even at low income levels then those consumers on low incomes will be very much affected by monopoly pricing practices. Thus if distributional considerations are to have any weight, regulation is more warranted in such cases. Therefore necessities (in the low income-elasticity sense) which constitute important industries (perhaps because of near-ubiquitous consumption) are commonly singled out from amongst natural monopolies for dedicated regulatory attention. Hence there is the widespread regulation of utility industries, gas, electricity and water.

Nevertheless it is important to note that regulation of an industry can take on a life of its own, and may outlive its purpose. As technology and tastes (demand) change, industries can change from being natural monopolies to being naturally oligopolistic. For example, long distance transmission of telephonic communication is no longer clearly a natural monopoly. Entrants can find they have some advantages over established firms locked into particular technologies but find their way blocked by regulation. Thus regulation should be selectively removed from time to time in response to such technology and taste changes and perhaps imposed in new areas where powerful monopolies arise.

CONCLUDING REMARKS

Monopoly power can lead to allocative inefficiency through monopoly pricing's distorting effect on consumption patterns. Thus people consume too few of the monopolist's goods, and monopoly welfare loss is created. The importance of the phenomenon varies from industry to industry. Particularly in cases of powerful natural monopolies, industry-based regulatory bodies to control price (and other matters) may be the best way of ameliorating the effects of monopoly. Lesser harms are probably better dealt with by broader agencies which are selective in their interventions.

REFERENCES

Akerlof, G.A. (1970) 'The market for "lemons": quality, uncertainty and the market mechanism', *Quarterly Journal of Economics* 84: 488–500.

Baumol, W.J., Panzar, J.C. and Willig, R.D. (1982) *Contestable Markets and the Theory of Industry Structure*, San Diego: Harcourt, Brace Jovanovich.

Borenstein, S. (1989) 'Hubs and high fares: dominance and market power in the US airline industry', *Rand Journal of Economics* 20: 344–65.

Brander, J.A. and Zhang, A. (1990) 'Market contestability in the airline industry: an empirical investigation', *Rand Journal of Economics* 21: 567–83.

Crew, M.A., Jones-Lee, M.W. and Rowley, C.K. (1971) 'X-theory versus management discretion theory', *Southern Economic Journal* 38: 173–84.

Dixit, A.K. (1982) 'Recent developments in oligopoly theory', *American Economic Review*, papers and proceedings 72: 12–17.

Harberger, A.C. (1954) 'Monopoly and resource allocation', *American Economic Review* 44: 77–87.

Hay, D.A. and Morris, D.J. (1991) *Industrial Economics and Organisation: Theory and Evidence* (2nd edn), Oxford: Oxford University Press.

Kay, J.A. (1983) 'A general equilibrium approach to the measurement of monopoly welfare loss', *International Journal of Industrial Organisation* 1: 317–31.

Leibenstein, H. (1966) 'Allocative efficiency vs "X-efficiency"', *American Economic Review* 56: 392–415.

Lipsey, R. and Lancaster, K. (1956) 'The general theory of the second best', *Review of Economic Studies* 24: 11–32.

Sawyer, M. (1980) 'Monopoly welfare loss in the United Kingdom', *Manchester School* 48: 331–54.

Sherman, R. (1989) *The Regulation of Monopoly*, Cambridge: Cambridge University Press.

Varian, H.R. (1987) *Intermediate Microeconomics: a Modern Approach*, New York: Norton.

Waterson, M. (1991) *Ownership and Regulation of the Major Utilities*, London: Fabian discussion paper no. 5.

Willig, R.D. (1976) 'Consumers' surplus without apology', *American Economic Review* 66: 589–97.

3

A STRATEGY FOR INDUSTRIAL DEVELOPMENT AS A BASIS FOR REGULATION

Keith Cowling and Roger Sugden

Until fairly recently, professional industrial economists' concern with policy was invariably confined to relatively narrow, albeit important issues such as monopolies and mergers regulation.[1] In the later 1980s, however, wider concerns began to receive great attention, particularly in the light of experience from Japan. This latter suggests that a comparatively broad and bold government industrial strategy can have an enormous influence on people's welfare because of its effect on industrial development.

In the spirit of this more recent work, our basic aim is to analyse the rationale for regulation within a framework of government strategies for fostering industrial development. In carrying out this analysis, we will be extending the scope for regulatory activity beyond its typical confines, at least for many countries.

The discussion will be divided into three substantive sections. The first will focus on a fundamental source of difficulties in so-called 'free market economies', namely concentrated decision-making within firms. Following Cowling (1990), we will identify and discuss three systemic, interrelated deficiencies which arise when government fails to take a planning, i.e. strategic, role: transnationalism, centripetalism and short-termism. The second will consider the remedy for these deficiencies. More specifically, given that the fundamental issue is concentrated decision-making power, the obvious solution is for government to introduce, facilitate and stimulate democratic decision-making.[2] In pursuing this, and again building from the first section, we will stress that the remedy is not accurately described as mere intervention in 'free markets'. Finally, the third section will focus on the nature of the regulation discussed in the second section. To emphasize our points, we will discuss how privatization and the consequent regulation of firms and industries – the dominant concern in British industrial policy throughout the 1980s – could be used as a mechanism for achieving democracy and how this contrasts with the policy which has actually been seen in Britain.

CONCENTRATED DECISION-MAKING

In a 'free market economy', the distribution and allocation of resources is essentially determined by the interplay of various actors operating within a set of ground rules implemented and policed by the state. The actors are either individuals acting *qua* individuals or forms of essentially non-government institutions, such as households and firms. Government's role is confined very much to the background, for instance to the drafting of laws of contract.

A popular perception is that such a system yields optimal results. Insofar as this perception is grounded in economic theory, neo-classical analysis is extremely influential. Within this, particularly important is the powerful and well-recognized theoretical conclusion that a complete set of perfectly competitive markets yields a Pareto efficient allocation. However, equally important but far less recognized is the idea of an even distribution of power. This is seen in the voluntary exchange concept, a tenet of neo-classicism that gives everyone the right of veto, nobody the power to force another into a worse position.

The reality of a 'free market economy', however, is that the markets and institutions acting within it are manipulated by a powerful subset of the population. These elite influence situations and events for their own benefit and hence observed outcomes will be optimal for some but not for society as a whole. This is not a problem of markets *per se*, rather a problem with the way markets can be used.

These points could be illustrated and explored from various angles. For example, consider the structure and activities of a typical large firm.[3] We do not have the space to develop a full justification and proof for our characterization but nevertheless will provide a detailed flavour of the analysis. In doing so, the discussion will draw heavily on Hymer's (1972) pathbreaking vision of the world economy; the work on control in, for instance, Zeitlin (1974) and Pitelis and Sugden (1986); and the theory of transnational corporations and their implications in Cowling (1986) and Cowling and Sugden (1987).

Decisions within firms can be classified into three types:

1 Strategic decisions – these concern broad corporate objectives, such

as a firm's relationship with its rivals and its geographical orientation.

2   Operational decisions – tactical, day-to-day options over the choice of a particular project from a subset of alternatives, etc.

3   Working decisions – for instance choices made by each person in a firm over their own work intensity.

All three categories of decision determine what actually happens in production but the strategic decisions are especially significant because, by definition, they essentially determine the direction of a firm. Moreover, the linkages between the three types are dominated by a hierarchy and, the further up the hierarchy, the less the number of people involved in making the decision. Everybody in a firm makes working decisions, which are severely constrained by both strategic and operational decisions. In contrast, only managers make operational decisions, albeit from a set of options largely determined by strategic decisions. Most importantly, the latter are made by an elite, despite resistance from others. Some managerialists argue that the elite are senior managers, others that they comprise senior shareholders, others that these two groups are effectively the same set of people anyway. Whatever, almost all but the purest neo-classical economists would accept that strategic decisions are effectively made by a subset of those involved in a firm.

The consequences of this are far reaching. For instance, it is commonly argued that senior managers seek maximum profits. If it is assumed that they control firms, we should hence expect firms to aim for product market monopolization. Consequently we should expect firms to manipulate markets by colluding, because this will suit the interests of those making strategic decisions. It may not suit others in society, for instance people seeking jobs or consumers seeking consumer surplus, but it will suit strategic decision-makers. Indeed this illustration is especially pertinent because a neo-classical alternative to our characterization is that appropriate market competition would remove any tendency for strategic decision-makers to impose their will. In the product market, for example, it could be argued that price competition amongst sellers would ensure that each can only obtain normal profits. However this misses the point. Profit seeking firms will avoid price competition that implies normal profits precisely because it implies normal profits. In the oligopoly case, this is recognized by Scherer, amongst others:

> When the number of sellers is small, each firm recognises that aggressive action such as price cutting will induce counteraction

from rivals which, in the end, leaves all members of the industry worse off. All may therefore exercise mutual restraint and prevent prices from falling to the competitive level.

(Scherer 1980: 514)

More generally, such collusion derives from recognition of interdependence amongst firms and thus characterizes all industries. The presence or absence of such conduct is not determined by, for instance, structure.[4] It is simply a given feature. After all, an industry by definition comprises firms producing goods which are substitutes for each other, and so interdependence is an unavoidable fact. There is no reason to think this is not recognized by firms and every reason to think that it is; can we really believe that firms could operate in an industry without recognizing their interdependence?

Similarly, when decisions are being made about a firm's geographical orientation, we should expect those decisions to be made in the interests of profit and nothing else. Thus when the conditions for accumulation weaken in any particular country, we should not be surprised to see deindustrialization and hence unemployment. The elite strategic decision-makers will ensure that a firm locates production wherever the conditions for accumulation are optimal. Shop-floor workers may object, as may deserted communities, but neither of these are making the crucial decisions. In short, concentrated decision-making power in a 'free market economy' results in the elite planning for their benefit and without regard to the costs imposed on others.

Perhaps a specific example will clarify some of our points. The outline of events leading to the closure of Ford's foundry at Dagenham is quite revealing (see GLC 1985). Apparently, senior management had a secret closure plan that was found out. As a consequence any intention to implement the plan was denied yet it was then carried out 'almost to the letter'. A particular problem for the shop-floor workers seems to have been that their role was limited to applying pressure on those making the decision; they were not decision-makers themselves. For many, to allow Ford's senior management to implement the plan would be to allow the 'free market' to reign. But this 'free market' was actually dictatorship by an elite for the benefit of the elite. Furthermore, any consequent problems for shop-floor workers would not have arisen because of the use of markets *per se*; they would have arisen because of an elite planning for its self-interest.

More generally, following Cowling's (1990) discussion of the imperatives for government to adopt a planning role, significant welfare consequences of concentrated decision-making power in 'free market economies' can be grouped into three sets of interrelated systemic deficiencies: transnationalism, centripetalism and short-termism.

We have effectively encountered the idea of transnationalism in the earlier discussions of deindustrialization and Ford. The basic idea is that transnational corporations have come to dominate economies, whose development is therefore threatened. The global perspective and ambitions of transnationals may cut across the interests of any particular nation state, or any particular community. Moreover, there is an asymmetry of power between corporation and community deriving from the corporation's transnationality, which can be exploited by its strategic decision-makers playing on the inherent locational rigidity of every specific community. To achieve its own objectives a transnational can switch investment and production, or credibly threaten to do so, wherever conditions in any one country or region appear disadvantageous. Thus transnationals which are left 'free' can impose their strategies on more or less enslaved communities.

Centripetalism is a closely related deficiency. It refers to the tendency for higher level economic, political and social activities to gravitate to the centre, away from the periphery. At the international level, this was explored most forcefully by Hymer (1972). He argued that a vertical division of labour within firms would produce a corresponding hierarchical division of labour between geographical regions. Thus amongst transnationals strategic decision-making is concentrated in a handful of major cities in the world, operational decision-making also extends to regional sub-capitals whereas the distribution of working decisions is more widespread, see also Dicken (1986) on Hymer (1972). Moreover the differences in wealth and power attached to these divisions of labour, as well as the differences in function for particular locations, produce a corresponding qualitative and quantitative distribution of other activities. For instance the best doctors, lawyers and entertainers gravitate to the major cities. Similarly, strategic decision-making in other firms serving transnationals and transnationals' employees is concentrated in particular areas, reflecting transnationals' uneven spread. In part this is due to the decision-makers choosing to enjoy the better standard of living available (for them) in, ideally, major cities, otherwise regional sub-capitals.

For any particular nation, this has far-reaching consequences. The nation's pattern of development depends crucially upon its position within the world order. Yet that position is essentially determined by firms' strategic decision-makers, not by the citizens of the nation as such. Furthermore, within any nation there will be uneven development across communities. Again, the position is determined by firms' strategic decision-makers, not by the citizens of communities.

A third set of deficiencies is problems of short-termism. By its very nature, a particular community is concerned with its long-term position and development; it has a vested interest in seeing that the location it occupies thrives and prospers into the future. However its basic difficulty is that the strategic decision-making of firms is based on the wishes of an elite, not the community. One view is that this may cause problems because the elite pursue short-term objectives, by choice or otherwise. In exploring the decline of British volume car manufacture, for instance, Lewchuk (1986) picks out the recurring theme of financial institutions demanding short-run returns at the expense of long-run development. More to the point, however, whether 'free market' firms plan short-term or long-term, they do so in the pursuit of their strategic decision-makers' wishes.[5] This is in no sense long-term planning for the communities in which they do or do not operate. This issue is especially seen where firms are transnationals with global strategies. Indeed it is dramatically illustrated by the deindustrialization argument. Firms will readily abandon particular nations to pursue profits elsewhere, regardless of the long-term consequences for those nations. Again this is well illustrated by events in the British car industry, as discussed in Cowling (1986). More generally, it is also a difficulty communities experience with other firms in all 'free market economies'.

DEMOCRATIC DECISION-MAKING

Faced by these difficulties, an obvious response is to tackle the issue head-on by addressing the most fundamental cause for concern. The basic argument is simple. A firm in which strategic decisions are taken by a subset of the population will serve the interests of that subset. Accordingly, a firm can only serve the interests of a community as a whole if all of the community's people make the strategic decisions, i.e. only if there is community control. Therefore a prime task for government is to establish, develop and stimulate a framework for community control. A prime task for economists is to analyse how this might be achieved.

Following Sugden (1990), underlying this analysis is the view that a community's people are generally capable of collectively deciding for themselves what best satisfies their objectives, although it is essential that they receive the appropriate education, etc. What this means in terms of such specific objectives as productive efficiency and growth, which are conventionally associated with industrial development, is in a sense irrelevant. For instance economists tend to presume increased growth is beneficial but if community control tends to give lower growth it does not really matter. If they can generally make the decision best suiting their objectives the observed outcome should generally be what the people want. Having said this, it seems reasonable to suggest that wealth creation is an important determinant of welfare. Hence the logic of our argument is to expect community control generally to imply successful wealth creation, i.e. increased productive efficiency and growth (other things being equal). Indeed there is considerable empirical support to suggest that this expectation will be fulfilled. See for instance Thomas's (1982) discussion of production in the Mondragon region of Spain. The region has a large co-operative sector in which the workforce has a considerable say over its own activity. Yet the co-operatives are 'more productive and more profitable' than conventional firms where decision-making is dominated by an elite few. (See also Knight and Sugden's (1990) more wide-ranging discussion of economic democracy).

Precisely how community control should be introduced is itself problematic, at least at the nationwide level. The issue is the subject of a large existing literature but it needs further attention. This is required both in terms of detail and imagination, in most ways beyond the scope of this paper. However, at a more general level four conceptual points warrant particular emphasis in this study:

1   Community control does not require central planning, which in fact suffers from similar problems to 'free markets'.
2   Community control does not entail the regulation of a 'free market economy', in the sense that we have been using the term 'free market'.
3   Community control does entail planning.
4   Community control does require a regulated market system that can be fairly accurately described as a 'democratic market economy'.

A system of central planning is in many ways diametrically opposed to the decentralized and devolved system that we are envisaging. This needs to be stressed if only to disassociate our suggestions from post-war failures in Eastern Europe and the Soviet Union. This matters in part because many people assume that a rejection of 'free markets' is an embrace of central planning, and vice versa. This assumption is wrong.

Although not advocating central planning, we are suggesting something other than a 'free market system'. Moreover, it would be inappropriate to characterize our suggestion as a regulated 'free market'. We are advocating a fundamental, radical change in decision-making structure: the inefficient and inequitable economy where the elite use markets and firms in plans designed for their benefit is being left behind as inadequate and unsuitable. To talk at all of 'free markets' would miss this basic change.

Having said this, there are two similarities between our suggestions and a 'free market system'. First, both are systems of planning. In one, communities do the planning whereas in the other, it is the elite. Second, both use markets. Like the elite, communities would use markets and firms to serve their objectives. This is a market economy because it is not being denied that markets would be a very effective mechanism for allocating scarce resources in certain circumstances. For instance they would be a useful tool for interaction and communication between firms and between firms and consumers. Most importantly, however, we are suggesting that markets should be a tool for communities. Hence what we are advocating can be fairly accurately described as a 'democratic market economy'. Furthermore, the thrust of our discussion is clearly that this would be a regulated system because government would need to play a vital, constant role in influencing economic activity. For example it is down to government to replace current systems with democratic control structures and constantly to scrutinize these new structures for their takeover by an elite.[6]

BRITISH INDUSTRIAL POLICY IN THE 1980s

To shed more light on the nature of this regulation, it is interesting to consider the dominant concern in British industrial policy over the 1980s, namely the privatization and consequent regulation of firms and industries. This is relevant both as a particular case study and because it typified a more general trend towards 'free market systems' in both capitalist and centrally administered economies throughout the world, a point seen in Vickers and Yarrow (1991). Indeed it has been argued that Britain provided the model for other countries to follow. The case study is significant because it reveals a missed opportunity, a lost chance to establish planning institutions which are central to economic success.

Throughout the 1980s, Britain saw numerous sales of publicly owned assets, see for example Vickers and Yarrow (1988, 1991) and Labour Research Department (1990) for details of companies, dates and the amounts of money involved. According to Labour Research Department (1990), between 1979 and 1989 privatization proceeds exceeded £24 billion. Over the same period, employment in nationalized industries and public corporations fell from 2.1 million (or 8 per cent of all UK employees) to 0.8 million (or 3 per cent of all UK employees), a drop of virtually 60 per cent. Thus privatization was undoubtedly a significant issue.

The basic idea is that firms were sold to the private sector. In some cases the focus was merely to create privately owned organizations regulated in the same way as the vast majority of other firms in Britain, for instance according to the Companies Act. However from the mid-1980s, with the privatization of British Telecom, regulatory concern was extended as it was felt that the major utilities posed different issues. Hence there has been debate over pricing formulae, for instance, and the likes of Oftel were born. See for example Kay, Mayer and Thompson (1986) and Vickers and Yarrow (1988, 1991). See also Chapter 6.

For our purposes, it is particularly relevant to consider the objectives of this process. These are discussed by Vickers and Yarrow (1988). Recognizing that objectives vary across government ministers and over time, they summarize seven principal aims:

1 reducing the public sector borrowing requirement;
2 easing problems of public sector pay determination;
3 gaining political advantage;
4 reducing government involvement in firm decision-making;
5 widening share ownership;
6 promoting employee share ownership;
7 improving efficiency.

Clearly the first three of these had nothing to do with promoting community control. What about the others?

In theory, decreasing government involvement in firm decision-making could be a reduction in community influence. This is because one method by which communities could control a firm is to use a democratically elected government as its instrument. Insofar as this might be a desirable mechanism in the particular cases under consideration, recent British policy may be a backward step. Nevertheless this is not a point we wish to press. To do so would entail arguing for public ownership as a means of community control. Whilst this may sometimes be reasonable, it is not necessarily the case and we do not want to give the wrong impression; public ownership and community control are not synonymous. In addition, a strategy based on public ownership is in some respects yesterday's argument. Our concern is today and tomorrow. It is also interesting to consider the way that Vickers and Yarrow (1988) expand on (4). They see it as designed to free firms from ministerial intervention for short-term political considerations. Such intervention is essentially not as an instrument of communities making strategic decisions. Accordingly, on this basis (4) also had nothing to do with promoting community control.

Objectives (5) and (6) – widening share ownership and promoting employee share ownership – could also be seen as instruments for promoting community control but again, in this instance, that was not a motive. The potential is discussed in Knight and Sugden (1990), which focuses on including employees in the 'membership' of British companies. The basic idea is that members have the right to influence a company's activities. For example a firm's directors may be dismissed by a majority vote of members; the significance of this is that directors are at the pinnacle of a firm's internal hierarchy and it is out of their meetings that a firm's strategy is given substance. Under the existing Companies Act members are shareholders. Thus one possibility for broadening involvement in firms' strategic decision-making is to broaden shareholding.

If it is to be effective in practice, this possibility raises wide-ranging and difficult problems that must be addressed. For instance, regulation would be needed to improve the quality of information received by the vast majority of shareholders. This is currently inadequate to enable effective control, see also Graham's (1991) analysis of accountability in privatized firms. Moreover the proportion of shares needed for the exercise of significant power is variable and uncertain, a point effectively established by a long line of literature dating back to Berle and Means (1932) and more recently seen in Cubbin and Leech (1983) for instance.

Consider a more specific illustration. One method of introducing community control would be initially to concentrate on involving all of its employees in a firm's strategic decision-making. Following Sugden (1990), this makes practical sense on the basis that everything cannot be changed at once and because the crucial welfare effect of a job makes employees the people most immediately affected by a firm's activities. They therefore warrant the most immediate attention. Accordingly, suppose each employee owned one share and thus had one vote in the election of directors. The chances are that employees' wishes would be swamped by other shareholders. With this in mind, serious consideration should be given to devising a system of regulation giving employees a significant collective voice and an incentive to participate as individuals in the exercise of that voice.

For example, one way to do this is to introduce an appropriate form of producer co-operative to exercise producer members' collective vote. Another is to establish a trust to exercise the vote. By its terms of reference, the trust would pursue employees' interests. All producers (subject to a qualifying period of employment) under a scheme of this kind would be entitled to equal voting rights in the election (by secret ballot) of the trustees. The accountability provided by this structure would need to be reinforced by regular trust meetings, and a communication system linking trustees to individual employees would be essential. Clearly this would require the trust to set up its own secretariat to do all of this properly and that may require public support.

Crucially, however, such considerations as the quality of shareholder information and the design of systems for giving employees a significant voice were not at the heart of British industrial policy in the 1980s. Part of the explanation for this is that, whatever the Thatcher Government had in mind with objectives (5) and (6), genuine community control was not on the agenda. Taking this view, insofar as share ownership can provide a useful mechanism for broader participation, the 1980s were therefore a lost opportunity. Another partial explanation stems from an argument by John Moore, a former Thatcher Minister and an architect of 1980s privatization:

> The extraordinary success that privatization now has in creating a wide distribution of shares produces shareholder pressures quite unlike those faced by nationalised industries or conventional companies. The existence of large numbers of shareholders who have both paid for their shares expecting a reasonable return and are customers interested in good service at a fair price is an irresistible combination and a powerful lobby in favour of both efficiency and price restraint.
>
> (Moore 1986: 95)

This undoubtedly suggests a desire to broaden control and, whilst it does not go as far as we are advocating, it suggests an unintentional step down that road. Taking this view, policy was unfortunately fatally flawed due to mistakes and/or misunderstandings, for instance a failure to regulate for appropriate information flows and to appreciate the complex relationship between share distribution and shareholder power. Without such flaws, the 1980s might have seen a useful step towards wider control.

The final aim identified by Vickers and Yarrow (1988) is improving efficiency. This is related to the other objectives, as Moore's (1986) argument illustrates, but especially interesting is the focus on promoting competitive pressures. If this had been pursued seriously, it could have provided another unintentional but useful step towards community control. As it was, Kay and Thompson (1986) argue that the forms of privatization in the 1980s were designed to suit dominant managers, who did not want increased competitive pressure. As such, not only was an opportunity missed, it was missed in a way which supports our earlier characterization of 'free market systems' and which reveals an industrial policy serving rather than challenging a system of concentrated decision-making power.

Improving efficiency by promoting competitive pressures is not the same as establishing community control. Following Kay and Thompson (1986), the efficiency idea is that appropriate competition ensures production costs are kept to a minimum (productive efficiency) and that prices are in line with costs (allocative efficiency). However a community is concerned with more than efficiency; distributional issues and the actual mechanisms for achieving outcomes are directly vital. Nevertheless, it is the case that increased competitive pressure can aid democratic control. Sugden (1990) argues that a concern with establishing, developing and stimulating a framework for community control identifies a well-focused but very complicated set of concerns. Yet unless successful industrial development is to be excessively delayed while all of these concerns are addressed, there is a need to concentrate immediately on a set of problems which can be solved relatively quickly. Accordingly it would be useful to focus in particular on two issues. One of these we have already discussed and justified, namely ensuring that firms' strategic decisions are collectively determined by every person working in the firm. The second is to guard against excessive monopoly or monopsony power, because this could totally undermine efforts to give employees strategic decision-making power and it recognizes the importance of other members of a community. For instance, a firm supplied by a pure monopolist must do as the monopolist bids. Such dictatorship would essentially remove employees' ability to make strategic decisions and is as unwanted as the dictatorship of a politician. However a firm's employees are not the only people in a community affected by a firm's activities. Thus dictatorship by producers with excessive monopoly or monopsony power must also be avoided. This is associated with the neo-classical view that appropriate competition removes any tendency for strategic decision-makers to impose their will, for example price competition in product markets guaranteeing that sellers can only obtain normal profits.

Although there are arguments for promoting competition, it seems that at least in the first half of the 1980s this has not featured as a significant aspect of recent British privatization policy, despite Government rhetoric. Kay and Thompson (1986) argue that competition was initially given more emphasis but that this degenerated into hollow words and subsequently the view that competition was undesirable. Their explanation is simple, revealing and damning:

> The clear theme to emerge from the political history of privatisation is that by far the most effective and influential of interest groups is the senior management of the potentially privatised industry. Their positive interest in privatisation is in being rid of what is seen as a burdensome form of Treasury control; their concurrent interests are in ensuring that this is achieved without change to the existing organisational structure and without a move to a more competitive environment.
>
> (Kay and Thompson 1986: 29)

The authors illustrate the success of senior management in achieving their aims by reference to British Telecom, British Airways and the British Airports Authority.

There is a claim in Vickers and Yarrow (1991) that competition re-emerged as a more important concern in the early 1990s, with electricity privatization.[7] Even so, the Kay and Thompson (1986) analysis clearly illustrates a stark inadequacy in recent policy. The British Government saw itself as extending the 'free market economy'. What this means is that the dominant elite within firms were able to influence situations and events for their own benefit. The community as a whole consequently suffered. It also means that the elite are in a secure position to impose their will both now and in the future.

The history of British privatization in the 1980s is thus a catalogue of missed opportunities. It was a time when large and important institutions received detailed attention. Yet the attention was not focused on fundamental areas. The Government was content to promote planning by the elite and a chance to introduce elements of a democratic market economy was lost. Supposing a case could be made for privatization, in line with democatizing the economy, escaping the clutches of the state bureaucracy, then the process has to be planned. What is needed is an overall strategy for transforming the structure of the economy. Whilst the regulation of the privatized state corporations appears today as a monopoly problem, the more fundamental issue is the planning problem. Structures appropriate to the evolution of a more democratic economy can be created most readily in the *ex ante* planning of a privatization process, rather than within the *ex post* regulation of its unplanned outcomes.

CONCLUSION

We have analysed the rationale for regulation within a framework of government strategies for fostering industrial development. The important parts of our discussion can be summarized in the following key points.

- Concentrated decision-making power in a 'free market economy' results in the elite planning for their benefit and without regard to the costs imposed on others.
- This planning system results in three sets of systemic deficiencies: transnationalism, centripetalism and short-termism.
- In seeking to overcome these deficiencies, government should establish, develop and stimulate a framework for community control.
- Community control entails an alternative planning framework, a regulated market system which can be fairly accurately described as a 'democratic market economy'.
- Using this rationale for regulatory activity, Britain's recent privatization and consequent regulation of firms and industries was an ill-conceived and inappropriately executed policy which favoured planning by the elite and thereby missed a valuable opportunity.

NOTES

1   The theoretical base for a wider concern with industrial policy was provided at a quite early date by Scitovsky's concept of pecuniary externalities, associated with economies operating away from equilibrium, see Scitovsky (1954). This had already been recognized as an issue of great practical significance in Rosenstein-Rodan's (1943) work on industrialization in Eastern and Southeast Europe and was developed as a doctrine of balanced growth or the big push by Nurkse (1953), Fleming (1955) and, most recently, Murphy *et al.* (1989). All these authors have focused on the industrialization of underdeveloped countries, but it will become apparent from our own analysis that their arguments and concepts have a similar resonance within the already advanced industrial countries. Linking the

two perspectives will form the basis of some of our future work.
2   We effectively assume that government is itself subject to democratic control. In practice, difficulties arising from concentrated decision-making power within the state apparatus must also be addressed.
3   We are actually characterizing a typical Anglo-American firm rather than a Japanese firm.
4   This is not to deny that structure is an important determinant of the consequences of collusion.
5   In this context Aoki (1990) makes an interesting distinction between the Japanese firm and the Anglo-American or hierarchical firm. In the former case, efficient and effective operation requires that incentives be related to firm's long-run organizational goals because all employees participate in decision-making, whereas in the latter case, since decisions are made elsewhere, this question does not arise. Which organizational mode actually works effectively in practice then becomes the central question. Aoki also theorizes the observed linkage between industrial firm and financial institution which again offers some insight into the issue of short-termism when contrasted with the linkage observed in the Anglo-American case. These matters will be pursued in future research.
6   The precise details of government's role are clearly something that need to be explored in considerable depth. We do not have the scope to do this here but it is worth emphasizing that we do not envisage a dominant role for the central state. See Chapter 8 by Chris Farrands and Peter Totterdill on this issue.
7   There is no suggestion that a greater concern with competition was motivated by the community control that we have been advocating.

REFERENCES

Aoki, Masahiko (1990) 'Toward an economic model of the Japanese firm', *Journal of Economic Literature*.

Berle, A.J. and Means, G.C. (1932) *The Modern Corporation and Private Property*, New York: Macmillan.

Cowling, Keith (1986) 'The internationalisation of production and de-industrialisation', in A. Amin and J. Goddard (eds) *Technological Change, Industrial Restructuring and Regional Development*, London: Allen & Unwin.

—— (1990) 'The strategic approach to economic and industrial policy', in Keith Cowling and Roger Sugden (eds) *A New Economic Policy for Britain*, Manchester: Manchester University Press.

Cowling, Keith and Sugden, Roger (1987) *Transnational Monopoly Capitalism*, Brighton: Wheatsheaf.

Cubbin, John and Leech, Dennis (1983) 'The effects of shareholding dispersion on the degree of control in British companies: theory and measurement', *Economic Journal*.

Dicken, Peter (1986) *Global Shift*, London: Harper & Row.

Fleming, J. Marcus (1955) 'External economies and the doctrine of balanced growth', *Economic Journal*.

GLC (1985) *London Industrial Strategy*, London: Greater London Council.

Graham, Cosmo (1991) 'Privatisation and company law', paper presented at *Workshop on Corporate Control and Accountability*, School of Law, University of Warwick.

Hymer, Stephen H. (1972) 'The Multinational corporation and the law of uneven development', in J.N. Bhagwati (ed.) *Economics and World Order*, London: Macmillan.

Kay, J., Mayer, C. and Thompson, D. (1986) *Privatisation and Regulation: The UK Experience*, Oxford: Clarendon Press.

Kay, J. and Thompson, D. (1986) 'Privatisation: a policy in search of a rationale', *Economic Journal*.

Knight, K.G. and Sugden, Roger (1990) 'Efficiency, economic democracy and company law', in Keith Cowling and Roger Sugden (eds) *A New Economic Policy for Britain*, Manchester: Manchester University Press.

Labour Research Department (1990) *Privatisation and Cuts: The Government Record*, London: Labour Research Department.

Lewchuck, W. (1986) 'The motor vehicle industry', in B. Elbaum and W. Lazonick (eds) *The Decline of the British Economy*, Oxford: Clarendon.

Moore, J. (1986) 'The success of privatisation', in J. Kay, C. Mayer and D. Thompson (eds) *Privatisation and Regulation*, Oxford: Clarendon Press.

Murphy, Kevin M., Shleifer, Andrei and Vishny, Robert W. (1989) 'Industrialization and the big push', *Journal of Political Economy*.

Nurkse, Ragnar, (1953) *Problems of Capital Formation in Underdeveloped Countries*, New York: Oxford University Press.

Pitelis, Christos and Sugden, Roger (1986) 'The separation of ownership and control in the theory of the firm: a reappraisal', *International Journal of Industrial Organization*.

Rosenstein-Rodan, Paul N. (1943), 'Problems of industrialisation of Eastern and South-eastern Europe', *Economic Journal*.

Scherer, F.M. (1980) *Industrial Market Structure and Economic Performance*, Chicago: Rand-McNally.

Scitovsky, Tibor (1954) 'Two concepts of external economies', *Journal of Political Economy*.

Sugden, Roger (1990) 'Strategic industries, community control and trans-national corporations', *International Review of Applied Economics*.

Thomas, H. (1982) 'The performance of the Mondragon cooperatives in Spain', in D.C. Jones and J. Svejnar (eds) *Participatory and Self-Managed Firms*, Lexington: Heath & Co.

Vickers, John and Yarrow, George (1988) *Privatisation and Economic Analysis*, Cambridge, Mass.: MIT Press.

—— (1991) 'Economic perspectives on privatisation', *Journal of Economic Perspectives*.

Zeitlin, M. (1974) 'Corporate ownership and control: the large corporations and the capitalist class', *American Journal of Sociology*.

Part III

INFORMATION

4

NATIONALIZATION AND THE BACKGROUND TO RECENT REGULATORY ISSUES

Martin Chick

In the literature on the economics of regulation, particular emphasis has been placed on the importance of the distribution of information between the regulator (principal) and the regulated (agent).[1] In Britain, asymmetries in the distribution of information within a principal–agent relationship were variously held to have affected the outcome, in terms of industrial structure, of the process of privatization, as well as acting as a significant influence on subsequent regulatory arrangements.[2] These asymmetries of information were seen as deriving from the monopoly structure of the nationalized industries. The purpose of this paper is to examine why British governments, in particular the 1945–51 Attlee Governments, took utility and basic sector industries into public ownership, and why the transfer to public ownership was frequently accompanied by the establishment of each nationalized industry as a monopoly with a centralized organization. Reading much of the principal–agent regulatory literature, the task of supervising national, centralized monopolies appears one that most economists would wish only on their worst enemies. In seeking to explain why British governments initiated such a series of principal–agent relationships between itself and publicly-owned monopoly industries, it is hoped to provide a background against which the more recent issues concerning regulation and information, considered elsewhere in this book, can be understood.

The increasing need of British governments to acquire information grew in line with their increasing political responsibility for the performance of basic sector and utility industries. Governments, perhaps aware of the limits of their effective powers, do not appear to have sought to increase the scope of their responsibilities. Rather, pressure from particular interest groups or widespread public concern about such issues as safety, pushed governments into accepting increased responsibility. In this sense, the nationalization programme of

63

1945–51 did not mark the beginning of public involvement in utility and basic sector industries,[3] but, in many ways, was the culmination of existing trends dating back to the nineteenth century. Concern with public safety and order had often provided an early occasion for the involvement of central and municipal authorities in utility industries. Firms wishing to lay underground gas pipes or electricity cables required certain statutory rights, with attendant obligations, from Parliament.[4] From the 1840s there had been an increasing tendency for legal provision to be made for the regulation of the tariffs, dividends and profit rates of utilities. Controls on the supply obligations of local gas and water utilities were also introduced,[5] these controls like the tariff, dividend and profit regulations largely coming in response to the emergence of *de facto* local monopolies in many towns and cities. From early on, there was an acceptance that utility monopolies would require some form of regulation, and that the operation of unregulated private monopolies in basic output, whether it be gas and water in the nineteenth century or salt in the seventeenth century, was politically unacceptable. Yet, in the nineteenth century, the effective arm's-length regulation of these privately-owned utilities proved difficult. Local interests closed ranks against perceived central interference and made both the monitoring and enforcement functions of regulation very difficult. This closing of ranks by producers denied government much of the information it required to regulate effectively. In addition, it became clear that the attempt to regulate so as to ensure a certain minimum quality (and availability) of service, in utilities like water, involved a more complex and closer form of regulation than controls on profits, dividends or certain physical aspects of production were likely to produce.

While the regulators may have been able to design a package of subsidies, profit controls and other incentives to draw a fuller service from private companies, their experience hitherto of arm's-length regulation disinclined local authorities to become involved with ever more complex regulatory arrangements. Dissatisfied with their experience of arm's-length regulation and lacking confidence in the willingness of private suppliers to meet their expectations, utility industries, beginning with water from the mid-nineteenth century, began to be characterized by a rising share of public ownership. By the twentieth century, the Labour Party was advocating public ownership as a means of obtaining much fuller information on the technical, financial and qualitative performance of utility industries and as a means of overcoming the apparent disinclination of private owners to extend the availability of their service beyond a certain point. Public ownership was presented as the answer to concerns which could be traced back to Joseph Chamberlain in 1874 and before.[6] As the Labour Party argued in 1946:

> In some cases it may be impossible to safeguard the public interest adequately without public ownership. Thus, it may be too dangerous, as with atomic energy or water (whose purity is all-important to health), to allow private capitalists to exploit a particular service; or at least the necessary inspectorate to supervise private industry may sometimes be far too expensive and cumbersome to tolerate.[7]

While the issues of safety and public health and dissatisfaction with the regulatory arrangements provided the main arguments for the public ownership of water, these concerns were not of equal importance in other industries. In the electricity industry, business and private consumer dissatisfaction with the inefficiency and consequent high prices of the industry pushed government into direct involvement in the industry in 1926, some twenty years before the Attlee Government's programme of nationalization. Again, interest group pressure forced a reluctant government to act. In the electricity industry, the municipalities' exercise of their statutory right to first option on the local supply franchise, meant that by the turn of the century they controlled twice as much of the industry's capacity as private enterprise.[8] Yet, this local public ownership of itself provided no guarantee of efficiency. With technological advances favouring larger-scale units, by the start of the twentieth century, many of the local supply areas were too small to exploit the optimum technology. Nevertheless, these local monopolies were doggedly defended by municipal authorities and private companies alike. It was the exposure of the industry's inefficiency during World War I, which prompted Parliament to establish the Electricity Commission in 1919, although the Commission had to rely on persuasion and encouragement to achieve the desired interconnection and bulk supply agreements. Without compulsory powers, progress was slow and within a few years, the Commissioners themselves were convinced that more positive government initiatives were needed.[9] Substantial reforms in the industry were planned by the minority Labour Government, and on returning to office in 1924, the Conservative Baldwin Government found itself faced with increasing dissatisfaction from industrial and other interest groups at the inefficiency and high prices of the electricity industry in Britain.

The political problem confronting the Baldwin Government was how to restructure the industry so as to exploit plant economies of scale but without forcibly transferring the generating section of the industry into public ownership. Its solution was to sanction the establishment of the Central Electricity Board (CEB) in 1926. The CEB was a state-financed body, which would be responsible for co-ordinating new power station planning and controlling power-station operation within 'the framework of a newly constructed national gridiron of high tension transmission lines'.[10] The advantage of constructing the grid network was that it would provide producers with the carrot of a potentially much larger market for an increased, cheaper output from larger sets, and the stick of facilitating competitive entry by other producers into each area's previously local monopoly. By vastly expanding both the market and the competition, the grid not only increased incentives but also increased the flow of information to both consumers (represented by the CEB) and producers through the operation of the competitive market. Indeed, if anything, the CEB as a monopsonist (sole purchaser) might well have been able to exploit the information asymmetries, both between itself and each generator, and also between the competing generators, to the CEB's advantage in its principal–agent relationship with each generator.

The ability to use a publicly-owned network to increase competition between previously local monopolies provided an important opportunity for government to promote efficiency through competition, but without stepping into the quagmire of issues surrounding ownership. Other industries, containing networks, where such a strategy might also be of use, included gas and telecommunications. However, there were other industries, like coal and steel, where such networks were not contained within the industry. In theory, the road system did provide a network for the two industries, but practical considerations of costs and speed of transport distinguished this network from that in telecommunications and electricity. Similar considerations of speed of use and the consequent capacity limits to extent of use also made the railway network less amenable to a CEB-style strategy.[11] However, the absence of internal networks did not prevent inter-war governments being drawn into involvement with such industries as iron and steel and, most notably, coal mining. Again, pressure from interest groups forced the government into greater involvement with each industry. In coal, the state proved responsive to lobbying on issues concerning labour and unemployment. As the official historian of the inter-war British coal industry has emphasized:

(Frequently) ... the ultimate roots of intervention lay in the desire to fend off a labour crisis ... (and) the government's consistent and perhaps overriding motive was to avoid any deepening of social distress or aggravation of industrial crisis.[12]

As in electricity, investigative commissions were employed to provide greater information to central government on the condition of the industry and the nature of its problems. Yet, while investigations 'laid bare'[13] the problems of the industry they did not make solutions any easier to find. In retrospect, the industry could be depicted as being in long-run decline across most of the twentieth century. Coal output was never again to be as high as in 1913, and the general trend across the inter-war period was for output to fall.[14] The response of owners was to place pressure both on manning and wage levels. When industrial disputes resulted, government often chose to ease their resolution by paying a subsidy. In 1921, following a previous subsidy of £34 million in 1917, a £10 million wage subsidy was provided as part of the efforts to resolve the national stoppage, with a further interim subsidy in 1924 being provided to resolve another industrial dispute. Yet subsidies could not prevent the continued fall in coal output, which by 1932 and 1933 was three-quarters of its 1913 level. Nor could subsidies remove the impact on employment within the industry. The average percentage of unemployed miners reached 34 per cent in 1932, and in some areas three out of four miners were out of work.[15] While the 1930s saw no equivalent of the wage subsidy of over £23 million of 1925–6, the government was steadily drawn ever deeper into involvement with the industry.[16]

Subsidies were not cheap and they neither addressed the fundamental problems of the industry nor bought its restructuring from the owners. A constant theme of the investigative reports on the coal industry was the industry's low productivity arising, in the main, from the fragmented structure of the industry. This point was re-echoed in internal Labour Party documents on the development of the coal industry[17] which pointed up the structural weaknesses of the industry. It noted that in the mid-1920s, of a total of 2,481 pits, one-third employed under 50 men, produced less than 1 per cent of total output and employed just over 1 per cent of total workers. Another third had from 50 to 500 workers, and produced one-sixth of total output. The 2,481 pits were owned by over 1,400 separate undertakings, and of these 685 employed under 100 workers each, and some 780 produced under 5,000 tons a year each. The mines were old and outworn – 4 of every

100 middle and large size pits were over 100 years old, 13 over 70 years, and another third over 50 years old. As a result, from the mid-1920s, when wartime declines had been overcome, to the cyclical maximum of 1936, output per man shift (OMS) rose by 118 per cent in The Netherlands, 81 per cent in the Ruhr, 54 per cent in Poland, but by only 14 per cent in Britain. By 1936, OMS averaged 35.94 cwt in The Netherlands and 33.66 cwt in the Ruhr, compared with only 23.54 cwt in Britain.[18] Improving the layout and organization of mines, as opposed to simply increasing mechanization, was seen as offering the greatest scope for productivity improvement in the British industry, facilitating as it would the concentration of production in the best mines and, within those mines, in the best seams, as well as extensive improvements in haulage and winding.[19]

The extent of government concern with the specific issue of efficiency in the coal industry should not, however, be over-emphasized. Unlike the electricity industry, consumers were not lobbying government about the level of coal prices. Moreover, any proposals for the rationalization of the industry threatened to exacerbate unemployment problems in the industry as mines were shut and more efficient mines made fewer calls on labour for similar levels of output. What forced government to address the problem of the restructuring of the industry was the political unacceptability of paying subsidies to private owners simply to enable them to prop up an inefficient industry.

Once political necessity had compelled government involvement in the issue of industrial restructuring, it also forced government to face the problem of the major obstacles to change presented by vested interests within the industry. The power of vested interests was of growing concern to political and economic commentators in the 1930s, as was implicitly acknowledged by Keynes in the now well-known concluding passage of *The General Theory*.

Practical men, who believe themselves to be quite exempt from any intellectual influences, are usually the slaves of some defunct economist. Madmen in authority, who hear voices in the air, are distiling their frenzy from some academic scribbler of a few years back. I am sure that the power of vested interests is vastly exaggerated compared with the gradual encroachment of ideas.... soon or late, it is ideas, not vested interests, which are dangerous for good or evil.[20]

The influence of vested interests in the coal industry was pervasive. Within Parliament, Part II of the Coal Mines Act of 1930, establishing the Coal Mines Reorganisation Commission which was to propound merger schemes which might become law, encountered sustained opposition from most owners. In the courts, the emergence of serious legal deficiencies in its powers, rendered it almost completely powerless. In 1935 a test case was heard before the Court of the Railway and Canal Commission whose decision made it clear that the powers of compulsion held by the Coal Mines Reorganisation Commission under the Coal Mines Act of 1930 were, in practice, non-existent.[21] Faced with the owners' general refusal to co-operate, the Commission found itself bereft of effective powers of enforcement. Much of the Commission's emasculation had occurred within Parliament, where the Bill to establish the Commission had taken a year and 88 Parliamentary Divisions to become law and emerged sadly mutilated (especially in the amalgamation clauses) at the hands of the opposition in both houses.[22] Further legislation attempted in 1936 encountered similar opposition, the first Bill raising such a storm that it was withdrawn. In short then, the instrument of amalgamation, the Reorganisation Commission, had encountered among coal owners 'a disposition to regard the Commission as a temporary inconvenience which need not be taken seriously'.[23] Only the semi-monopoly powers given by the Act were taken seriously, becoming permanent, not temporary features of the industry. In 1938, the number of firms was still 1,034 and the number of mines, 1,870.[24]

Such blocking by vested interests of proposed structural change was by no means confined to the coal mining industry. In the iron and steel industry, aspirant reformers like William Firth encountered very similar obstruction. Steel masters, sheltering behind tariffs, and establishing cost-pooling arrangements, preferred to preserve their own private financial interests ahead of any national interest. As one of the few and ultimately frustrated entrepreneurs within the industry, William Firth, remarked in 1934:

> Thirty years' close contact with the trade entitles me to believe that I understand its mentality ... and it is my recognition of the futility of hoping that individuals will subordinate their private interests to national interests that causes me to criticise the present scheme.[25]

The increasing concern with the power of vested interests during the 1930s and their ability to obstruct reforms within struggling industries led to a slow but mounting frustration with the activities of owners and a growing public and government disposition to listen more sympathetically to such groups as the mining unions. As Sir Ernest Gowers,[26] the oft-frustrated Chairman of the Coal Mines Reorganisation Commission reported to government in April 1935: 'public opinion is now ... sick of the obstructiveness of the old school of employers in coal, cotton and iron and steel.'[27] Increasing public and government familiarity with the blocking activities of vested interests increased the profile of the issue of ownership. Indicative of a toughening attitude towards the private owners was the passing of legislation in 1938, which transformed the powerless Coal Mines Reorganisation Commission into the Coal Commission and charged it with overseeing the public acquisition of mineral royalties, a task which it completed in 1942.

The outbreak of World War II intensified the relationship between government and industry and brought government into almost day-to-day contact with the industry's personnel and problems.[28] The wartime experience had the effect of steadily turning government and expert minds ever more towards the compulsory reform of the industry. Above all, the involvement of government with the industry, steadily drew officials into considering the industry's post-war future. Sir Ernest Gowers continued during the war to press the case for greater government intervention in the industry after the war.[29] The war strengthened the role of the Ministry of Fuel and Power, and brought in such temporary civil servants as John Fulton and Harold Wilson, who were less inclined to be circumspect in expressing their thoughts on the industry and its future than were perhaps permanent career civil servants. The general influx of Labour Party politicians into the wartime Cabinet in quite crucial positions meant that sitting below Churchill were supporters of the public ownership of the industry.

The war, by intensifying government–industry relations within the industry, also increased the availability of information about the industry within government. The information on the technical problems of the industry was increased by the publication of the Reid Report in 1945. This independent report, written by a committee of technical engineers who also had some senior managerial experience, re-emphasized the impact which the archaic layout of mines was having on the transport of coal and men and its consequent crippling effects on labour productivity. The impact of the Report lay not so much in what it reported about the industry as in the implications which many drew for what would have to be done if the condition of the industry was to be improved. To many the required improvement of the industry needed to be planned on a national basis, and this, with considerable restructuring and new investment, seemed to suggest that public ownership was a technical requirement for the reform of the industry.[30] As the Reid Report argued:

> It is evident to us that it is not possible to provide for the soundest and most efficient development and working of an area unless the conflicting interests of the individual colliery companies working the area are merged together into one compact and unified command of manageable size.[31]

The Reid Report itself did not advocate public ownership, but it did urge that a national authority be established to supervise the reorganization of the industry into optimum units. The election of the Labour Government ensured that such an authority would be provided through the nationalization of the industry.[32] Supported by railway, coal mining and other unions, there was little doubt that once in power, the Attlee Government would seek to push on with its plans for nationalization. Certainly, the Labour Party gave little thought to any possibility of realizing the necessary restructuring of the industry without transferring the industry from private to public ownership:

> Can this huge recasting of the industry's structure, demanded by the Reid Committee, the Scottish Coalfields Committee and others, ever be realised by the mine owners? The whole history of the industry since 1930 makes the idea laughable.... Nor will a revived, strengthened Coal Commission fit our needs. For if such bodies at last become effective, the coal-owners become useless appendages, playing no useful part in the industry but retaining some of their power to hamper and harass the controlling authorities.[33]

The transfer of ownership was seen by the Labour Government as providing one of the few remaining means of combating the obstruction of vested interest groups. This was true not only of coal, but also of other industries like electricity where wartime attempts to rationalize the supply industry foundered on the sharp political fact that 'rationalisation (though the necessity of it was now widely accepted) could not appeal to those who were to be rationalized out of existence'.[34] Iron and steel, textiles, and other basic sector and utility industries were all displaying similar symptoms to worrying degrees. On the one hand, encouragement of industries with tariff protection and price support was failing to persuade many existing owners to work towards a restructuring of their industries, and rationalization through collective agreement within federations was inevitably breaking down in the face of opposition from those threatened with closure. On the other hand, market forces were not driving small inefficient producers out of business, in part because of the tariff protection and price support being offered, but also because of the tenacious ability of small long-established firms with financial reserves and low debt gearing to survive difficult times and, at the same time, offer few attractions in terms of market share to stimulate attempted acquisitions by other firms.[35] If anything, as was evident in the iron and steel industry at the end of the 1920s, the firms most likely to be driven out of business were those attempting to expand and progress when, faced with a collapse in demand, they were still carrying very high debt commitments.[36]

When nationalization came, it came with a certain air of inevitability. In a sense, it was one of the few ideas which had not yet been tried or rejected by one or other influential body of opinion. It was common for such benefits as the provision of finance, better working conditions, and improved industrial relations to be associated with the coming of nationalization, but there was no logical reason why such benefits could not be achieved without transferring ownership. As has been seen, the inter-war period was riddled with instances of government's ability to provide finance and wage subsidies to privately owned industries. Ultimately, the main reason for transferring ownership was that by doing so government was able to break the power of vested private interests which had for so long blocked the restructuring of industries. In turn, the rationale for such restructuring was the perceived need to improve the technical efficiency of industries. Yet, considerations of technical efficiency had not been what had first occasioned government contact with these industries. Rather, the beginnings of such sustained contact often came in response to lobbying by interest groups, whether industrialists concerned at the price of electricity or miners worried about wage levels and employment prospects. It was only as government was steadily drawn into clearer and more frequent contact with the industries that the issue of efficiency began to come to the fore. In its transfer of ownership, nationalization could make an important one-off contribution to the attempt to improve efficiency. But in its dominant concern for the issue of ownership, nationalization had little to contribute to the more long-term question of how to operate and organize nationalized industries. The act of nationalization represented the culmination of over half a century of increased government involvement in basic sector and utility industries. While nationalization reflected much of what had happened in the past, it had reflected little on what might happen in the future.

In retrospect, two central features of the structure and organization of the newly nationalized industries merit particular consideration. Firstly, why was it that when nationalization occurred, the entire industry was taken into public ownership, and why were the industries established as monopolies, which minimized the use of market mechanisms, both internally and externally? Did a transfer of ownership also have to mean an extension of monopoly? Secondly, having established a national, monopoly industry, why was the organization of that industry on a centralized basis preferred to some more decentralized alternative? The retrospective interest in these two questions stems from the fact that, from the principal–agent viewpoint, the state (principal) would appear to have actively sought to create not only a series of monopoly industries (agents) but also highly centralized industries in which information was asymmetrically distributed strongly in favour of the agent.

The issue of why the act of nationalizing an industry was frequently accompanied by its establishment as a monopoly is related in part to the issue of ownership. When, as with coal, the transfer of the entire industry into public ownership was in part taken to break the resistance of vested interests to the restructuring of the industry, it did leave the state as sole owner of the industry. Ostensibly, a monopoly existed to the extent that there was no competition for the provision of coal within Britain. However, if the issue of ownership was itself a driving force behind the nationalization of the coal industry in monopoly form, this was not true of all the industries which were taken into public ownership as newly-formed monopolies. The establishment of the CEB in 1926 had demonstrated the scope which existed for overcoming vested interests impediments to increased efficiency in industries containing networks by promoting competition amongst producers but without changing ownership. However, where industries – gas, telecommunications – contained such networks, there does not appear to have been extensive discussion among the Labour Party or immediate post-war government committees of the idea of extending the CEB model to other industries. If anything, the existence of a natural monopoly network within an industry was sometimes sloppily taken as indicating that the entire industry was therefore a monopoly. There were not long discussions as to which natural monopolies could facilitate competition among suppliers to the network (electricity, gas, telecommunications) and those which could not (rail). To a considerable extent, this reflects differences in outlook and attitude towards markets, competition and monopoly between those existing today and those which prevailed in the 1940s.

That the Attlee Government was aware of the danger of the abuse of monopoly power seems reasonably clear. It was the Attlee Government which established the Monopolies and Restrictive Practices Commission in 1948, thereby enacting a promise made in the Employment Policy White Paper[37] of 1944 which noted the 'growing tendency' in recent years towards price, output and market agreements among manufacturers, although 'such agreements or combines do not necessarily operate against the public interest; the power to do so is there.'[38] The persistence of cartels, vested interests quotas and price-fixing inclined many, within and outside the Labour Party, to identify the growth of effective monopoly as an important characteristic of economic development during the first half of the twentieth century:

> The growth of monopoly and the decline of competition have been significant and persistent features of the British economy for the past half century. Apart from different forms of imperfect competition, two principal types of monopolistic organisations are customarily distinguished. The first of these is the giant combine or trust, created by amalgamations, by the formation of holding companies or, more loosely, by interlocking directorates and joint working agreements. The second type of organisation is the restrictive trade association or cartel, a grouping of independent firms employing such restrictive practices as price fixing, output allocation, the scrapping of productive capacity, restriction of entry into the trade, or other penal practices designed to secure the enforcement of agreements.[39]

The iron and steel industry was frequently cited as an example of the first type of monopolistic organization, that which was characterized by interlocking directorates. The 1948 Labour Party internal research paper on the iron and steel industry argued that the ramifications of these interlocking directorates were 'widespread':

> The Directors of the Big Six control about 100 subsidiaries and hold about 600 seats on the boards of other companies. For example, the Earl of Dudley holds 21 Directorships, Lord Greenwood 17, Menzies-Wilson 21, A G Steward 19, S R Beale 20, Sir James Craig 21.[40]

Both the iron and steel industry and the inter-war coal industry could be cited as examples of the second type of monopolistic organization, the restrictive trade association or cartel. Moreover, within industries like iron and steel, the increasing capital intensity of production and the increasing cost of plant were held to increase the tendencies for producers to come to price and output agreements.[41] Allied to this concern with cartels, there was also scepticism about the scope for, and effectiveness of, the operation of 'free markets'. With the inter-war experience of unemployment and the failure of self-reform in many basic sector industries as a background, the traditional advantages and capabilities claimed for market mechanisms were regarded by many with some scepticism. Faith in competition as an agent of change and spur to efficiency was reduced by the view that genuine competition often did not exist. Any concern that might have existed at the state establishment of industrial monopolies was tempered by the view that 'free markets' already and increasingly contained informal monopolies. The Labour Party did not regard the abandonment of competition and the 'free market' system as major losses, since the 'free market' system frequently did not operate as its supporters claimed.

There was also the continued suspicion of the influence of vested interests which reached into the civil service and prompted civil servants to press for the extension of publicly-owned monopolies across industrial sectors. In arguing for the National Transport Commission (NTC) to be established as a monopoly, civil servants in 1946 were stressing the danger that otherwise might be expected from outside vested interests:

> The argument of the first school is that unless NTC has the widest possible monopoly from the outset independent vested interests (with the present anomalies of different bases of charges) will be perpetuated and strengthened and effective co-ordination made progressively more difficult; it follows, therefore, that the NTC must have an initial and absolute monopoly.[42]

Thus, while the Attlee Government presided over the formal establishment of monopolies, the abandonment of competition was held to be a theoretical rather than a practical loss. While strongly alive to the dangers of monopoly, the Attlee Government was prepared to establish nationalized industries as monopolies, because monopoly was in many cases, almost regarded as being inevitable. If monopoly was inevitable, then better that it be transferred into the hands of government and operated in the public interest. As an internal Labour Party research paper put it in 1946, 'for economic and political reasons monopolies are objectionable and should, other things being equal, be transferred to public ownership'.[43]

Implicit in such arguments was the assumption that by transferring a monopoly into public ownership, the fact of ownership would provide the means of effective control. That, in short, if you owned something, you also controlled it. This assumption of ownership providing control also suffused much of the thinking on the counter-cyclical use of the nationalized industries' capital investment programmes so as to help maintain the level of effective demand within the economy.[44] Early assumptions concerning the ability of government to check monopoly abuse by nationalized industries also influenced the Attlee Government's decisions to centralize the organization of most nationalized industries and discouraged the greater development of market mechanisms within the nationalized monopolies, thereby denying itself a source of information on such matters as the level and structure of demand, future capacity requirements and the comparative technical efficiency of component operations within the industry.

The questions of how the industries should be organized and of how much use should be made of market mechanisms, were, to some extent, related. In the persistent arguments over the appropriate mix of administrative and planning mechanisms which characterized much of the Attlee Government's period in office, the advocates of making greater use of market mechanisms also favoured more decentralized forms of organization. Such thinking, notably by James Meade, one-time Director of the Cabinet Economic Section and by the civil servant, Philip Chantler, at the Ministry of Fuel and Power, did on occasions draw wavering support from the Treasury and from the likes of Hugh Gaitskell. The Treasury was certainly prepared to consider a less strongly centralized nationalized electricity industry than the one which emerged.[45] Yet, such decentralized views were firmly and effectively opposed by Herbert Morrison, who, as Lord President, had overall responsibility for the nationalization programme. Morrison not only favoured a strongly centralist form of organization, but was also withering in his attacks on economists who suggested that more use might be made of pricing mechanisms in guiding resource allocation.

Morrison's opposition to the greater use of market mechanisms explicitly stemmed from his wish to secure outcomes in the pricing and distribution of public utility output which might well not arise from a freer operation of market mechanisms. In general, he wished to make the output of many of the newly nationalized industries widely accessible at relatively low uniform prices. This was not simply a private concern of Morrison's but had been a long-standing aim of the Labour Party. Ever since the 1920s the Labour Party had looked to industries like electricity as providing the means of freeing workers from the drudgery of repetitive, manual work, and of encouraging a leveling process between classes within society.[46] Moreover, promises of cheap domestic electricity for the working classes and the spread of electrification to the rural areas were thought likely to win votes for the Labour Party. This keenness to see reasonably uniform prices and the extension of supply to more difficult areas had led Morrison in his 1932 proposals for the merger of the electricity industry to favour a national organization for the industry.[47] One means of facilitating the uniformity of prices was to establish a cental fund for price equalization and standardization. By 1942, when such an idea was seriously considered by industrialists like Sir Andrew Duncan,[48] the wartime Minister of Supply, middle opinion was beginning to edge closer to Morrison's thinking. Although such central pooling of prices and cost information with its perceived blurring of some efficiency data within the industry had its contemporary critics,[49] it can be seen as merely a continuation and extension of pre-war and wartime developments.

In the coal industry, moves towards cost pooling, price arrangements and national wage-bargaining had been occurring since at least the start of the 1930s. The Coal Mines Act had introduced schemes for the control of output and sales, thereby opening the way to cartelization and price maintenance, while by 1935–6 the government was prepared to lend support to calls from the Miners' Federation of Great Britain for national wage-determination.[50] This general drift towards national pooling arrangements was intensified during World War II. Government took an active interest in restraining the wartime price of coal, and in the autumn of 1940, the War Emergency Assistance Scheme 'provided for a levy on coal to form a fund to compensate those collieries which, by reason of the War, produced less than their pre-war share of output.'[51] Then, in June 1942 the creation of the Coal Charges Account transferred the administration of levies and allocations from the owners to the Ministry of Fuel and Power. Moreover, as in World War I, the industry's prices were adjusted to cover its costs, proceeds and profits were pooled, and high-cost districts were helped by a transfer of funds from the more profitable areas.[52]

During the war, it also became clear that whatever new system was devised for settling miners' wages, these wages would be settled by a national body.[53] With wage disputes between the miners and the owners continuing during the war, the War Cabinet was persuaded by the Ministry of Fuel and Power that the government would need to intervene in the determination of a new wage structure, especially as wage settlements had to be paid for by the Coal Charges Account, and thereby passed on in increased coal prices. The result was the national wages agreement (signed on 20 April 1944) which not only drew the government into direct involvement in the industry, but also marked the abandonment of the procedure for wage determination which had been created in 1921, and which had both related wage levels to the profitability of the industry and allowed them to be determined within the various districts.[54] In turn, the development of national wage agreements encouraged union organization on a national basis, the National Union of Mineworkers coming into existence on 1 January 1945. Thus, both prices and wages had been further removed from having any relation to local costs and efficiency. Subsidies were paid automatically on the basis of output thereby ignoring the differing profit potential of the recipient firms. The flat-rate addition to wages which followed the Greene Board's recommendations had very unequal effects on the tonnage costs of different enterprises and rather than attempt to cover these by differential price increases, firms were compensated for costs actually incurred from an industry-wide levy. As district costs of production rose unevenly, these costs were met not by allowing varying price increases on a district basis, but by increasing the national levy and price, pooling the proceeds in the Coal Charges Account, and paying 'price allowances' to the weaker districts.

The nationalization programme of the Attlee Government had not simply involved the transfer of ownership, but also the establishment of publicly-owned industries as monopolies with a generally strong centralized organization. In part, this move towards national, centralized pricing and wage structures can be discerned in inter-war and wartime developments in such industries as coal mining. Given the scepticism with which market mechanisms were viewed by many, ministers like Morrison and Shinwell (Minister of Fuel and Power) were able to push for centralized, national organizations, often with accompanying national wage, cost and price pooling arrangements. This form of centralized organization did of course place increased weight on the administrative capabilities and functions of managers, who were effectively left to operate an organization in which information on local costs and efficiency had, to some extent, been suppressed. It also placed much of the information on the internal operation of the industry in the hands of central managers.

In the balance of relations between ministers and the managers of the nationalized industries, there was a distinct asymmetry in the distribution of information in the managers' favour. The suppression of market mechanisms within the nationalized industries increased the number of matters which came before central managers for their administrative decision, as well as making it difficult for a minister to obtain information from other than the industry's managers with which to question their decisions. In part, this had not been foreseen as a problem since the very public corporation form of Minister–industry relationship not only emphasized the right of managers to manage at 'arm's-length' from government, but also seemed to imply that the public-spirit of nationalized industry managers would not lead them to exploit their monopoly position. Information asymmetries were not a problem so long as minister and industry were in agreement. Problems arose when, as in the electricity industry, the minister, Hugh Gaitskell, thought that the electricity industry managers were using low prices to inflate demand and their own capital investment programme in a period of shortages of capital investment resources. In the subsequent struggle to reform the industry's tariff structure, Gaitskell was effectively defeated by the industry. Not only would the industry not release information on price elasticities which Gaitskell needed to fight his case, but the managers lack of co-operation in publicising the half-hearted seasonal differential which was introduced, ensured the failure of Gaitskell's attempt to price out some excess demand.[55]

Many of these issues increasingly vexed politicians and managers after 1951. The issue of the appropriate organization for the nationalized industries and the search for a suitable mix of centralized and decentralized structures rumbled on for years. Even during the very first years of the National Coal Board's existence the issue helped to provoke resignations from the Board, while in 1958, in response to fears of 'over-centralization' the British Electricity Authority was split into the Electricity Council (with powers similar to those of the Gas Council) and the Central Electricity Generating Board (which controlled the production and distribution of electricity).[56] Similarly, such issues as the appropriate pricing and financing arrangements for the nationalized industries were to continue to provoke argument well beyond the 1940s.

In time, the problems implicit in Morrison's public corporation arrangement became explicit. The difficulties of legislatively expecting a minister to conduct effective 'arm's-length' supervision of a monopoly industry became apparent, but did not precipitate any fundamental reforms. Although the Select Committee on Nationalised Industries reported in 1968 of 'lack of clarity', 'confusion of responsibilities' and of 'a failure to understand and to work towards the fulfilment of the basic purposes of Ministerial control in respect of industries',[57] little was done to dispel the confusion. Indeed, it is questionable whether Parliament, and to lesser extent, ministers, ever really sought effective supervisory powers over nationalized industries. The Select Committee on Nationalised Industries which, after much hesitation, was established by the House of Commons in 1955, was originally intended simply to provide a means of improving the parliamentary accountability of the industries. Again, as with the inter-war coal industry, what moves there were towards a closer monitoring of the industries and an analysis of fundamental issues like pricing policies were driven by the Treasury's concern at the cost of providing finance to certain nationalized industries. Yet, such financial reviews did not directly address such issues as productivity. Proposals that a more independent Efficiency Audit Commission[58] be established to take scrutiny of the nationalized industries' performance beyond a financial assessment were opposed by the industries.[59] While the Treasury and Ministers variously attempted to change investment levels in the interests of countercyclical stability,[60] they exhibited little interest in monitoring individual project decisions even when pressed to do so by the Select Committee.[61] Significantly, when privatization did come in the 1980s, it was prompted more by financial than productivity considerations, priorities which were explicit in the sale of industries as monopolies and duopolies.

It might be tempting to conclude that history has simply come full circle. Once again, utilities have returned to a private, regulated existence, even if in a more concentrated form than those of Victorian Britain. Public ownership may come and go, but concentrated industrial structures would appear to persist, and with them all of the informational problems afflicting their regulation. Yet, such a quick reading of history may prove misleading. While it is true that many industries were transferred into private ownership as monopolies and duopolies, the subsequent activities of a distinctly unusual and determined group of regulators has made it seem more likely that many utility industries will contain a greater degree of competition than seemed likely when they were privatized. What is striking in this respect is the current move back towards 1926 CEB-style solutions, most notably in the privatization of electricity itself, but also as suggested in recent papers from the Department of Trade and Industry concerning the longer-term structure of the telecommunications industry. Of interest here also, is the increasing use made by Ofgas and some other regulators of the British legal system as a means both of extracting information from the regulated industry and of drawing attention to the concentrated structure of the regulated industry. Such use of the judicial system is relatively new, and marks a move towards an American-style use of courts as a counter-balance to the lobby power of concentrated industries.

Lying behind much of these moves towards securing increased competition is the greater faith placed in market mechanisms by current politicians compared with their equivalents in the 1940s. Whether or not such a view of market mechanisms is as optimistic as that in the 1940s was pessimistic, the indications are that government is keen to shed responsibility for the performance of industries which it cannot control. However, the irony may be that while the issue of structure proves less enduring than first appeared, that concerning responsibility and ownership may continue to dog governments. The drift to public ownership came in part in response to increasing dissatisfaction with the regulation of utility industries. The public minimum requirements of utility industries, in particular, in terms of quality, price, and availability of service, proved too complex for regulators to meet. If, despite shedding ownership, government is still held to have some responsibility for the economic and qualitative performance of utility industries, and if regulatory structures cannot be designed which satisfy public expectations, then it is not inconceivable that the drift towards some form of public or municipal ownership may begin again. History may not repeat itself, but its fundamental issues and problems have a nasty habit of recurring.

NOTES AND REFERENCES

1 Early contributions to the development of the principal–agent approach with its concern with information included: S. Ross 'The economic theory of agency: the principal's problem'. *American Economic Review*, 1973, 63(2) May, pp. 134–9; J. Mirrlees, 1974, 'Notes on welfare economics, information and uncertainty', in M.S. Balch, D.L. McFadden and S.Y. Wu (eds) *Contributions to Economic Analysis*. Amsterdam: North Holland; J. Mirrlees, 1976. 'The optimal structure of incentives and authority within an organisation', *Bell Journal of Economics*, 7(1) Spring, 105–31; J.E. Stiglitz (1975) 'Incentives, risk and information: notes towards a theory of hierarchy', *Bell Journal of Economics* 6(2) Autumn, 552–79. More recently, see J. Vickers and G. Yarrow, *Privatisation: An Economic Analysis*, MIT Press, London 1988.

2 J. Kay and D. Thompson, 'Privatisation: a policy in search of a rationale', *Economic Journal*, 1986, 96, pp. 18–32.

3 In 1944, 36.8 per cent of gas sales were made by local authorities, while in the electricity supply industry the publicly owned sector accounted for some 60 per cent of the industry measured in terms of employment. Sir Norman Chester, *The Nationalisation of British Industry, 1945–51*, HMSO London, 1975, pp. 16–17.

4 Op. cit.

5 Robert Millward and Robert Ward, 'The Costs of Public and Private Gas Enterprises in late-nineteenth century Britain', *Oxford Economic Papers*, 39, (1987), no. 4, 719–37.

6 Bob Millward, 'Emergence of gas and water monopolies in nineteenth century Britain: contested markets and public control' in James Foreman-Peck (ed), *New Perspectives on the late-Victorian economy*, (Cambridge University Press, 1991).

7 Labour Party Archive, R.D. 33/November 1946, *Criteria for Nationalisation*. The passage continued 'Then the Government may want to prevent excessive profiteering in "industries" like football pools or greyhound racing but be unable to do so, without an unduly large central apparatus except through public ownership.'

8 L. Hannah, 'A Pioneer of Public Enterprise: The CEB and the National Grid, 1927–40' in Barry Supple, *Essays in British Business History* (Clarendon, Oxford 1977).

9 Ibid., p. 208.

10 Ibid., p. 210.

11 The idea of operating a 'leasing' scheme in the railway industry in the nineteenth century did not make much progress. Even if contractors had been allowed to run trains on railways owned by a 'common carrier', the remaining problem of regulation appeared to be considerable. J.S. Foreman-Peck, 'Natural Monopoly and Railway Policy in the Nineteenth Century', *Oxford Economic Papers*, 39 (1987) no. 4, 699–718.

12 Barry Supple, *The History of the British Coal Industry, vol. 4* (Oxford, Clarendon Press) 1987, pp. 339–41.

13 Labour Party, 'Coal', R.D. 8/November, 1945.

14 C.H. Feinstein, *Statistical Tables of National Income, Expenditure and Output of the U.K., 1855–1965*, Cambridge, University Press, 1976, Table 51.

15 Supple 1987 op. cit., p. 274.

16 Ibid., p. 284.

17 Labour Party, *Coal*, R.D. 8/November, 1945.

18 Ministry of Fuel and Power, *Coal Mining: Report of the Technical Advisory Committee*, Cmd. 6610 (Reid Report), 1945, p. 29. See William Ashworth. *The History of the British Coal Industry, vol. 5, 1946–1982: The Nationalised Industry*. (Oxford, Clarendon Press, 1986).

19 Supple 1987 op. cit., p. 285. He also notes that the *Reid Report*, 16–18, pointed out that improvements in OMS did not depend on intensified mechanization.

20 John Maynard Keynes, *The General Theory of Employment, Interest and Money*, (Macmillan, Cambridge University Press, London and Basingstoke, 1981 reprint of 1974 paperback edition), pp. 383–4.

21 Ben Fine, *The Coal Question: Political Economy and Industrial Change from the Nineteenth Century to the Present Day* (Routledge, London and New York) 1990, p. 20.

22 Labour party, R.D. 8/November, 1945. *Coal*.

23 Ibid.

24 Supple 1987 op. cit., p. 302.

25 Labour Party, *British Steel at Britain's Service*, R.D. 140/August 1948.

William Firth, letter to *The Times*, 22 February 1934.

26 Chairman of both the Coal Mines Reorganisation Commission from 1930 and of its successor, the Coal Commission, from 1938.

27 Supple 1987 op. cit., p. 347. Public Record Office. COAL 12/12.

28 Legislation in June 1942 provided a wartime system of dual control for the industry. Collieries remained in private ownership but the Ministry of Fuel and Power became responsible for the general oversight of the industry, a role which included providing technical advice to pits on the best means of improving efficiency and production.

29 Supple 1987 op. cit., p. 612.

30 Ibid., pp. 617–8.

31 Reid Report, 137–8. Quoted in Ashworth, *British Coal* vol. 5, p. 8.

32 Since January 1918. Clause IV of the Labour Party's constitution had stated the party's commitment: 'To secure for the producers by hand and brain the full fruits of their industry, and the most equitable distribution thereof that may be possible, upon the basis of the common ownership of the means of production and the best obtainable system of popular administration and control of each industry or service.'

33 Labour Party, R.D. 8/November 1945, *Coal*.

34 Hannah, *Electricity Before Nationalisation*, Macmillan, London, 1979, p. 342.

35 Supple 1987 op. cit., pp. 310–11.

36 P.L. Payne, *Colvilles and the Scottish Steel Industry* (Oxford, Clarendon Press, 1979), pp. 225–7.

37 *Employment Policy*, Cmd. 6527, May 1944.

38 Ibid., para. 54. Margaret Hall, 'Monopoly policy' in G.D.N. Worswick and P.H. Ady, *The British Economy, 1945–50* (Oxford, Clarendon Press) 1952, p. 399.

39 Labour Party, *The Public Control of Monopoly*, R.D. 44/February 1947.

40 Labour Party, *British Steel at Britain's Service*, R. D. 140/August 1948.

41 Ibid.

42 Quoted in Chester 1975 op. cit., p. 396. Minute to the Permanent Secretary 8/1/46.

43 Labour Party, R.D. 33/November 1946, *Criteria for Nationalisation*.

44 Such an idea was contained, for example, in the memorandum written by the Economic Section of the Cabinet at the end of 1945, and in which the hand of James Meade was clearly present. See 'The socialisation of industries. Memorandum by the Economic Section of the Cabinet Secretariat' in Susan Howson (ed.), *The Collected Papers of James Meade, vol. II: Value, Distribution and Growth.* (Unwin, Hyman, London 1988) p. 75.

45 See Chester 1975, op. cit., p. 418.

46 Hannah 1979 op. cit., p. 330.

47 Ibid., p. 332.

48 Duncan had previously been Chairman of the CEB before becoming Chairman of the British Iron and Steel Federation in 1935.

49 Meade 1988 op. cit., p. 73.

50 Supple 1987 op. cit., p. 340.

51 Ibid., 518.

52 Ibid.
53 Ibid., p. 534.
54 Ibid., p. 577.
55 See Martin Chick, 'Marginal Cost Pricing and the Peak-Hour Demand for Electricity', in Martin Chick (ed.) *Governments, Industries and Markets* (Aldershot, Elgar) 1990.
56 The change was recommended in the Herbert Committee's *Report of the Committee of Inquiry into the Electricity Supply Industry* (1956) Cmd. 9672. For criticism of the split see A.E. Thompson in 'Organisation in Two Nationalised Industries: Fleck vz. Herbert', *Scottish Journal of Political Economy* 4, (1957) 81–100.
57 Select Committee on National Industries, session 1967–8, para. 875. See Leonard Tivey (ed.) *The Nationalised Industries Since 1960* (London, George Allen & Unwin) 1973, p. 205.
58 Professor W.A. Robson was one keen advocate of the establishment of an Efficiency Audit Commission. In his evidence to the Select Committee on Nationalised Industries, session 1967–8, pp. 534–6, para 15, he stated: 'I do not believe that the professional audit used for the nationalised industries serves any important purpose beyond ensuring that financial regulatory and honesty are observed in their administration.'
59 See Select Committee on Nationalised Industries session 1967/8) for nationalized industries' objections to an Efficiency Audit Commission. (Vol. III, Appendices 32, 33, 35, 37, 38, 40).
60 As proposed in the 1944 White Paper on Employment Policy.
61 William Shepherd, *Economic Performance Under Public Ownership*, (New Haven and London, Yale University Press, 1965) p. 31. In a footnote Shepherd notes how the Select Committee has grown quite critical of the Treasury's and the Ministry's reluctance to monitor and thereby accept partial responsibility for individual investment projects; see especially, the reports on coal and British Railways; also the Committee's report, *Outcome of Recommendations and Conclusions*, House of Commons. 116 (1962).

5

REGULATORS' NEED FOR QUALITY INFORMATION AND THE PROVISION OF BUS SERVICES IN SCOTLAND

George Harte

This chapter examines the general question of regulators' need for quality information by focusing on an industry which was regulated from 1930, but which was partially deregulated (particularly in respect of economic matters) in 1985. By focusing on an industry which has been, and still is to some extent, regulated, it is hoped to cover matters of interest and relevance to the regulation of bus services as well as more general contemporary developments in economic regulation.

Unlike most of the contributions to this book, the focus of this chapter will be on the accounting information used in regulation. The contribution of accounting information in regulation of the private sector has not previously been widely researched. Searches of traditional accounting indexing services such as Anbar and The Accountant's Index revealed very little on the topic of accounting information in regulation. In addition further searching of economics literature indices, focusing particularly on the regulators of the bus industry, the Traffic Commissioners, was as unfruitful.

In one of the few references to the subject Tinker (1985: 110) suggests that accounting research has excluded enquiries into the role of accounting in regulatory economic activity, despite the fact that 'accounting data has superseded competition as the chief arbiter of society's resources' (Scott 1933: 225). Thus despite its apparent increased importance in economic activity in a regulated environment, particularly where resource allocation and prices are to depend on accounting costs or balance sheet asset values, this subject has received relatively little attention in accounting circles. This chapter is an attempt to redress this imbalance.

Although it may be tempting to do so, this chapter does not attempt to develop a model of accounting for regulators' needs. Rather it focuses on what has been reported to regulators in a particular industry, examining this in light of recent debates concerning the nature and form (quality) of accounting information. Our main concern is with the difficulties of developing a model of accounting for regulators' needs. Since there is little or no previous empirical work on which to draw, and, as we will see, because of changes in the organization and staffing of the regulators, this chapter concentrates on what legislation has specified in terms of accounting information, and what accounting information has been contained in annual reports and accounts.

Although the research conducted is limited I will suggest that there is evidence to support Scott's view that accounting data is in less demand in a deregulated environment. In the case of the Scottish bus industry it would appear that accounting reports played a greater role prior to 1985. It would seem that increased competition and partial deregulation have resulted in a reduction in the collection of accounting information. However as our discussion of the nature and form (quality) of accounting information will suggest, there is scope for addressing the question of the very focus of financial accounting for economic regulation, in particular the way in which accounting defines the agenda for debate and discussion in a particularly narrow financial and quantitative manner. We will examine the case for a more sensitive accounting which attempts to portray a fuller picture of economic and social activity, which in the case of the bus industry would cover the wider economic, social and environmental impact of individual bus companies.

We must also recognize that the bus industry differs from many of the privatized ex-nationalized industries, where Scott's view seems likely to fit new regulated circumstances. In those cases where there has been privatization without the introduction of substantial competition, the issues discussed here would appear to take on added significance. Our focus on the Scottish bus industry reveals change from a more highly regulated industry to one which is effectively deregulated in economic terms. For many of the privatized nationalized industries we have seen continued regulation, rather than reduced, in the context of limited competition.

REGULATION

Regulation has grown in importance in this country since the spate of privatizations of the 1980s which reduced the extent of public sector ownership. The creation of huge private monopolies has been accompanied by new forms of government control, with the creation of Ofwat, Ofgas etc. In many respects privatization and deregulation have been major planks of economic policy of recent Conservative Governments, appearing to illustrate Gramsci's passive revolution from above developed through the apparatus of the state (Humphrey and Scapens 1990). Such policies have stressed the economic over the social, and further emphasized the importance of economic calculation (Hopwood 1986), and so not surprisingly intensified the focus on accounting numbers and accountants as providing solutions.

I do not intend exploring the subject of economic regulation in great depth, since many of the other chapters will do so. However for our purposes we can see economic regulation as 'control of an industrial activity by government' (Waterson 1988: 2). Schultz and Alexandroff (1985) discuss the meaning of economic regulation further by referring to various definitions which draw on matters such as the setting of rules by government regarding economic activity, the essential function of government, an attempt to modify economic behaviour significantly, an attempt to affect the relationships in and results of private markets, and public intervention by way of non-market controls.

It seems likely that regulation can take various forms, particularly as a result of different intentions. Some regulation may be designed to benefit consumers, whereas other regulation would seem to protect the interests of (parts of) the industry concerned, whether by design or otherwise (see, for instance, the discussion of regulatory capture in Chapter 1). And logically therefore we would expect the accounting information collected to vary according to the purpose.

In general in Britain today there appears to be an emphasis on consumers' interests, with rate of return and price regulation most prominent, particularly where there is an attempt to control monopoly power (see for instance Chapter 6). Both would seem likely to be of interest to accountants, and to some extent rely on accounting information to be effective, particularly as accounting reports concentrate substantially on matters such as costs, revenues, investment in assets and finance (capital and liabilities). However, the extent of collection and use of accounting information in regulation is an empirical question which appears surprisingly to have been rarely addressed by accounting researchers. The increasing importance and potential for economic regulation, and the importance of economic calculation in society would lead one to expect a great deal more interest than is evident.

Regulation has often stemmed from the (lack of) impact of privatization

tion on competition and the (continued) existence of imperfect competition in particular (see for example Chapter 3). By imperfect competition we may mean incomplete competition, or perhaps a concern that parties operating in the market and dealing with a 'monopoly' may not be fully informed. For example consumers and workers must rely on companies to provide relevant information for their needs (Peacock 1984). More recently public concern has raised the possibility of companies having to disclose details of their environmental impact. Thus information availability is seen as an important aspect of market operation.

In addition the intention of some regulation may be to focus on externalities imposed by a monopoly supplier, a subject which is always likely to cause some difficulty to traditional accounting. Although externalities would not feature in traditional accounting reports, there have over the years been attempts to account for these in various ways as part of a social audit or social report (see Gray *et al.* 1987, chapters 5–7). Recently however externalities have become a matter of importance to even accountants in practice. In particular the need to recognize the possible future financial consequences which could arise from current actions which are harmful to the environment brings such externalities, and their financial consequences in particular, within the scope of traditional financial accounting (Gray 1991).

This chapter is primarily concerned with the role of accounting information in the economic regulation of Scottish bus services by the State. In some respects this interest can be seen to parallel the more popular concern in accounting research with understanding the operation of management accounting in organizations. Here concern with the potential for accounting information systems to facilitate control from the centre, at a distance, suggests that although there has been relatively little concern shown by researchers in accounting and economic regulation we can use some of the ideas of such critical management accounting research to examine what little we do know about accounting and economic regulation. In addition critical debates concerning the portrayal of economic reality in external corporate accounting reports are also of interest, since our focus on quality of accounting information in regulation can be expressed as a concern with the extent to which such financial accounting portrays an acceptable picture of economic reality. The following section discusses the quality of information for regulation by drawing on both of these areas of accounting research. In particular we focus on the accounting profession's concern with the relationship between economic reality and financial accounting, as illustrated by the conceptual framework debate.

QUALITY OF INFORMATION FOR REGULATION

Although there has apparently been little research conducted on the quality of accounting information for regulation, there has been recognition of the importance of regulators as users of accounting information (e.g. American Accounting Association 1966; Accounting Standards Steering Committee 1975; and Solomons 1991a). As with all professional accounting attempts to develop standards for external reporting by organizations, in economic regulation it is felt necessary to develop rules and regulations since there is insufficient incentive for firms to disclose, and interested parties have insufficient power to enforce their requirements. (The principal–agent problem.) Sappington and Stiglitz (1987) also stress the problem of getting firms to tell the truth, suggesting that an audit is needed, in order to enable the regulator to rely on the information supplied. The issue of accounting information to be used in regulation seems therefore to be something one would expect the accounting profession to be concerned about.

We shall not consider the audit question in detail here since no matter how good an audit is, if it and the original accounting focus on the wrong issues they will be of little value. The accounting information may be easily verified (though even this is unlikely) but of questionable use if it covers the wrong issues, or does so in the wrong way. Thus quality of information should not be assessed solely on criteria of reliability, objectivity etc., but should also reflect issues such as fitness for purpose and relevance. For example, Peacock is critical of the quantity and quality of technical information available on a range of matters regarding business performance, such as health and safety (Peacock 1984: 4). Thus our discussion of quality will focus more on how appropriate the coverage of accounting reports is, and in particular the links between financial accounting and economic reality.

If information is not collected or reported it is not likely to have as significant an impact on defining 'reality'. However once you define something as 'real/the truth' it has real consequences (Handel 1982 quoted in Hines 1989: 56). In this respect accounting, as the language for defining economic reality, can be seen to be contributing to the setting of the agenda, not only for regulation but also for wider debate and discussion of economic and social policy. The nature and form of accounting reports can be crucial in enabling regulators to function and in contributing to wider debate of a regulated company or industry. A narrow focus in the reporting of accounting information might well be of interest to both regulators and the regulated (making their job easier), though not necessarily in the interest of those dependent on the industry, such as consumers, workers and the community. In this respect traditional financial accounting reports are said to be partial, favouring the interests of owners of capital rather than other interest groups (Cooper and Sherer 1984). The focus of traditional financial accounting reports on the financial performance (rather than the impact) of the reporting entity (its revenues and expenses, its assets and liabilities) precludes reporting on the wider impact. Thus in the case of profit maximizing firms we can expect accounting reports to provide us with turnover, costs, profits and asset details, enabling us to judge the financial performance by means of, say, ratio analysis. However such reporting would not reveal much detail of the wider economic (including financial), social and environmental impact such as pollution levels, alienation and exploitation, industrial relations, product quality, health and safety at work and so on.

We are clearly aware of the many criticisms of the traditional accounting model based on historic costs (e.g. its subjectivity and flexibility particularly in cost allocation, its failure to reflect changing prices or be based on an acceptable capital maintenance concept, and its related failure to reflect future consequences in full) and its many related unresolved debates e.g. regarding intangible assets such as brands and goodwill. Yet accounting information would seem to play an important part in the functioning of society (and not solely in the traditional economic sphere), perhaps as a result of its apparent simplicity, often involving a bottom line or single figure answer (Miller 1991). In this respect the twin concepts of profit and net present value perhaps represent the best examples of such 'simplicity' and objectivity.

Of particular significance to our discussion of the quality of information are the various professional attempts to define the objectives and the desirable characteristics of externally reported financial accounting information. Whilst most such studies stress the importance of considering in any given situation the user and the purpose for which accounting is intended, nevertheless there have been, and continue to be attempts to develop a single conceptual framework for external reporting of accounting information. 'Such attempts must imply a ranking of interests (e.g. shareholders' interests are more important than workers' etc.), or a view that a general purpose reporting would be suitable. For example, following on from a fundamental objective 'to communicate economic measurements of and information about the resources and performance of the reporting entity useful to those having reasonable rights to such information' it has been suggested that the following are desirable characteristics; reports should be relevant, understandable, reliable, complete, objective, timely and comparable (ASSC 1975). Although the report from which this view is drawn proposed a number of different developments to corporate reporting, it did so very much within the framework of general purpose reporting, and had very little to say about ranking or even conflicts of interest.

It is not so relevant for our purposes to consider each attempt to determine a conceptual framework, nor to identify what are in this author's view desirable characteristics of accounting information. Instead we will concentrate on the difficulty of developing a conceptual framework, and so as a consequence the difficulty of deciding what we mean by quality of accounting information.

To some extent a cursory glance at Table 5.1 indicates some of the difficulties. This shows that in a number of the major attempts to develop a conceptual framework or identify desirable characteristics of accounting information, we can see lists of varying length and content, though with some similarity.

To some extent this table simplifies the contents of the various studies. To begin with it fails to distinguish between the scale and the significance of each project, and within projects there have been contrasting approaches. Whereas some reports simply focus on desirable characteristics, having identified an objective for external reporting, other studies, particularly the American Financial Accounting Standards Board (FASB)'s project have identified a ranking by means of a hierarchy which begins with users, considers a pervasive constraint (benefits must exceed costs), user specific qualities (understandability and decision usefulness), primary decision specific qualities (relevance and reliability) which are ingredients of primary qualities (predictive value, feedback value, timeliness, verifiability and representational faithfulness), secondary and interactive qualities (comparability, consistency and neutrality) and finally a threshold for recognition (materiality).

Focusing on the FASB's project allows us to consider the most extensive attempt to define what we might mean by quality of accounting information. Most recently the FASB's conceptual framework (CF) project has dominated discussion of the nature and purpose of external financial accounting. However Hines (1991) describes the impasse which has been reached with the development of the latest Statement of Financial Accounting Concept (SFAC) number 5 on recognition and valuation. Whereas the CF project originally set out to identify and prescribe the nature and purpose of external reporting,

Table 5.1 Desirable characteristics of accounting information

	A	B	C	D	E	F	G	H
Understandability/intelligibility/clarity	*	*	*	*	*	*	*	
Decision usefulness					*			
Relevance	*	*	*		*	*	*	*
Reliability		*	*	*	*	*		*
Timeliness			*		*	*	*	*
Predictive value						*	*	*
Feedback value						*	*	
Verifiability/objectivity	*		*	*		*	*	
Representational faithfulness/isomorphism						*	*	
Neutrality/freedom from bias	*	*				*	*	*
Comparability	*	*	*	*	*	*	*	*
Consistency	*	*		*		*	*	*
Quantifiability	*							
Appropriateness of use	*							
Materiality	*	*				*	*	*
Inclusion of environmental information	*							
Quantity					*			
Cost/cost–benefit			*		*	*	*	*
Form and substance		*					*	*
Completeness			*		*		*	
Confidentiality			*					
Realism					*			
Prudence/conservatism					*		*	*
Ease and economy of preparation					*			
Precision						*		
Rationality						*		
Non-arbitrariness						*		
Uniformity						*		
Flexibility						*		
Data availability						*		
Choice of aspect								*
Valid description and measurement								*
Disclosure								*
Users' abilities								*
Presentation								*
Compliance with accounting standards								*
Balance between relevance and reliability								*

Key A American Accounting Association (1966)
  B American Institute of Certified Public Accountants (1973)
  C Accounting Standards Steering Committee (1975)
  D Inflation Accounting Committee (1975)
  E American Accounting Association (1977)
  F Financial Accounting Standards Board (1980)
  G Canadian Institute of Chartered Accountants (1980)
  H Accounting Standards Board (1991)

publication of SFAC 5 has confirmed the shift from prescriptive to descriptive, by failing to indicate a value system to be used in external reporting. Thus a multi-million dollar project has failed to agree on a value system (e.g. the choice between historic cost, replacement cost and sale value etc.) as the basis for external reporting. To this extent it must be seen to have failed in its original objective. But more importantly it suggests a difficulty in defining and applying economic reality to financial accounting.

Elsewhere Hines has suggested that CF projects in general maintain a professional myth that accounting practices are or can be based on a cohesive knowledge core (the search for the Holy Grail), and so play an important role in legitimizing the monopoly privileges of the accounting profession (Hines 1989). The FASB CF project assumes that financial accounting can reflect economic reality, and that the causal direction is from economic reality to financial accounting (Hines 1991). However, Hines suggests such CFs generally fall back on an appeal to the informed reader (such as the investment analyst) when exploring the desirable characteristics of accounting information, and that ultimately despite the lengthy discussions of desirable characteristics, the form of financial accounting should be determined by what such well informed users indicate is of use. Hines sees CFs as world forming devices. Yet despite the incentives of structuring and retaining control of accounting practice the accounting profession appears unable to agree on a central value system. It continues to be criticized, particularly in the financial media, for failing to devise an accounting system which provides useful information to investors in particular.

Further, more critical views suggest that accountants create partial and one sided accounts of the world (Morgan 1988). Clearly this partiality is of some importance if, as Morgan suggests, the accountant's view is an important and influential one. Tinker goes further by likening accounting theory to social beliefs (Morgan's reference is to perspectives), but suggesting that financial accounting is not merely a passive representation of reality, rather accounting is an agent in changing or perpetuating reality (Tinker 1985).

In a rare mention of accounting information in regulation Geroski and Mueller (1990) stress that accounting and economic profits will differ noticeably at any point in time, and warn against using the former to estimate the latter. In many respects they express concern with what Morgenstern had described as 'the single most important source of information about the economic activity of the nation' (Morgenstern 1967: 70). But their concern is limited and apparently entirely within the neo-classical, marginalist paradigm. Such differences between the neo-classical economist's definition of profit and the accountant's are well known and stressed at an early stage in accounting education (e.g. Whittington (1984) who refers, amongst other things, to the difference in terms of the backward looking accountant and the forward looking economist). Yet despite numerous attempts to introduce changes to corporate external accounting we are still operating the same basic system based on historic costs as was used in the last century. There seems little doubt that traditional historic costs are a practical alternative, suited to the accounting profession and its audit service in particular. Yet as our discussion above concerning the development of a conceptual framework has suggested, there are numerous problems in accounting which remain unresolved, and which are likely to lead one to question the calculation of important accounting figures such as profit, capital or asset values even where one accepts the constraints of recording only market transactions (see Tinker 1985, chapter 6, for a discussion of the problem of accounting for deferred tax and the impact on utility pricing, through both the impact on the utilities' profits but also in terms of the impact on the financial structure of the utility).

Thus the influence of neo-classical economics is not to be directly equated with accounting practice, but rather seen as a dominant influence, which leads to a focus in accounting on objective market transactions expressed in financial terms (the money measurement concept) and restricted largely to those transactions and events which have an impact on the organization's bank balance (the entity concept). Accounting practice appears to be constrained by 'an overarching metaphor encouraging a numerical view of reality' (Morgan 1988: 48), though only some financial numbers enter the equation. Such numerical views are seen as objective, rather than as an interpretation of a complex reality, which relies for its focus on what accounting is able to measure and chooses to measure (Morgan 1988). What Morgan and other critics are suggesting is that not only does financial accounting practice reflect a particular definition of economic reality, but that financial accounting may actually influence our perception of economic reality. The suggestion is that something is real if it can be accounted for.

Thus neo-classical/marginalist economists are not likely to be satisfied with traditional accounting reports, nor are those who adhere to a critical school of thought. The capture of the terrain of economic regulation by practising accountants would be of concern to both.

In terms of our earlier discussion those critical economists and accountants not subscribing to neo-classical economics are likely to wish to see accountings which are not based solely on the money measurement concept, and are not restricted to traditional accounting's entity concept. In the latter case accountings for the wider economic and social impact of the entity (rather than accountings which concentrate on events affecting the entity bank balance) would be expected. Contemporary concerns with the environmental impact of business, and concern with the broader economic and social consequences of business appear to be relevant here. Certainly if one takes the view that transport is, for instance, of central importance to people's lives, that everyone depends on public transport, and that travellers 'live with it, they love it, they hate it' (Campbell 1989) then these broader concerns should inform our discussion of the role of accounting information in the regulation of the Scottish bus services.

There seems little doubt that transport is a matter of great concern to both industry and the public, that it raises various economic, social and environmental issues which are unlikely to be reflected by the traditional accounting reports of any subsection of the industry. In the case of the bus industry recent concerns have included the financial and environmental consequences of traffic congestion, the performance of old fleets compared to new 'green' buses, and wider social questions of access for the disadvantaged and women (particularly regarding design of buses and night travel). Although these additional matters rarely enter the debates concerning the nature of accounting and its attempts to capture economic reality, there seems little doubt that to particular groups in society safety, quality, environmental impact, etc. are as much part of their reality as is the performance portrayed by financial accounting.

THE SCOTTISH BUS INDUSTRY

The main reason for the regulation of the bus industry (initially with the Road Traffic Act 1930) appears to have been concerns with safety (particularly with the use of surplus ex-army lorries after World War I). However an important consequence of the legislation was consolidation of the industry, in addition to increased comfort in travel and greater seating capacity (Bagwell 1974).

Savage refers to the fierce competition between rival bus companies using war surplus vehicles before 1930, resulting in a high accident rate thought likely to have been caused by poor driving and maintenance of vehicles, in part as a result of intense competition (Mulley 1983 referred to in Savage 1985). White (1988) also describes the consequences of the 1930 Act as including quality control (with driver and vehicle licensing introduced, though not operator licensing) and quantity control by the use of route licensing (including registration of route, timetable and fare scale with the newly created Traffic Commissioners). Regulatory powers were delegated to a regional level in the form of Traffic Commissioners (TCs), who administered the new licensing system. The entrance of new operators to the market was controlled, and the TCs controlled route and fare changes. The TCs were appointed to cover a particular geographical area, and were expected to make decisions with the interests of their area uppermost. This often led to sanctioned cross-subsidization of services (Button 1988).

Thus the 1930 Act introduced tight control over operations of the bus service market. As a consequence a consolidation of the industry took place, with surviving operators offered a security of tenure (Sleeman 1953). In some cases agreements were reached with local authorities e.g. SMT and Edinburgh Corporation, where the agreement signed in 1920 lasted until 1954, enabling the company to offer a monopoly service in the city, with a levy per bus mile being paid to the Corporation (Hunter 1987).

However concern with growing subsidies and cross-subsidization, particularly with services not being adjusted for falling demand, appears to have encouraged deregulation and privatization. One of the first actions of the 1979 Conservative Government affecting the bus industry was the 1980 deregulation of coaches. This did not in itself mean increased competition. Rather this involved new quality controls, especially safety standards, with quantity controls being removed for all scheduled services. However the monopoly strength of the Scottish Bus Group and the National Bus Company ensured that further legislation privatizing these companies followed. Deregulation of buses followed in 1985 (see White 1988: 22) for a number of damning criticisms of the selective use of data to make a case for deregulation).

The major changes introduced by the Transport Act 1985 concerned the abolition of road service licences (replaced by the registration of services with the TC), non-commercial services now had to be put out to competitive tender by local authorities, and TCs no longer had any responsibility for levels of fares charged by operators. This is now left to the market. In general the TCs have been left with the task of ensuring maintenance and health and safety standards are met in the industry, accepting registration of services and dealing with complaints concerning particular services. In general they seek to uphold competition in the bus industry.

The 1985 Act was intended, according to the White Paper, to

increase consumer choice, increase supply, reduce fares, eliminate cross-subsidization, expose subsidies, reduce government revenue support, maintain safety, encourage innovation and maintain services in areas of social need (Farrington and Mackay 1987). It attempted to do so by a mixture of deregulation, competitive tendering (for subsidized services), privatization and reduction of government subsidy (Gwilliam 1990), with the overall intention to end a period of public interest regulation by government (Gwilliam 1989). The consequences of the Act are less clear, since six years is a short period compared with the 55 years of regulation. In addition there are difficulties identifying any decline due to the legislation compared to the long run decline in bus use. Cost savings of 31 per cent have been calculated, largely due to increased productivity (19 per cent) and wage reductions (7.5 per cent) (Heseltine and Silcock 1990). However one author has suggested that it will not be clear what the consequences will be until the industry settles down (after some consolidation of operators), and then we might better estimate the impact of the power of monopoly suppliers (Evans 1990). Yet there seems little doubt that accounting for the performance of the individual bus companies which constitute the industry will remain largely unchanged and follow the traditional model. The wider economic and social objectives of even the 1985 Act seem unlikely to have much impact on the way accounting reports present the performance of bus companies.

Other changes, of more relevance to a focus on more traditional financial accounting information, included the application for an operator's licence, which includes the need to satisfy a requirement on financial resources and satisfaction of technical fitness. It is this need to satisfy a requirement on financial resources which illustrates one of the few examples of traditional financial accounting information being considered by the TCs nowadays.

ACCOUNTING INFORMATION USED IN REGULATION

I have taken two approaches to researching the question of the role of accounting information in the regulation of Scottish Bus Services. Much of this section of the chapter is based on interviews conducted with staff at a Traffic Commissioner's office (including the Clerk to the TC) and management of a large bus company. Prior to the 1985 Act a great deal of accounting information appears to have been collected by the TCs in order to assess the reasonableness of proposed fares increases. Although

I could find no academic references in economics and accounting literature to such work, conversations with staff in a TC's office referred to the involvement of accountants as expert witnesses on occasions where fares were considered, and on some occasions when matters went to a public inquiry (and this is still a possibility, though not in terms of financial standing). Since the view was that practising accountants were called on as expert witnesses, it seems most likely that their focus would be very much on traditional financial accounting information, and in particular cost structure, with all of the difficulties that our earlier discussion suggested attached to such accounting. Unfortunately the influence of accountants and accounting reports is an empirical question which will be very difficult to address, since many relevant staff appear to have left the TCs following the introduction of deregulation, and records will likely not have been kept (in the opinion of TC staff).

However in general it is safe to say that post-1985 and the deregulation of the bus industry we have seen a reduced contribution of (traditional) accounting information. Now the main reporting of accounting information arises when applicants for new routes must satisfy the need to be of 'appropriate financial standing.... having available sufficient financial resources to ensure the establishment and proper administration of the business carried on or proposed ...' (Transport Act 1985). Once again there appears to be no academic research concerning what has actually been collected and used by the TCs. One indication of what may be being done is contained in the Guidance Notes issued by the TCs. These interpret and question of financial standing as requiring at least a banker's or accountant's reference. New applicants for a Standard International Public Service Vehicle Operator's Licence must also provide evidence of financial standing of an amount at least equal to the number of vehicles times £2,000 or the number of passenger seats times £100. The Department of Transport's Application for a Public Service Vehicle Operator's Licence (PSV 421) requests that in order to show that there is sufficient money to start up and maintain your business you must submit audited accounts, or a statement of income and expenditure or a bank reference, although this is not necessary for applicants who held a PSV Operator's Licence before 1 January 1978. Finally in a letter intended for general circulation to applicants from one TC's office it is suggested that bank statements or a corroborative statement of assets and liabilities may suffice.

Since the 1985 Act responsibility for setting fares has rested with the market and the TCs do not collect information to consider fares increases. The TCs role is primarily to help the operations of the market. While public inquiries and investigations by the TCs still take place, these are now largely concerned with issues such as service reliability, maintenance and safety etc. Accounting information appears to be collected as indicated above and on an *ad hoc* basis, such as where a matter is reported in the media or reported direct to the TCs, usually by a competitor rather than the general public. Interestingly the TCs office contacted would appear to connect the financial performance of bus companies to their non-financial performance, by using information on maintenance, safety etc. as a basis for investigating the financial affairs of a bus company, and vice versa. However there does not appear to be collection of data on a systematic basis, other than concerning applications referred to above. And it would appear that information collected on an *ad hoc* basis is based on traditional accounting reports, such as those lodged at Companies House, rather than a detailed investigation of a company's finances. There seems to be no encourage-ment in the legislation for TCs to monitor bus companies on a regular basis, whether by traditional financial accounting information or by some wider accounting.

Clearly there is some scope for researching the question of how information has been collected, what was collected, how it was used, and contrasting before and after legislative changes. And it would appear that despite overall government control, TCs have been known to be fiercely independent and notoriously inconsistent. Such are perhaps ideal conditions to compare and contrast approaches (though perhaps it is likely that no real difference would be discovered), although the absence of research may reflect practical difficulties as suggested above.

A second approach to assessing the contribution of accounting information concerned an examination of bus company financial state-ments and annual reports. Although there was and still is not a require-ment for bus companies to send their annual report and accounts to the TC, it does seem possible that such reports reflect what is considered accountable and therefore important about company performance.

Annual reports and accounts are frequently used as the basis of accounting research, though often the conclusions from such research are questioned because of doubts over the significance or use/usefulness of the accounts. Justifiably, criticism is made where accounting is equated with annual corporate financial reporting, and in many respects there was in the past an imbalance of research effort into such reporting rather than management accounting in organizations. Annual corporate reports are after all a convenient source of information, can be collected easily and avoid the difficulties and very substantial demands on one's time often associated with conducting research by interview and observation.

However there is a danger that one dismisses annual reports as a suitable basis for research altogether. Of some importance would seem to be the extent to which such a visible accounting chooses to focus on certain issues and not others, and so contributes to (and reflect) thinking in society (setting the agenda). For example, recent research by Tinker and Neimark on the struggle over meaning in accounting research 'rejects the view of annual reports, either as neutral reflection of reality, or as downright falsification intended to manipulate a passive audience' (Tinker and Neimark 1988: 59). They attempt to 'delineate the active part that reports play in social conflict, by showing how these documents may down play, reinterpret and reconstruct a history of social and economic events' (ibid.: 59). Clearly Tinker and Neimark are concerned not only with what is reported and how, but also what is excluded (censored). It should be stressed that there is no evidence that annual reports play a role in the economic regulation of bus services by TCs. Instead such reports may be of more general interest as a reflection of the matters considered of most significance in bus company performance.

A major Scottish bus company was contacted and asked to supply a copy of each of its last ten years' annual reports and accounts. Normally such a request would be dealt with in full by a large quoted company. In this case the finance director was only willing to send two years' reports, and some four years' accounting reports prepared for distribution to employees. A further request for the missing reports was turned down, and a request for access to the company's own file of accounts was also turned down.

An analysis of the annual reports revealed interesting changes in what is reported. Although the analysis relies on the 1981 and 1990 reports, it does offer limited opportunity of contrast. Whereas nowadays the bus company is a limited liability company (owned by the local authority), and so prepares an annual report (based in part on replacement cost accounting) which is audited for presentation to the owners, a few years ago, before deregulation, the same 'company' reported similar financial information in addition to various non-financial statistical details of performance, primarily to the local authority. The report was published then as the *Accounts and statistics*, in contrast to the current *Report and accounts*. It must be emphasized that in neither case is it clear what contribution the accounts made to the regulation of that bus company. It is known that the ICs did receive copies of each year's annual report, and copies were prepared for the benefit of the local authority, which controlled and still controls the company.

For example, the 1990 annual report and accounts appears to be typical of the financial statements produced by large private companies, with sections on company information (bankers, auditors etc.), report of the directors, profit and loss account, balance sheet, funds statement, accounting policies, notes to the accounts and report of the auditors. In all, there seems to be very little of note reported which is not required by company law. The only point worth mentioning is the use by the company of replacement cost accounting for public service vehicles. Such practice was quite common in many nationalized industries during the 1970s as the accounting profession struggled to find a solution for the private sector, and is to this day still relatively uncommon in company reporting.

In contrast, the 1981 accounts and statistics detail the membership of the transportation committee of the local authority, management, income and expenditure (including figures expressed per mile), balance sheet (with public service vehicles at depreciated historic cost), analysis of income, analysis of expenditure, capital account items, season ticket sales, tickets sold data, traffic revenue and passenger analysis, passengers carried and mileage run (including graphs), statistics (including population served, route mileage etc.), ratios (26, including passengers per bus mile, staff per bus, variable cost per mile), staffing, passenger and mileage statistics per route and bus fleet. Yet there are no details of accounting policies, no 'directors' report and no auditor's report. However, in general what is revealed is a wider accounting of the performance of the bus company. Although not covering matters such as environmental impact, energy consumption, customer satisfaction, exploitation and alienation etc., such reporting indicates a concern with more than simply the financial performance of the company. The accounting report does not concentrate solely on financial statements, but includes a range of non-financial measures of performance.

Subsequent attempts to interview the finance director, in addition to seeing the missing accounts, were unsuccessful. The main reason given was the new competitive climate the company was now operating in, despite assurances of complete confidentiality and anonymity. Although it was stressed that the author's interest was more in the form of reporting and the contribution and use of the figures, rather than the meaning of the figures *per se*, the finance director would not agree to be interviewed.

As a consequence it is not clear how significant these accounting and reporting differences are. It is not known why such changes took place. They would appear to signal a shift from the public sector, with some emphasis on financial and non-financial performance indicators, to a more private sector emphasis on financial accounting numbers such as profit calculations. It was not possible to discover what differences there were regarding the intentions of reporting, the recipients, the possibility that the 1981 statistics were not used, or that they are now reported elsewhere. Answers to these and other questions are clearly significant to our understanding of accounting information prepared. However on the surface there does appear to be a change in what is defined as the business annual report, similar to that discovered in a review of water authority/company annual reports pre- and post-privatization (Harte and Owen 1991). Such narrowing of focus to a manner more consistent with private sector reporting, should not be too surprising. Yet it may be that this coincides with an increased power of traditional financial accounting. And that although the annual reports of the bus company are not called for by the TC they are sent, and may be seen as an indicator of the change in the focus of the annual report and of performance measurement since deregulation. Accounting, and the focus of reporting, would appear to have changed due to deregulation, becoming more like the financial accounting associated with private companies, as required by law, the stock exchange (where applicable) and the accounting profession.

CONCLUSION

This chapter appears to indicate a declining role for accounting information on one level (the operation of the TCs, and in particular their no longer being concerned with the issue of fares) and an apparent increase in importance for the traditional accounting financial statements in annual reporting. The wider reporting in the statistical analysis of earlier years no longer appears in the annual report. To this extent it would appear that economic reality has been redefined in a manner more consistent with private companies' financial accounting. Despite the concerns discussed earlier with regard to environmental and social performance, such non-financial performance indicators as did exist in previous years have been removed from the accounting. Rather than seeing a development of accounting to reflect contemporary social and environmental concerns we have seen a consolidation of the emphasis on (some aspects of) financial performance.

In general accounting would appear to have been relegated in importance to competition, despite the continued existence of an albeit limited economic regulation. The market is now the price and rate of return regulator for bus services, and even traditional accounting reports are not collected on a regular basis by TCs. Yet clearly the existence of wider economic, social and environmental impacts suggests that a reality to workers, consumers and the community is being ignored by accounting reports.

The role and form of accounting in the regulation of Scottish bus services would appear to be largely shaped by government legislation. However the influence of traditional accounting's form, as shaped in part by the profession and individual accountants is of interest. Clearly one way of accounting is also a way of not accounting, whether we are referring to the measurement techniques used or the focus. Accounting research and practice has long been dominated by a common sense and more recently positivist line of enquiry, where reality is seen to be concrete, where those accounts produced and considered to be true set the agenda for debate and decision making (Hines 1989). Traditional, though still reforming, views of accounting see its role as to provide information as free from bias as is possible, so as to be useful to decision makers, and have as an overall objective the improvement of social welfare (Solomons 1991a). Such a view accepts some of the problems of accounting for economic reality, but stresses that to account for social reality complicates matters further, and is outside the scope of accounting and the expertise of accountants. In this respect it is often seen that to measure externalities involves intractable problems (Benston 1982 and Solomons 1991a). On the other hand to raise the Nirvana argument whilst still advocating a partial and subjective alternative has been criticized (Schreuder and Ramanathan 1984).

Selection in traditional accounting is not denied, yet is not thought, particularly by practitioners and the many academic accountants working with the profession, to affect neutrality (Tinker 1991: 299). Neutrality seems to be equated with a state of mind, that of the professional. Tinker suggests that epistemological and accounting considerations are embedded in social reality (e.g. representational faithfulness, CCA (Current Cost Accounting) and HCA (Historic Cost Accounting)). Such concepts and principles are seen as social constructions and socially enactive phenomena (Tinker 1991: 301), and so are based upon a choice of focus. The suggestion is that the way accounting is is not the only way it can and perhaps should be.

Of particular note in the case of accounting for the Scottish bus industry is the absence of any accounting for externalities, a matter of concern particularly where these may be disproportionately borne by already disadvantaged sections of society, as may be the case with transport (see Galvel 1986; Glaister 1985a, b; and Nash 1985). Objections to the incorporation of externalities in accounting reports should not be left to imply that traditional accounting is free of measurement problems as we suggested earlier in this paper. All systems of accounting are selective in their focus and most are subjective in their measurement.

Critical academics are themselves criticized for failing to posit an alternative model of accounting (e.g. Solomons 1991b: 301). Tinker appears to see his text as offering a number of alternatives. Yet he too is critical of what is often seen as the main alternative to accounting practice, namely social accounting, particularly where this is seen as simply marginalism plus externalities, with the latter relying on market prices (Tinker 1985).

However the solution to the accounting problem may not lie in proposing a rigid alternative. Instead the idea of a new epistemology of accounting which will emphasize the interpretive, where accounting should be approached as a form of dialogue is suggested (Morgan 1988: 477). Morgan suggests accountants need to be sensitive to the many dimensions of the realities which they are attempting to account for (ibid.: 484). In the case of the contribution of accounting to the regulation of the Scottish bus industry and to its portrayal of the performance of the industry, we appear to have seen a narrowing of the focus, rather than an increase in the dimensions. In particular we noted the indication of change in annual reporting of a large bus company, from 1981's inclusion of some non-financial statistical data to the 1990 report which appeared no different to that of any other large private company. In this case it would appear that the accounting report has become less sensitive, appearing to redefine economic reality in a particularly narrow manner. In light of increased concerns regarding the importance of a reliable transport infrastructure and the environmental impact of the industry, it seems insensitive for accounting reports to narrow their focus at the very time that we are hearing calls for the development of corporate accountability.

In many respects economic regulation can be expected to increase the significance of accounting information, particularly where the focus is on the rate of return or prices and profitability. Consistent with this, this study illustrates a situation where partial deregulation and the introduction of competition has reduced the role of accounting information.

Yet in relation to the accounting which continues to be done we appear to be seeing an increased emphasis on traditional financial accounting reports and information. Such a narrow, one dimensional account is unlikely to satisfy calls for a more sensitive accounting which reflects the complexities of organizational and social reality.

REFERENCES

Accounting Standards Board (1991) *The Objective of Financial Statements and the Qualitative Characteristics of Financial Information* (Exposure Draft), London: ASB.

Accounting Standards Steering Committee (1975) *The Corporate Report*, London: ASSC.

American Accounting Association, Committee to Prepare a Statement of Basic Accounting Theory (1966) *A Statement of Basic Accounting Theory*, Sarasota: AAA.

American Accounting Association, Committee on Concepts and Standards for External Financial Reports (1977) *Statement on Accounting Theory and Theory Acceptance*, Sarasota: AAA.

American Institute of Certified Public Accountants, Study Group on The Objectives of Financial Statements (1973) *Objectives of Financial Statements*, New York: AICPA.

Bagwell, P.S. (1974/1988 reprint) *The Transport Revolution*, London: Routledge.

Benston, G.J. (1982) 'Accounting and corporate accountability', *Accounting, Organizations and Society* 7(2): 87–105.

Button, K. (1988) 'Contestability in the U.K. Bus Industry, Experience Goods and Economies of Experience', in J.S. Dodgson and N. Topham (eds) *Bus Deregulation and Privatisation*, Aldershot: Gower.

Campbell, B. (1989) 'Summer of Discontent', *Marxism Today*, August, pp. 16–17.

Canadian Institute of Chartered Accountants. (1980) *Corporate Reporting: Its Future Evolution*, Toronto: CICA.

Cooper, D. and Sherer, M. (1984) 'The value of corporate accounting reports: arguments for a political economy of accounting', *Accounting, Organizations and Society* 9(3/4): 207–32.

Evans, A. 'Competition and the structure of local bus markets', *Journal of Transport Economics and Policy* 24(3).

Farrington, J. and Mackay, T. (1987) 'Bus deregulation in Scotland – a review of the first six months', *Fraser of Allander Quarterly Economic Commentary*, August.

Financial Accounting Standards Board (1980) *Statement of Financial Accounting Concepts No. 2: Qualitative Characteristics of Accounting Information*, Stamford Connecticut: FASB.

Galvel, T.E. (1986) 'A comment', *Journal of Transport Economics and Policy* 20(1).

Geroski, P.A. and Mueller, D.C. (1990) 'The persistence of profits in perspective', in D. Mueller (ed.) *The Dynamics of Company Profits*, Cambridge: Cambridge University Press.

Glaister, S. (1985a) 'Competition on an urban bus route', *Journal of Transport Economics and Policy* 19(1).

—— (1985b) 'A Rejoinder', *Journal of Transport Economics and Policy* 19(3).

Gray, R.H. (1991) *The Greening of Accountancy: The Profession After Pearce*, London: Chartered Association of Certified Accountants.

Gray, R., Owen, D. and Maunders, K. (1987) *Corporate Social Reporting*, London: Prentice/Hall.

Gwilliam, K.M. (1987) 'Setting the market free: deregulation of the bus industry', *Journal of Transport Economics and Policy* 23(1).

—— (1990) 'Bus deregulation – editorial', *Journal of Transport Economics and Policy* 24(3).

Handel, W. (1982) *Ethnomethodology: How People Make Sense*, Englewood Cliffs: Prentice/Hall.

Harte, G. and Owen, D. (1991) 'Current trends in the reporting of green issues in the annual reports of United Kingdom companies' in D. Owen (ed.) *Green Reporting: Accountancy and the Challenge of the Nineties*, London: Chapman & Hall.

Heseltine, P.M. and Silcock, D.T. (1990) 'The effects of bus deregulation on costs', *Journal of Transport Economics and Policy* 24(3).

Hines, R.D. (1989) 'The sociopolitical paradigm in financial accounting research', *Accounting, Auditing and Accountability Journal* 2(1): 52–76.

—— (1991) 'The FASB's conceptual framework, financial accounting and the maintenance of the social world', *Accounting, Organizations and Society* 16(4): 313–31.

Hopwood, A. (1986) 'Economics and the regime of the calculative', in S. Boddington, M. George and J. Michaelson (eds) *Developing the Socially Useful Economy*, London: Macmillan.

Humphrey, C. and Scapens, R.W. (1990) *Whatever Happened to the Liontamers? An Examination of Accounting Change in the Public Sector.* Mimeo.

Hunter, D.L.G. (1987) *From SMT to Eastern Scottish*, Edinburgh: John Donald.

Inflation Accounting Committee (1975) *Report of the Inflation Accounting Committee*, Cmnd 6225, London: HMSO.

Miller, P. (1992) 'Accounting and objectivity: the invention of calculating selves and calculable spaces', *Annals of Scholarship* 9(1–2).

Morgan, G. (1988) 'Accounting as reality construction: towards a new epistemology for accounting practice', *Accounting, Organizations and Society* 13(5): 477–85.

Morgenstern, O. (1967) *On the Accuracy of Economic Observations* (2nd edn), Princeton: Princeton University Press.

Mulley, C. (1983) 'The background to bus regulation in the 1930 Road Traffic Act: economics, politics and personalities in the 1920s', *Journal of Transport History* 4(2): 1–19.

Nash, C.A. (1985) 'Competition on an urban bus route – a comment', *Journal of Transport Economics and Policy* 19(3).

Peacock, A. (1984) *The Regulation Game – How British and West German*

Companies Bargain With Government, Oxford: Blackwell.

Power, M. (1991) 'Auditing and environmental expertise: between protest and professionalisation', *Accounting, Auditing and Accountability Journal* 4(3): 30–42.

Sappington, D.E.M. and Stiglitz, J.E. (1987) 'Information and regulation', in E.E. Bailey (ed.) *Public Regulation; New Perspectives on Institutions and Policies*, Cambridge, Mass.: MIT Press.

Savage, I. (1985) *The Deregulation of Bus Services*, Aldershot: Gower.

Schreuder, H. and Ramanathan, K.V. (1984) 'Accounting and corporate accountability – an extended comment', *Accounting, Organizations and Society* 9(3/4): 409–15.

Schultz, R. and Alexandroff, A. (1985) *Economic Regulation and the Federal System*, Canada: Ministry of Supply and Services.

Scott, D.R. (reprint 1933/1973) *The Cultural Significance of Accounts*, Houston, Texas: Scholars Books.

Sleeman, J.F. (1953) *British Public Utilities*, London: Pitman.

Solomons, D. (1991a) 'Accounting and social change: a neutralist view', *Accounting, Organizations and Society* 16(3): 287–95.

—— (1991b)'A rejoinder', *Accounting, Organizations and Society* 16(3): 311–12.

Tinker, T. (1985) *Paper Prophets: A Social Critique of Accounting*, Eastbourne: Holt Rinhart and Winston.

—— (1991) 'The Accountant as partisan', *Accounting, Organizations and Society* 16(3): 297–310.

Tinker, T. and Neimark, M. (1988) 'The struggle over meaning in accounting and corporate reporting: a comparative evaluation of conservative and critical historiography', *Accounting, Auditing and Accountability Journal* 1(1): 55–74.

Transport Act (1985), London: HMSO.

Waterston, M. (1988) *Regulation of the Firm and Natural Monopoly*, Oxford: Blackwell.

White, P.R. (1988) 'British experience with deregulation of local bus services', in J.S. Dodgson and N. Topham (eds) *Bus Deregulation and Privatisation*, Aldershot: Gower.

Whittington, G. (1984) 'Accountancy and economics', in B.V. Carsberg and T. Hope (eds) *Current Issues in Accountancy* (2nd edn), London: Philip Allan.

Part IV

REGULATORY INSTRUMENTS

6

REGULATING FIRMS WITH MONOPOLY POWER

Chris Doyle

Industry and commerce function most successfully in environments where there exist clear regulatory rules governing conduct and structure. A good example of regulatory rules are accounting principles which enable investors and tax authorities to understand more easily the activities of companies. In general regulation is imposed in two ways. First, it may be self-imposed or voluntary, and secondly it may be enforced by an external agent such as the government. In this chapter I shall focus on externally imposed regulation through government agencies.[1]

By its very nature government is intimately connected with regulation in that it establishes and maintains many of the explicit codes of conduct within which all firms must operate. Such general rules impinge upon the structure, conduct and performance of firms and they embrace a wide range of issues, including the maintenance of property rights, the regulation of mergers and acquisitions (see the contribution of Ajit Singh in the following chapter), the monitoring of trading practices and the control of monopoly power, etc. All these areas constitute governance structures for industry.

I focus on how some firms, notably natural monopolies and firms with considerable monopoly (market) power, are subject to additional or special forms of regulation imposed by government. As noted in Michael Waterson's account in Chapter 2, privately owned monopolies that are not fully contested will, by pursuing profit maximization, produce output levels that result in a deadweight loss to society. In these circumstances there is a justification for government regulation on efficiency grounds. Regulation of this kind may take the form of instructions requiring monopolies to increase output levels beyond the profit maximizing levels, but for a natural monopoly this may result in a loss, despite there being a net gain to society. It is unlikely to be the case

111

that shareholders will tolerate such losses, but a subsidy in the form of a non-distorting (that is, no deadweight loss) lump-sum transfer could be made.

Lump-sum redistributive taxes are typically unobserved and difficult to implement in practice and therefore governments may not be able to regulate natural monopolies via instructions. For this reason it may be preferable for government to assume ownership through nationalization. This has traditionally been the case for those industries with capital intensive supply networks such as electricity, gas, telecommunications, railways and water. In the period after the second world war, it was perceived by many that government ownership would dominate private ownership in terms of achieving social welfare objectives.[2]

Government regulation imposed as a result of acquisition, however, has met with considerable criticism in recent years, especially in the UK, and this has led to a change in attitudes towards industrial regulation.[3] The ownership by government of firms that participate in competitive markets has in particular received considerable criticism, which is not surprising given the difficulties of justifying this on efficiency grounds.[4] Increasingly governments around the world are reappraising the merits of owning companies, including natural monopolies. This has resulted in the privatization of many companies, including a large number that were formerly acknowledged to be natural monopolies.[5]

The privatization of some natural monopolies has been feasible because many produce a multitude of goods and services, some of which can be supplied within competitive market structures. But the main impetus for the privatization of natural monopolies has derived from the view that private ownership when combined with an arm's length approach to regulation is superior to state ownership. Thus the privatization of large public utilities has been accompanied by the construction of new regulatory auspices. The recent and ongoing behaviour on the part of many governments with respect to natural monopolies thus represents a marked shift in industrial regulation in favour of more distant and market oriented regulation.

In the remainder of this chapter I outline and examine the ways in which a natural monopoly or dominant firm can be regulated. The analysis is entirely theoretical and normative in nature.[6] I commence by outlining the benchmark case, that of direct control or regulation via instruction. In this section I show how a regulator should set prices in order to achieve a constrained welfare maximizing allocation. This could possibly involve choosing Ramsey prices or two-part tariffs. I then examine the case of regulation by design of rules rather than through the imposition of instructions. This form of regulation involves the setting of decentralized mechanisms by the regulator. The two most common forms of regulation are then discussed, rate-of-return and price-capping. In the next section, problems to do with asymmetric information are raised and the implications of this on various forms of regulation are discussed. I conclude by examining briefly some aspects of regulation not focused on in the previous section.

REGULATING A NATURAL MONOPOLY BY INSTRUCTION: THE CASE OF FULL INFORMATION

Let us suppose that there exists some regulator who is charged with the responsibility to ensure that a multi-product natural monopoly does not impose any unnecessary deadweight loss on society. I assume that the firm is not contested in the Baumol *et al.* (1982) sense. I assume also that the regulator is omniscient and omnipotent, and is thus always capable of computing and enforcing any instruction sent to a firm. Regulation of this kind could be viewed as equivalent to regulation through acquisition and direct control. Private ownership and shareholder monitoring, however, may result in lower X-inefficiency than public ownership. If this were the case, then private ownership is preferable given the existence of a powerful regulator. I assume that if the firm is publicly owned that the regulator can observe X-inefficiency and instructs the firm to set this at zero and implement the price schedule chosen by the regulator. This is the case of regulation by instruction or centralized regulation. Public ownership and regulated private ownership, in this case, are indistinguishable.

Constrained welfare maximizing prices

Given the virtual impossibility of attaining first best outcomes, the regulator will have to seek second best solutions; that is, choose a set of prices that maximize welfare subject to a non-loss-making constraint.[7] The price chosen by the regulator will necessarily reflect the weights attached to efficiency and equity by the policy maker. A major problem confronting the regulator is how to design price schedules that cover fixed or common costs. For example, if local and long distance telephone calls use the same local exchange, then how does the regulator apportion depreciation of the fixed capital across the different services? The regulator can choose a set of prices that cover costs from a number of different alternatives. For example, prices may be set so that they are subsidy free, meaning that taking any subset of products supplied to the market generates revenue that meets their incremental costs or stand-alone costs.[8] A pricing policy that may lead to subsidy free prices is fully distributed cost-pricing (FDC). Under FDC a regulator will normally allocate common costs according to some allocator function, which may be in terms of relative quantities, relative revenues or relative attributable costs. If it is possible to devise 'internal' subsidy free prices that fully allocate variable costs, then one can devise a set of prices that are subsidy free for any arbitrary distribution of fixed costs. It does not matter, therefore, how fixed costs are allocated but in practice a regulator may care about equity and therefore require a fair allocation of common costs.

Ramsey prices

A regulator choosing prices that are subsidy-free may do better instead to choose second best optimal or Ramsey prices.[9] I assume that the regulator is seeking to maximize the utility of a representative agent. The regulator is seeking a price vector p to maximize $v(p, y)$, the agent's indirect utility function, where y is income.[10]

$$\max \ W(p) \equiv v(p, y) \tag{6.1}$$

$$\text{s.t.} \ \Pi(p) = 0$$

where $W(p)$ is the social welfare function and $\Pi(p)$ is the monopoly's profit function. Both are assumed to be twice continuously differentiable. The first order conditions of the optimization problem are as follows:

$$\frac{\partial v}{\partial p_i} (p^*, y) - \lambda \frac{\partial \Pi(p^*)}{\partial p_i} = 0 \quad \forall \, i=1, \ldots, n, \tag{6.2}$$

where λ is the Lagrange multiplier. I will assume that marginal utility of income is constant and normalized to equal one, thus $\partial v/\partial y = 1$. By Roy's identity we then have

$$\frac{\partial v}{\partial p_i} = -q_i \ \left(\Rightarrow -\lambda = \frac{q_i}{\partial \Pi/\partial p_i} \right)$$

which upon substitution yields

$$- q_i - \lambda \, (\partial \Pi(p^*)/\partial p_i) = 0 \quad \forall \; i = 1, \ldots, n. \tag{6.3}$$

The profit function is defined as follows:

$$\Pi(p) = \sum_{i=1}^{n} q_i(p)p_i - C(q(p)). \tag{6.4}$$

I will make the following simplifying assumption: $\partial q_i(p)/\partial p_j = 0$ $\forall \; i \neq j$. Thus cross price effects are ruled out but they can be incorporated without any great difficulty. Differentiating the profit function with respect to each price yields:

$$\frac{\partial \Pi(p)}{\partial p_i} = q_i\,(p) + p_i \frac{\partial q_i}{\partial p_i} - \frac{\partial C(q(p))}{\partial q_i} \frac{\partial q_i}{\partial p_i} \quad \forall \; i = 1, \ldots, n. \tag{6.5}$$

Note that (6.5) implies that $\lambda < -1$, reflecting the deadweight loss. Substituting the above into (6.3) yields

$$- q_i = \lambda q_i + \lambda \left(p_i - \frac{\partial C}{\partial q_i} \right) \frac{\partial q_i}{\partial p_i}$$

or

$$- \frac{1 + \lambda}{\lambda} \frac{q_i}{\partial q_i/\partial p_i} = p_i - \frac{\partial C}{\partial q_i}. \tag{6.6}$$

Dividing through by p_i and denoting the own price elasticity of demand as

$$\varepsilon_i = - \frac{\partial q_i}{\partial p_i} \frac{p_i}{q_i}$$

implies the following:

$$\frac{1 + \lambda}{\lambda} \frac{1}{\varepsilon_i} = R_i = \frac{p_i^* - \dfrac{\partial C(q^*)}{\partial q_i}}{p_i^*} = L_i \quad \forall \; i = 1, \ldots, n, \tag{6.7}$$

where L_i is the Lerner index and R_i is the Ramsey index. This is the familiar Ramsey mark-up pricing rule where the price of each product i is marked up over marginal cost inversely proportional to the absolute value of the elasticity of demand in the ith market. It differs from the conventional monopoly result which would omit $(1 + \lambda)/\lambda$ from the expression in (6.7). Thus the monopoly generates revenue in a profit maximizing way but only fractionally in comparison to an unconstrained monopolist. Ramsey prices are an example of value based linear price schedules that result in a second best solution.[11]

Two-part tariffs

Different forms of pricing, such as two-part tariffs and non-linear tariffs can further improve upon welfare, particularly where there exists a heterogeneity of consumer types.[12] In most of the UK public utilities within the public sector it was common for pricing to be based on two-part or multi-part tariffs. The most familiar are telephone bills where there is a rental component and separate user charges. An interesting variant of the two-part tariff model was considered by Willig (1978). He considered a scheme where all consumers can be better off by choosing a two-part tariff rather than a pricing schedule based on average cost.[13] Of course, those who would benefit by paying a lump sum and a lower price tend to be those consumers who buy larger quantities of the product. A firm, in principle, can always design schedules that generate Pareto-superior outcomes to non-optional two-part tariffs. In principle it is feasible to design multi-part (or even non-linear) tariffs which can be optimal and result in the marginal customer paying marginal costs for the product.[14]

IMPLEMENTING DECENTRALIZED REGULATORY MECHANISMS: SOME THEORY

Principal–agent relationships

From hereon the discussion will focus exclusively on privately owned firms. Regulation of privately owned firms is an illustration of a principal–agent relationship.[15] The regulator is the principal and the managers of a regulated firm are the agents. It is the regulator acting as the principal that designs the rules and the managers acting as the agent that act on any rules set. The principal or regulator's objective is to select rules that maximize some combination of the consumers and shareholders (the regulated firm's utility) welfare, knowing that the rules it sets affect the behaviour of the producer and therefore affect the welfare of consumers and shareholders alike. When a regulator sets rules and the agent chooses a response, then we say that the regulatory environment is decentralized.

In this section I shall focus on two common forms of regulation that have been employed by regulators in Europe and in the United States. These are price capping (PC) and rate of return (ROR) regulation. Each share the feature that they are implemented in a decentralized manner. This is, the regulator transmits to the firm a set of rules, rather than instructions, and the firm maximizes profits incorporating the rules as constraints into its optimization problem. They are not, however, mechanisms necessarily designed to maximize the principal's payoff, but are simple ways of limiting the losses associated with natural monopoly and dominant firms. In the analysis in the remainder of this section I assume that the regulator has complete information. In other words, the regulator can solve the regulated firm's optimization problem and can therefore observe costlessly whether the firm abides by the rules set.[16] I will deal with problems of asymmetric information in the next section.

Rate of return regulation

The classic early work on ROR regulation and its impact on firm behaviour is Averch and Johnson (1962). They addressed the issue of how a regulated firm responds optimally to a ROR constraint, which until recently was a popular way of regulating utilities in the United States. A simple version of the model (the single output case) is outlined here.[17] A monopoly seeks to maximize profit and produces a single output q using two inputs L and K, where $q = F(L,K)$ and the price of each input is w and r respectively. Let total revenue be given as $R(L,K)$ and total costs be $wL + rK$. The firm faces a rate of return constraint, where $R(L,K) - wL$ divided by the value of the capital base cannot exceed s, where $s > r$, for otherwise the firm would not operate. Formally,

$$\max \Pi(L, K) = R(L, K) - wL - rK \tag{6.8}$$

$$\text{s.t.} \quad \frac{R(K, L) - wL}{K} \leq s. \tag{6.9}$$

The constraint is assumed to be binding, for otherwise the firm could always choose the monopoly price. Setting up the Lagrangian results in the following:

$$H(L, K, \lambda) = \Pi(L, K) - \lambda[R(L, K) - wL - sK].\quad (6.10)$$

The associated first order conditions for this problem are

$$(1 - \lambda) \left(\frac{\partial R}{\partial L} - w \right) = 0 \qquad (6.11)$$

(the second order condition gives $0 < \lambda < 1$) and

$$\frac{\partial R}{\partial K}(1 - \lambda) - r + \lambda s = 0 \quad \Rightarrow \quad \frac{\partial R}{\partial K} = r + \frac{\lambda(r - s)}{1 - \lambda} < r. \quad (6.12)$$

Inspection of (6.11) shows that labour is chosen where the wage rate is set equal to the marginal revenue product of labour and (6.12) shows that constraint (6.9) induces an excess amount of capital to be employed, relative to the cost minimizing input mix. Essentially a ROR regulated firm inflates the capital base and by so doing attains higher absolute profits for a given output level than at the cost minimizing input mix. Thus ROR regulation encourages gold-plating. In a situation where a multi-product ROR regulated firm may sell some of its output on competitive markets, then this may lead to pricing below marginal cost in some of those markets as a way of expanding the rate base. The latter will occur when losses in the competitive market are more than offset by the gains through higher prices in monopolized markets.

In the Averch and Johnson (1962) (A-J) model it is assumed that the rate of return will be larger than the cost of capital. If it is equal to the cost of capital, then the model is degenerate in that a firm will be indifferent across any output that results in zero profits. Braeutigam and Panzar (B-P, 1989) in a model of ROR regulation set the base rate s equal to the cost of capital.[18] They show that a partially regulated firm (one where the revenues generated from sales on competitive markets are excluded from regulation) will be inefficient if it operates under a ROR constraint with FDC. This arises because a firm will find that cutting back production in the competitive market, resulting in more of the common costs to be allocated to the non-competitive regulated market, is profitable at the point where marginal costs equal price in the competitive market. By expanding the rate base in the regulated sector the firm can force higher prices.

The partial ROR in the B-P analysis differs from the A-J model where there is complete regulation. B-P show, however, that where the revenues from a competitive sector are included in the ROR constraint, as in the A-J model, then this leads to over-production in that market. The reason for over production differs to the A-J effect, where it is due to the regulated rate of return exceeding the cost of capital. In the B-P model it occurs because at the margin expanding output beyond the social optimal level in the regulated competitive sector adds to the allocation of common costs. This enables the firm to increase its prices in the regulated monopolized sectors and more than offset losses in the competitive sector. A drawback of both models, however, is their static nature and as a consequence they do not account for any strategic interaction which might take place with respect to the setting of s.[19]

The A-J model suggests that a firm facing a ROR constraint faces no incentive to minimize cost or care about X-efficiency, first raised by Cross (1970).[20] This is because once s is established a firm can always adjust prices to attain a return on capital equal to s. Thus if costs rise the firm can compensate for this by raising prices. ROR regulation has in practice, however, been implemented in terms of past data, thus leading to the phenomenon of regulatory lag. The rate base s is set by applying the ROR constraint on past cost and quantity data, thus providing an incentive for a regulated monopoly to become more efficient for the duration of the lag between cost reduction and the setting of a new base rate. ROR regulation therefore does provide some incentive for cost reduction. The length over which a base rate applies is similar to the issue of patent length, the longer the lag the greater are allocative efficiency losses but the higher the rewards for cost reductions.

The justification for ROR regulation is couched largely in terms of allocative efficiency but its implementation may induce other inefficiencies. For example, it may encourage accounting practices that overstate capital valuations and thus mislead investors. Another drawback is that it requires substantial information about cost and demand to be made available to the regulator. This could induce bureaucratic inefficiencies and may lead to revelation problems (see pages 124–8). An issue that arises under ROR regulation is rate base selection, what is an appropriate choice for s? For these and other reasons there has been a shift towards less informationally demanding regulation through what is termed price cap regulatory mechanisms.

Price capping regulation

Price capping has come into prominence largely as a consequence of the UK Government's privatization of public utilities.[21] The first such utility to be divested was British Telecom (BT). The UK Government was sceptical of the merits of ROR regulation and commissioned Stephen Littlechild to consider all options with regard to regulating British Telecom's profitability.[22] Littlechild advocated the adoption of a PC form of regulation, which he claimed dominated ROR regulation in terms of restraining monopoly power, promoting competition, reducing X-inefficiency and by providing incentives for cost reductions. It was also argued to be more likely to lead firms to efficient price schedules.

Acton and Vogelsang (1989) define PC regulation as having four characteristics. First, a regulator constrains (typically through an upper bound) the set of feasible prices. Secondly, price constraints (usually expressed as price indices) are set with reference to a basket of services or goods, but subsets of goods and services may be subject to different constraints. Thirdly, price constraints are adjusted periodically by a pre-announced factor that is exogenous to the firm. Fourthly, over a longer period the constituents of a PC can be adjusted. The third of these characteristics seems at odds with the practice of PC as the regulated firm is often involved with the setting of the variables within the constraint.[23] The third characteristic might be better described as follows. Price constraints are adjusted periodically as the outcome to a game played between the regulator and the regulatee. A key outcome to the game might be the time over which price-capping endures.

In the B-P model discussed above, the consequences of introducing PC are analysed. As the model is very simple in structure the consequences of an upper bound on the price that can be charged in the regulated sector are rather obvious. The firm will produce output at a cost minimizing point because the constraint removes cost interdependency. Thus the incentive to innovate in all markets and price at marginal cost in the competitive market also holds. In practice, however, PC has not been applied in such a simple way and below I discuss the theory lying behind more complicated schemes.

RPI-X price capping regulation

RPI-X can be applied directly to tariffs, as in the case of BT where the weighted average of the price increases for regulated services is constrained to lie within RPI-X. The weights are revenue shares generated in the previous year and are thus backward looking and known with certainty at the beginning of the year. RPI-X can also be applied on revenue yield, as in the case of British Airports Authority (BAA), British Gas and the National Grid Company (NGC). A revenue yield is defined as the revenue generated from the regulated sector divided by some measure of the volume of business in that sector. Thus there is an average price constraint applied to a common unit. For British Gas an upper bound on the average revenue per therm on customers purchasing less than 25,000 therms per year is established, and it is the upper bound that is subject to RPI-X. The weights in a revenue yield constraint are some measure of current quantity and can therefore be influenced by the firm's pricing policy. In this case the weights are current and are not known until the year end.[24]

Revenue weighted form of RPI-X

RPI-X as applied to BT is a Laspeyre index constraint on tariffs. Thus BT's tariffs are constrained as follows:

$$\sum_i \frac{p_{i,1} - p_{i,0}}{p_{i,0}} \frac{p_{i,0} q_{i,0}}{\Sigma_i \, p_{i,0} q_{i,0}} \le \frac{RPI_1}{RPI_0} - X - 1, \qquad (6.13)$$

where the 0 and 1 subscripts refer to time, RPI is the retail price index and X is an incentive factor. X is chosen by the regulator, usually after consulting the regulatee, and is intended to reflect expectations about cost changes and also takes into account return on capital, see Oftel (1992). Thus for telecommunications, technological advances are lowering costs and this is reflected in the setting of positive values for X. Rearranging (6.13) yields

$$\frac{p_1 q_0}{p_0 q_0} \le \frac{RPI_1}{RPI_0} - X. \qquad (6.14)$$

The left hand side of (6.14) is a Laspeyre index on prices. Thus the price cap has a backward looking component. For positive values of X there is likely to be an improvement in efficiency over time. To consider this, assume that inflation is zero, then the increase in consumer surplus will be at least as great as $X p_0 q_0$. The firm will choose prices so that $p_1 q_0 \le (1 - X) p_0 q_0$ and it will set prices to make this hold as an equality. If it is assumed that $q_1 \gg q_0$, then if sales were q_0 in period 1 the fall in profits would be equivalent to the rise in consumer surplus. But assuming profits remain positive and ray average costs are decreasing, then additional sales must add to total profit.[25] Thus the imposition of RPI-X on tariffs can generate an increase in welfare and it can lead to Ramsey prices as the scheme has the same property as a regulatory device suggested by Vogelsang and Finsinger (1979), discussed on pages 124–9.

The revenue yield form of RPI-X

The revenue yield form of RPI-X establishes weights in current terms and does not have the same properties as the tariff based scheme. The firm's optimization problem when faced with a revenue yield constraint is given as follows:

$$\max \Pi(q) = \sum_i p_i(q)q_i - C(q) \tag{6.15}$$

$$\text{s.t.} \quad \frac{\sum_i p_i(q)q_i}{\sum q_i} \leq \bar{p} \tag{6.16}$$

where $p_i(q)$ is the inverse demand function for each good or service $i = 1, \ldots, n$. As the purpose of regulation is to prevent monopoly behaviour, it follows that the constraint will be binding. Setting up the Lagrangian and differentiating yields the following first order conditions:

$$\text{MR}_i \left[= \frac{\sum_i \partial p_i}{\partial q_i} q_i + p_i(q) \right] - \text{MC}_i \left[= \frac{\partial C}{\partial q_i} \right]$$

$$- \eta \left[\frac{\text{MR}_i (\sum_i q_i) + \sum_i p_i(q)q_i}{(\sum_i q_i)^2} \right] = 0 \quad \forall \ i=1, \ldots, n. \tag{6.17}$$

where $\eta \geq 0$ is the Lagrange multiplier. After algebraic manipulation this results in the following:

$$\text{MR}_i - \text{MC}_i = \frac{-\gamma}{1 - \gamma} (\bar{p} - \text{MC}_i) \tag{6.18}$$

where

$$\gamma(\bar{p}) = \frac{\eta(\bar{p})}{Q(\bar{p})} \, \varepsilon \, (0,1)$$

for $\bar{p}$ between the average price under perfect competition and the average price under pure monopoly and $Q = \sum_i q_i$. This appears to be similar to the Ramsey condition for prices implied in (6.3) and given below in a slightly different form to (6.7).

$$MR_i - MC_i = (1 + \lambda)^{-1}(p_i - MC_i) \qquad (6.19)$$

The left hand sides of (6.18) and (6.19) are the marginal profits. The revenue yield constraint leads the firm to have marginal profit proportional to the difference between marginal cost and the average price, whereas an overall profit constraint leads to it being proportional to the difference between the price in the ith market and marginal cost. Thus marginal profitability is likely to be higher in higher marginal cost markets under a revenue yield constraint. Indeed, it could even be positive, in which case the firm would supply output below the unconstrained monopoly level.

A revenue yield constraint encourages a firm to expand its production in elastic markets in an effort to lower the weight on prices charged in the more profitable markets with inelastic demands. The consequence of this leads to overproduction in the elastic markets relative to the inelastic markets and may even result in pricing below marginal cost. This effect is identical to that experienced under ROR with FDC, as discussed above. In an intertemporal setting a revenue yield constraint encourages high pricing in expanding markets. Few detailed welfare statements have been derived on comparing revenue yields with other regulatory constraints but Bradley and Price (1988) present some comparisons for a simple case.

Optimal regulation

One of the problems with the many analyses on ROR and PC regulation is the omission of welfare comparisons between the two different regulatory mechanisms. Clemenz (1991) goes some way to doing this, building on earlier work by Cabral and Riordan (1989). He shows that PC achieves a higher social welfare than ROR regulation. He considers a simple model of a single good monopoly that can expend resources on research and development (R&D) that yields reductions in production costs probabilistically. He assumes that a firm produces over three periods and that R&D only occurs in period one. ROR regulation is assumed to take the form of setting the price in periods 1 and 2 equal to period 1 marginal costs, and the price in period 3 is set equal to period 3 marginal costs. PC regulation sets price in period 1 at period 1 marginal costs and then in periods 2 and 3 it is set equal to some number below period 1 marginal costs.

The structure of the model implies that benefits flowing to the firm due to innovations under ROR regulation occur only in period 2, whereas under PC they arise in both periods 2 and 3. Thus a firm is likely to devote more resources to cost cutting behaviour under PC than under ROR regulation, a point first shown by Cabral and Riordan (1989). By generating higher R&D expenditures a monopolist may well produce higher output levels, as costs would be expected to be lower than in the case of ROR regulation. Clemenz (1991) shows that under full information PC will always be expected to yield a higher consumer surplus than that expected under ROR regulation. It is pointed out, however, that the superiority of PC is dependent on the regulator possessing full information; once this assumption is removed then the outcome may well change. The case of imperfect information is taken up in the next section.

INFORMATION AND INCENTIVES

In the previous section I ignored the issue of information and its role in the design of decentralized mechanisms. In practice the regulated firms' managers know more about demand and cost conditions than the regulator. This is the case of asymmetric information. In a world of asymmetric information the main constraint falling on the regulator, when trying to implement regulatory policy, is an incentive problem.[26] For example, a regulator will require information about demand and costs from the firm if it wants to implement welfare maximizing prices. As the firm knows that the regulator will rely on information it supplies, then it may find it advantageous to misinform the regulator. This is the incentive problem; that is there may be incentives for managers to transmit false information to the regulator. Incentive problems give rise to moral hazard and adverse selection problems.

Something known as the revelation principle, however, enables a regulator to obtain the same outcome when the agent lies under an alternative set of rules where truth as a (weakly) dominant strategy is obtained.[27] The revelation principle is very powerful because it means that where a firm might find it advantageous to lie, the regulator can always design another contract that will get truth revealed which will be at least as good in terms of the regulator's objectives. Therefore the regulator need only ever consider truth revealing or incentive compatible contracts.

Implementing regulation under asymmetric information: direct mechanisms

A direct mechanism implements a rule as a function of the regulators' priors (beliefs) about the private information of the regulated firm. This type of mechanism works by requesting the firm to reveal information to the regulator. The regulated firm knows that any reported value will directly affect its payoff, as the contract is a function of the reported value. Because of this the firm will obtain some informational rents on its private information. For example, a firm might prefer to be thought of as a high cost firm when in truth it is a low cost firm; so that the regulator may treat it leniently. The regulator, knowing that the firm might lie, could correct for this by designing an incentive compatible mechanism that gets the firm to reveal truthfully its type without doing any worse than a non-incentive compatible contract. The benefit of doing this is that the regulator could design a scheme that gets the firm to behave in a way that is socially desirable. The downside is that to get truth it might entail a cost because of possible incentive effects on other variables which might be present in the firm's cost function; such as research and development expenditures or effort.

I will commence by examining the mechanism proposed by Baron and Myerson (B-M 1982).[28] B-M consider a model of a monopolist with unknown costs. The cost function posited is as follows; $C(q, \theta)$, where θ is a cost parameter known imperfectly to the regulator and is described by a density function $f(\theta)$. The regulator has to determine a subsidy (to cover fixed costs and to provide an incentive for production) and a price as a function of the reported value of θ, where $\hat{\theta}$ will be used to denote reported value. The B-M model extends the simpler framework of Leob and Magat (L-M, 1979), which describes the construction of what is termed an indirect mechanism (described more fully in the next sub-section).

The L-M approach considers a monopolist with unknown cost but where demand is common knowledge. Their solution is an example of what is known as an anonymous mechanism. An anonymous mechanism is an indirect mechanism relying on observables like accounting profits.[29] The L-M mechanism is straightforward. The firm is asked to announce to the regulator its price and the regulator then writes a cheque equal to the consumer surplus. In addition the firm is allowed to keep any operating profit. Under this scheme the firm obtains the whole of the surplus and it will be maximized when price equals marginal cost. Hence the first best outcome is achieved.

Although the L-M scheme is simple it relies critically on knowing the demand function and it inevitably involves the transfer of funds from the regulator to the firm. This transfer requires funding and may itself be distortionary. Under the L-M mechanism the distributional consequences are entirely in the firm's favour and this is unlikely to be optimal in a more general setting. Indeed, consumers would be better off under monopoly pricing because at least some surplus is obtained. Loeb and Magat do suggest, however, that to overcome any adverse distributional consequences an auction could be organized for the monopoly rights. The problem with this solution is that to obtain an efficient outcome there ought to be many players in the auction game, which is unlikely to be so in practice if the industry is characterized by large sunk costs.

B-M consider a more general framework where the regulator attaches a unit weight on consumer surplus in the social welfare function and a weight no greater than unity on shareholder profits or producer surplus. The regulator maximizes expected social welfare by choosing a price function $p(\hat{\theta})$ and a subsidy function $s(\hat{\theta})$. (The B-M model also admits a probability function for operating or closure.) The regulator chooses the control variables subject to an individual rationality constraint (that the firm makes a profit) and an incentive compatibility constraint (the firm finds truth to be a weakly dominant strategy). The solution results in the optimal price generally lying above the firm's marginal costs (except at the lowest value of θ) and in some cases may even exceed the unregulated monopoly price. *Ex post* this might appear to be inefficient, but it is a consequence of the truth telling constraint. The regulator wants the firm to reveal low marginal costs when this is so, to enable a low price to be set that generates a large consumer surplus. To prevent overstatement of costs in this case the regulator can either reward the firm with a subsidy for announcing a low cost or it can penalize the firm for announcing high costs. For example, the regulator may set $p(\hat{\theta})$ such that the price is above the monopoly price when announced costs are high.

The B-M optimal strategy has $p^*(\hat{\theta})$ non-decreasing in $\hat{\theta}$, where the asterisk denotes optimal. As a corollary, if the regulator places an equal weight on consumer and producer surplus, then the solution equates with the mechanism devised by Loeb and Magat. This is explained by the indifference over distributional effects.

Laffont and Tirole (L-T 1990a, 1990b) derive a more general solution to the problem of regulating a multi-product monopolist under asymmetric information. They specify a cost function that also contains the managers' cost reducing effort. Thus the function looks as follows $C(q, e, \theta)$, where e denotes effort which cannot be observed by the regulator and θ is the firm type drawn on $[\underline{\theta}, \bar{\theta}]$. It is assumed that $C_\theta > 0$ and $C_e < 0$. The managers' disutility function of effort is described by the function $\psi(e)$, where $\psi'(e) > 0$, $\psi''(e) > 0$ and $\psi'''(e) \geq 0$.

The regulator has a utilitarian social welfare function containing the shadow price of public funds. The firm receives a payment from the regulator equal to t, making the overall payoff the firm receives equal to $U = t - \psi(e)$.[30] The regulator maximizes social welfare by choosing $e(\hat{\theta})$, $t(\hat{\theta})$ and $q(\hat{\theta})$. The programme is as follows:

$$\max \int_{\underline{\theta}}^{\bar{\theta}} [V(q) + \gamma R(q) - (1 + \gamma)(\psi(e) + C(\theta, e, q)) - \gamma U]f(\theta)d\theta$$
(6.20)

subject to

$$U(\bar{\theta}) = 0 \tag{6.21}$$

and

$$\dot{U}(\theta) = -\psi'(e)E_\theta(\theta, C(\theta, e, q), q) \tag{6.22}$$

where $E(\theta, C, q)$ denotes the effort required for a firm of type θ to produce q at cost C, $V(q)$ is consumer surplus, $R(q)$ is total revenue and γ is the shadow price of public funds. In this framework the firm faces a trade-off between extracting informational rent and effort, and it is this that constitutes the incentive compatibility constraint (6.22). The problem facing the regulator is that to get truth revealed it has to penalize the firm for lying (or reward the firm for truth telling). But consider a firm type $\theta - d\theta$. This firm could produce the same output vector and obtain the same transfer as a firm with type θ simply by lowering its effort by $de = E_\theta(\theta, C(\theta, e, q), q)d\theta$. Therefore the gradient of the firm's rent with respect to effort is $\dot{U}(\theta) \equiv dU/d\theta = -\psi'(e)de/d\theta$. Thus the regulator takes this into account and this is reflected in the incentive compatibility condition in (6.22). The term in (6.21) is the individual rationality constraint, the highest cost firm is constrained to get zero informational rent. This follows immediately from the direction of the incentive, lower values of θ obtain higher rents because they would try to be higher cost firms (thus lowering effort needed) in a non-incentive compatible scheme.

The generalized optimal scheme is as follows:

$$V_{q,i} + \gamma R_{q,i} = (1 + \gamma)C_{q,i} + I_i. \qquad (6.23)$$

The I_i term is the information incentive correction term for good i. The left hand side of (6.23) is the marginal social benefit for production and the right hand side the marginal social cost. For the case of linear prices and independent demands, as derived in (6.7), the optimal pricing results in each product's Lerner index being equal to the sum of a Ramsey term and an incentive correction.

$$L_i = R_i + I_i \qquad (6.24)$$

In the full information Ramsey case studied on pages 114–16 $R_i = L_i$, implying that $I_i = 0$. The expression in (6.24) differs from the traditional Ramsey set of prices in two respects. First, the shadow price of public funds appears rather than a Lagrangian dependent on the firm's (unknown) cost function. This means that the regulator can compute this from publicly available data, using estimates on demand elasticities etc.. This contrasts with the traditional Ramsey structure where the term is dependent on the firm's cost structure. The incentive correction term is determined entirely by the firm's cost. This term implies that overall the firm will set higher prices than in the conventional Ramsey result. The price of the ith good is higher than the conventional Ramsey solution when the following condition is satisfied,

$$\frac{\partial}{\partial q_i} \left(-\frac{C_\theta}{C_e} \right) > 0. \qquad (6.25)$$

The optimal mechanisms derived are intermediate forms lying between cost-plus contracts, which induces $\psi'(e) = 0$ and fixed price contracts where $\psi'(e) = -C_e$.

Implementing regulation under asymmetric information: indirect mechanisms

In this type of regulation the firm is not requested to disclose private information. Instead the regulator imposes rules that are based on observables, such as past output levels, prices and profits. These mechanisms do not require the regulator to ascertain detailed information about costs or demands. If, as will typically be the case, the regulator cannot observe costs and demand perfectly, then RPI-X PC schemes fall into this category. The Loeb and Magat (1979) model discussed above is an example of an indirect mechanism which obtains marginal cost pricing. Another indirect mechanism that leads to Ramsey prices was proposed by Vogelsang and Finsinger (V–F 1979). V–F proposed a decentralized mechanism allowing the firm to engage in profit maximization in each period subject to a constraint that overall it could choose only prices in the current period that would not generate positive profits using last period's costs and outputs.[31] Within their framework the existence of decreasing ray average costs ensure convergence to Ramsey prices.

The V–F mechanism constrains prices in period t to generate nonpositive profits if applied to period $t-1$ quantities and costs, that is

$$p_t q_{t-1} - C(q_{t-1}) \leq 0. \tag{6.26}$$

Dividing through by $p_{t-1} q_{t-1}$ leads to the following:

$$\frac{p_t q_{t-1}}{p_{t-1} q_{t-1}} \leq \frac{C(q_{t-1})}{p_{t-1} q_{t-1}} = 1 - \frac{\Pi_{t-1}}{p_{t-1} q_{t-1}}. \tag{6.27}$$

Ignoring any intended incentive effects, this inequality results in a monotonically decreasing Laspeyres chain index. Note that (6.27) has the same form as the revenue weighted RPI-X scheme in (6.14), where instead profits perform the role of X. Thus the revenue weighted form of RPI-X has the same properties as the V–F mechanism.

Building on the foundation of the Loeb and Magat idea, Finsinger and Vogelsang (F–V 1985) and Sappington and Sibley (1988) present anonymous mechanisms to be implemented by regulators. Sappington and Sibley introduce what they term ISS or increment in social surplus regulation. Their model is identical to L–M's except that the regulator cannot observe current accounting profits. They propose an incentive scheme which states that in any period t the firm can retain current profits and the firm will receive a subsidy equal to

$$S_t = \int_{p_t}^{p_{t-1}} q(p)\mathrm{d}p - R_{t-1}, \tag{6.28}$$

where $R_t = p_t q_t - E_t$ and $E_t \geq C(q_t)$ are the firm's expenditures. If the firm engages in wasteful expenditures such that it does not minimize cost, then the latter inequality holds as a strict inequality. S_t is equal to the change in consumer surplus less last period's profits, this being the increment to social surplus. Therefore this mechanism leads to the firm obtaining the true increment in social surplus between $t-1$ and t. If the price were to remain unchanged across two periods, then the firm would be taxed by an amount equivalent to last period's profits. Thus excess profits are taxed away in the following period. This implies that the firm can only gain by changing the true social surplus. The firm solves the following problem.

$$\max \sum_{t=0}^{\infty} \beta^t \Pi_t \tag{6.29}$$

subject to

$$E_t - C(q_t) \geq 0 \tag{6.30}$$

and

$$S_t = \int_{p_t}^{p_{t-1}} q(p)\mathrm{d}p - R_{t-1} \qquad \text{for all} \quad t \geq 1 \tag{6.31}$$

where $\beta < 1$ is the discount factor, and $\Pi_t = R_t + S_t$. Given an initial price $p_0 > C'(q_0)$, then the solution to the problem results in the firm jumping immediately to marginal cost pricing. This is because as the firm faces a tax, then the best that it can do is to set p_1 equal to marginal cost to obtain the whole of the consumer surplus obtaining period zero profits and deadweight loss, while losing the profit earned at time zero. This gives the firm the true increment in social surplus. The presence of the discount factor makes any slower approach to marginal cost pricing have an overall lower return. After period 1 the firm avoids paying a tax, as price and quantity remain constant.[32] Informational rents occur in the first period only, which is an improvement over the L–M mechanism.

The problem with the ISS mechanism is that it relies on the regulator knowing the demand function. In practice this is unlikely to be the case. The F–V mechanism in contrast is designed without assuming common knowledge about demand. F–V propose that the regulator can only observe the quantity of output with a lag and as it is assumed that the regulator does not know the demand function, the current price cannot be used to identify demand in the current period. The firm receives a subsidy equal to the following:

$$F_t = q_{t-1}(p_{t-1} - p_t) - R_{t-1} = \Pi_t - \Pi_{t-1} + q_{t-1}(p_{t-1} - p_t). \tag{6.32}$$

The subsidy F_t is an approximation to the true increment in social surplus given in by S_t in (6.31). Replacing S_t with F_t in the programme given in (6.29)–(6.31) leads to a solution which has p_t declining gradually over time to marginal cost. The mechanism does not get an immediate move to marginal cost pricing because this would leave the firm with zero profit overall. The firm would not derive any of the increment to social surplus, its informational rent, because the approximation rules out appropriation of the deadweight loss. The firm can do better by gradually lowering price, as the approximation allows it to obtain some informational rent over time.

These mechanisms are interesting as they can be interpreted as price cap forms of regulation. They are equivalent to regulation by imposition of a two-part tariff, as suggested by Vogelsang (1989). In this case we interpret the S_t and F_t as entry fees (the fixed component) and p_t the price (the variable components). In the ISS model the customer is offered the option of choosing (S_t, p_t) or (S_{t-1}, p_{t-1}). As (S_t, p_t) weakly dominates any past bundle, then the customer will choose it. This results in the firm extracting the increment to social surplus, as the customer is willing to part with the gain in consumer surplus. This however, happens only once. In the F–V model, the mechanism also leads the customer to always choose the current two-part tariff. Thus (S_{t-1}, p_{t-1}) and (F_{t-1}, p_{t-1}) can be viewed as the price ceilings in period t.

Sibley (1989) proposed a modification of the ISS scheme which does not require the regulator to know the demand function $q(p)$. Sibley calls the modification ISS–R, where R denotes revelation. The mechanism works by setting the rules such that the firm always has an incentive to reveal truthfully the demand function. In other words the regulator designs an incentive compatible scheme. This works as follows. Consumers pay an entry fee based on what the firm reports to be the demand function. Let this be denoted as follows.

$$\hat{S}_t = \int_{p_t}^{p_{t-1}} \hat{q}'(p)\mathrm{d}p - R_{t-1}. \qquad (6.33)$$

If demand is revealed truthfully, then the scheme is identical to the ISS scheme. The firm offers consumers (all identical) a choice of tariffs: either $(\hat{S}_t, p_t)$ or $(-R_{t-1}, p_{t-1})$. The consumer will choose that which yields the greater consumer surplus. It is obvious that the consumer will always choose the new two-part tariff if reported demand is no greater than actual demand and will choose the old 'ceiling' two-part tariff if the opposite is the case. The firm faces a slightly modified version of the problem outlined in (6.29)–(6.31) above. In the ISS–R problem the firm has an extra choice variable in $\hat{S}_t$. Sibley shows that the solution to the modified problem generates an outcome identical to that in the ISS scheme. In other words, the consumer is willing to pay an amount equal

131

to the increment in social surplus (last period's deadweight loss). Thus the informational burden on the part of the regulator is lightened considerably.

Sappington (1980) highlighted that when the firm's cost function contains effort as a choice variable, and $C_e < 0$ then these schemes have poor incentive mechanisms. If (6.32) is considered once more, in a stationary equilibrium where $\Pi_{t-1} = \Pi_t$, the firm does not gain by reducing costs. Laffont and Tirole (1990b) propose a simple regulatory mechanism similar to these schemes, basing it on price changes and historical data. Their approach is to tax the firm for price increases (the F–V scheme rewards firms for price cuts) and it leads to socially optimal prices in the steady state.

CONCLUSION

Several issues were not examined in the analysis above and will be discussed briefly below. The first area concerns the position of asymmetric regulation. An example of asymmetric regulation is the case of British Telecom in the United Kingdom. British Telecom has imposed on it a RPI-X constraint on a subset of the services it provides. Its main competitor Mercury Communications does not face such a constraint. A similar situation arises in Japan where NTT, the dominant domestic telecommunications company, faces a price floor on a range of services while new operators are free to choose their tariffs. These asymmetries exist because the regulation is perceived as temporary and one of its primary functions is to ensure that entry takes place. In the long run new competitors would mitigate the need for externally imposed regulation. Caillaud (1990) and Laffont and Tirole (1990b) provide some theoretical insights to the question of asymmetric regulation.

When there exist several companies in an industry but only one or a small number are viable in any one geographical area, then there is available to the regulator the possibility of exercising yardstick regulation.[33] Yardstick regulation is feasible where comparison of performance across several similar companies can be made. In the United Kingdom the water companies are to some extent regulated in this manner. The obvious problem that might arise in this context is collusion. Another problem facing a weak regulator is the possibility of the companies deliberately engaging in strategies that lead to differentiation.

It is sometimes remarked that regulation can be captured (see also the discussion by Jim Tomlinson in Chapter 1). A seminal contribution in this area was made by Stigler (1971).[34] His contribution was non-normative in nature, being more concerned with distributional consequences of regulatory mechanisms and the likely evolution of proposed mechanisms. His thesis is premised on the notion that 'as a rule, regulation is acquired by the industry and is designed and operated primarily for its benefit.' Company pension funds in the United Kingdom have recently borne testimony to the persuasiveness of Stigler's point. The way in which company pension funds are managed in the United Kingdom is through a system based on self-imposed regulation. Commenting on the regulators, Mr Frank Field, Chairman of the House of Commons Select Committee reporting on City Regulation, states if the regulators had 'acted with proper degree of suspicion.... and its professional advisers' care had been commensurate with their fees.... then the Maxwell pension funds would have been secure.'[35] Regulatory capture is more likely to occur under self-imposed regulatory structures, but occasionally claims are made that official bodies are captured.

Another important dimension to regulation is quality.[36] In the analysis above the quality of a good was assumed to be known and deterministic. In many instances, however, it might be difficult for the regulator to detect deliberate quality under-provision as a way of lowering costs. It is clear that within the RPI-X price capping framework, quality is not explicitly considered. Indeed, there is an incentive to lower quality if this is difficult to detect and can result in large cost savings. A good example of quality and the problems of regulation surfaced in the United Kingdom telecommunications sector in the middle 1980s. The regulated company British Telecom experienced a decline in the quality of its services after privatization. Some claimed that this was a deliberate measure aimed at boosting profits, while the company rejected this and cited the occurrence of industrial disputes and other adverse factors. The regulatory body Oftel required BT in October 1987 to introduce regular six-monthly reports on measurements of its quality of service. This response highlighted the weakness of price capping forms of regulation.[37]

In this chapter I have outlined a variety of approaches to regulating a natural monopoly or dominant firm. The material presented has been theoretical in nature and has concentrated on normative measures. The analysis aimed to illustrate the feasibility of designing socially enhancing welfare schemes and some of the flaws and advantages of present regulatory policy were discussed. It was shown that regulation is most complex when the information environment is asymmetric.

NOTES

1 At various stages during the writing of this chapter I have benefited from discussions with Professor Sir Bryan Carsberg, Professor David Newbery, Professor Geoffrey Whittington, Richard Green and Maria Maher. I should also like to acknowledge financial support from the Economic and Social Research Council under the project *Privatisation and re-regulation of the Network Utilities*, based in the Department of Applied Economics, University of Cambridge.

2 This was the view of Morrison (1933) and Hotelling (1938) who were influential in steering attitudes prior to the post-Second World War nationalizations in the United Kingdom. See also Chapter 4.

3 The work of Pryke (1981, 1982) demonstrated the relative inefficiency of state run enterprises in the United Kingdom. This work and other research was influential in steering the government of the United Kingdom in the early 1980s towards the view that regulated privately owned monopolies were preferable to nationalization, see Moore (1983). Kay and Thompson (1986) point out that it is the nature of competition, rather than ownership, that is the significant factor influencing the behaviour of a firm. See also Chapter 3 of this volume.

4 There may be a strong case for public ownership if one considers equity. For example, a government concerned either about regional or employment matters might use these concerns to justify the nationalization of a company facing bankruptcy.

5 In the United Kingdom the government has privatized over fifty companies, including companies in the gas supply industry, the electricity generation and supply industry, the telecommunications sector and the water supply industry.

6 For analyses focusing on the experience of regulation see Armstrong and Vickers (1992), Beesley and Littlechild (1991), Bishop *et al.* (editors) (1992), Veljanovski (editor) (1991) and Vogelsang (editor) (1992).

7 I am ruling out as infeasible the possibility of engaging in lump-sum transfers. On pp. 124–32 we shall see that asymmetric information also leads to the emergence of constrained (non-first best) welfare maximizing prices.

8 Faulhaber (1975) introduced the term subsidy free prices. Incremental costs of good i are the difference between the costs for a firm of producing a vector of all goods $j = 1, \ldots, n$ and the cost of producing all goods except i.

9 Ramsey prices were first solved in the context of taxation, see Ramsey (1927). Baumol and Bradford (1970) provide a historical survey and Sherman (1989) provides a good summary of recent developments.

10 It is assumed that income effects are negligible and are therefore ignored.

11 Models of Ramsey pricing have been extended to include the possible existence of a competitive fringe, see Braeutigam (1979, 1984), the presence of externalities, see Willig and Bailey (1977), the presence of uncertainty, see Sherman and Visscher (1978) and over time, see Brock and Dechert (1985).

12 For a single output monopolist Coase (1946) demonstrated that a simple

134

two-part tariff that sets the price at marginal cost and distributes fixed costs across consumers as a lump-sum charge will be optimal. The scheme, however, is premised on the assumption that all consumers can afford to pay the fixed charge, which may not always hold. The consequence of such a pricing strategy is a distribution from customers to the firm through the levying of the fixed charge. Ng and Weisser (1974) extend the Coase result to show that two-part tariffs are socially preferable to uniform prices where a firm faces a break even constraint. If consumers are heterogenous, then it is possible that two-part tariffs may disadvantage low income groups, which may be relevant if the policy maker is concerned about equity.

13 Ordover and Panzar (1980) show that this is not necessarily the case if some buyers are not final consumers.

14 A multi-part tariff can be replicated by a set of two-part tariffs, thus allowing for a finer partition over the heterogenous consumer base. For example see Mirrlees (1971, 1976), Roberts (1979) and Spence (1977). For a good discussion on this literature see Brown and Sibley (1986) and more recently by Mitchell and Vogelsang (1991). Mirman and Sibley (1980) extend the analysis to the multi-product monopoly case and this has recently been analysed by Armstrong (1991).

15 In a principal–agent relationship the principal sets rules (implements mechanisms or contracts) which reward the agent for actions taken. The agent's actions, as well as affecting his own utility, affect the well-being of the principal. The principal attempts to design a reward function that maximizes her (expected) payoff. For an interesting non-technical discussion of agency problems, see Arrow (1985).

16 This is an extreme assumption because in practice it is doubtful whether the managers of a firm themselves can calculate precise estimates on demands and costs, a point raised by Weitzman (1978).

17 See Baumol and Klevorick (1970) for a more complete exposition.

18 It was remarked on by Joskow (1974) that there is no reason why the return on capital for a regulated firm should be any greater than the cost of capital.

19 Extensions of the basic model to incorporate stochastic and dynamic features have been undertaken by Klevorick (1973) and Bawa and Sibley (1980). Interesting game theoretic models of rate base selection can be found in Greenwald (1984) and Gilbert and Newbery (1991).

20 Cabral and Riordan (1989) in a theoretical model contrast the incentives for cost reduction under both price capping and ROR regulation, showing the former to be superior.

21 One of the first theoretical enquiries into price-capping regulation was presented by Vogelsang and Finsinger (1979).

22 See the Littlechild Report (1983).

23 See Oftel (1992).

24 See Department of Transport (1986), Bos (1991) and Bradley and Price (1988) and Oftel (1992) for discussions on RPI-X regulation.

25 A cost function $c(q)$ has decreasing ray average costs if $c(kq) < kc(q)$ for $k > 1$.

26 The regulator will choose an optimal rule but this will depart from the first best solution because of the welfare loss associated with the information asymmetry.

27 In other words the revelation principle states that if a contract (the rules) leads to an agent lying (mis-reporting), another contract can be designed by the principal, that takes this into account, yet gets the agent to reveal the truth. Although I have stated that the revelation principle ensures truth can become a dominant strategy, in a multi-agent situation (I deal with only one agent) this becomes a Bayesian mechanism. For a thorough discussion on these issues see Fudenberg and Tirole (1991).

28 A complete description of regulating a multi-product monopolist under asymmetric information can be found in the excellent survey by Laffont and Tirole (1990a, b). See also Caillaud *et al.* (1988), Mirrlees (1971, 1976) and Roberts (1979).

29 An indirect mechanism does not depend on the regulator's priors about the firm's private information. Anonymity indicates that the firm's type does not affect its payoff; another firm generating the same observables will obtain the same payoff irrespective of unobservables which might affect the regulator's priors. Pages 128–32 focus in more detail on indirect mechanisms.

30 The firm's revenues $R(q)$ are paid over to the regulator and the costs $C(q)$ are covered by the regulator.

31 Vogelsang and Finsinger (1979) assume, however, that the firm maximizes profits myopically. If this assumption is relaxed, then the problem becomes more complex and the solution is not immediately apparent.

32 The firm may obtain a subsidy each period if the price lies below average costs.

33 For a very interesting model on yardstick competition see Shleifer (1985).

34 See also Laffont and Tirole (1991).

35 See the *Financial Times*, 10 March 1992.

36 For some discussion on quality and regulation see Besanko and Donnenfeld (1988), who focus on ROR regulation and product variety, Laffont and Tirole (1989) and Mussa and Rosen (1978).

37 See Armstrong and Vickers (1992) and Doyle (1992) for more detailed discussions on the privatization and regulation of telecommunications in the United Kingdom.

REFERENCES

Acton, Jan Paul and Vogelsang, Ingo (1989) ' "Introduction" to the Symposium on Price-Cap Regulation', *Rand Journal of Economics* 20: 369–72.

Armstrong, C. Mark (1991) 'Optimal nonlinear pricing by a multiproduct monopolist' chapter in D. Phil. Thesis, in preparation, Oxford University.

Armstrong, C. Mark and Vickers, John (1992) 'Competition and regulation in telecommunications' forthcoming in Matthew Bishop, John Kay, Colin Mayer and David Thompson (eds) *Privatization and Regulation – The UK Experience*, Oxford: Oxford University Press.

Arrow, Kenneth J. (1985) 'The economics of agency', in John Pratt and Richard Zeckhauser (eds) *Principals and Agents: The Structure of Business*, Cambridge, Mass.: Harvard University Press.

Averch, Harvey and Johnson, Leland (1962) 'Behavior of the firm under regulatory constraint', *American Economic Review* 52: 1052–69.

Baron, David P. and Besanko, D. (1984) 'Regulation, asymmetric information and auditing', *Rand Journal of Economics* 15: 447–70.

Baron, David P. and Myerson, Roger (1982) 'Regulating a monopolist with unknown costs', *Econometrica* 50: 911–30.

Baumol, William J. and Bradford, D. (1970) 'Optimal departures from marginal cost pricing', *American Economic Review* 60: 265–83.

Baumol, William J. and Klevorick, Alvin K. (1970) 'Input choices and rate of return regulation: an overview of the discussion', *Bell Journal of Economics* 1: 162–90.

Baumol, William J., Panzar, J.C. and Willig, Robert D. (1982) *Contestable Markets and the Theory of Industry Structure*, New York: Harcourt Brace Jovanovich.

Bawa, V.S. and Sibley, David S. (1980) 'Dynamic behaviour of a firm subject to stochastic regulatory review', *International Economic Review* 21: 627–42.

Beesley, Michael E. and Littlechild, Stephen C. (1991) 'The regulation of privatized monopolies in the United Kingdom', in C. Veljanovski (ed.) *Regulators and the Market: an Assessment of the Growth of Regulation in the UK*, London: Institute of Economic Affairs.

Berg, V. Sanford and Tschirhart, John (1988) *Natural Monopoly Regulation: Principles and Practice*, Cambridge: Cambridge University Press.

Besanko, David and Donenfeld, Shabtai (1988) 'Rate of return regulation and product variety', *Journal of Public Economics* 36: 293–304.

Bishop, M., Kay, J., Mayer, C. and Thompson, D. (1992) *Privatisation and Regulation – The UK Experience* (2nd edn), Oxford: Oxford University Press.

Bos, Dieter (1991) *Privatization: A Theoretical Treatment*, Oxford: Clarendon Press.

Bradley, Ian and Price, Catherine (1988) 'The economic regulation of private industries by price constraints', *Journal of Industrial Economics* 37: 99–106.

Braeutigam, Ronald R. (1979) 'Optimal pricing with intermodal competition', *American Economic Review* 69: 38–49.

—— (1984) 'Socially optimal pricing with rivalry and economies of scale', *Rand Journal of Economics* 15: 127–34.

Braeutigam, Ronald R. and Panzar, John C. (1989) 'Diversification incentives under "price-based" and "cost-based" regulation', *Rand Journal of Economics* 20: 373–91.

Brock, W.A. and Dechert, W.D. (1985) 'Dynamic Ramsey Pricing', *International Economic Review* 26: 569–91.

Brown, Stephen J. and Sibley, David S. (1986) *The Theory of Public Utility Pricing*, Cambridge: Cambridge University Press.

Cabral, L.M.B. and Riordan, Michael H. (1989) 'Incentives for cost reduction under price cap regulation', *Journal of Regulatory Economics* 1: 133–47.

Caillaud, Bernard (1990) 'Regulation, competition and asymmetric information', *Journal of Economic Theory* 52: 87–110.

Caillaud, Bernard, Guesnerie, Roger, Rey, Patrick and Tirole, Jean (1998) 'Government intervention in production and incentives theory: a review of recent contributions', *Rand Journal of Economics* 19: 1–26.

Clemenz, Gerhard (1991) 'Optimal price-cap regulation', *Journal of Industrial Economics* 34: 391–408.

Coase, Ronald H. (1937) 'The nature of the firm', *Economica* 4: 386–405.

—— (1946) 'The marginal cost controversy', *Economica* 13: 169–89.

Cross, John G. (1970) 'Incentive pricing and utility regulation', *Quarterly Journal of Economics* 84: 236–53.

Demsetz, H. (1968) 'Why regulate utilities?', *Journal of Law and Economics* 11: 55–65.

Department of Transport (1986) *Economic Regulation of the British Airports Authority plc*, London: HMSO.

Doyle, Christopher (1992) 'British Telecom: historical and institutional analysis', forthcoming in I. Vogelsang (ed.) *Divestiture in the UK: A Cost-Benefit Case Study*, World Bank.

Faulhaber, Gerald R. (1975) 'Cross-subsidization: pricing in public enterprises', *American Economic Review* 65: 966–77.

Finsinger, J. and Vogelsang, Ingo (1985) 'Strategic management behaviour under reward structures in a planned economy', *Quarterly Journal of Economics* 100: 263–70.

Fudenberg, Drew and Tirole, Jean (1991) *Game Theory*, Cambridge, Mass.: MIT Press.

Gilbert, Richard and Newbery, David (1991) 'Regulation Games' mimeo, University of Cambridge.

Greenwald, B.C. (1984) 'Rate base selection and the structure of regulation', *Rand Journal of Economics* 15: 85–95.

Hotelling, H. (1938) 'The general welfare in relation to problems of taxation and of railway and utility rates', *Econometrica* 6: 242–69.

Joskow, P.L. (1974) 'Inflation and environmental concern: structural change in the process of public utility price regulation', *Journal of Law and Economics* 17: 291–327.

Kay, John A. and Thompson, David J. (1986) 'Privatisation: a policy in search of a rationale', *Economic Journal* 96: 18–32.

Kay, John and Vickers, John (1988) 'Regulatory reform in Britain', *Economic Policy* 7: 285–352.

Klevorick, Alvin (1973) 'The behaviour of a firm subject to stochastic regulatory review', *Bell Journal of Economics* 4: 57–88.

Laffont, Jean-Jacques and Tirole, Jean (1989) *'Provision of Quality and Power of Incentive Schemes in Regulated Industries'*, MIT working paper, Department of Economics, number 528, Cambridge, Mass.

—— (1990a) 'The regulation of multiproduct firms, Part I: theory', *Journal of Public Economics* 43: 1–36.

—— (1990b) 'The regulation of multiproduct firms, Part II: applications to competitive environments and policy analysis', *Journal of Public Economics* 43: 37–66.

—— (1991) 'The politics of government decision making: a theory of regulatory capture', *Quarterly Journal of Economics* 1089–127.

Lewis, Tracy and Sappington, David E.M. (1989) 'Regulatory options and price-cap regulation', *Rand Journal of Economics* 20: 405–16.

Littlechild, Stephen C. (1983) *'Regulation of British Telecom's Profitability'* Report to the Secretary of State, Department of Industry, London: HMSO.

Loeb, M. and Magat, W.A. (1979) 'A decentralized method for utility regulation', *Journal of Law and Economics* 22: 399–404.

Mirman, L.J. and Sibley, David S. (1980) 'Optimal nonlinear prices for multiproduct monopolies', *Bell Journal of Economics* 11: 659–70.

Mirrlees, James M. (1971) 'An exploration in the theory of optimal taxation', *Review of Economic Studies* 38: 175–208.

—— (1976) 'Optimal tax theory: a synthesis', *Journal of Public Economics*.

Mitchell, Bridger M. and Vogelsang, Ingo (1991) *Telecommunications Pricing: Theory and Practice*, Rand Corporation manuscript, Cambridge: Cambridge University Press.

Moore, John (1983) 'Why privatise?', in John Kay, Colin Mayer and David Thompson (eds) (1986) *Privatisation and Regulation – the UK Experience*, Oxford: Clarendon Press.

Morrison, Herbert (1933) *Socialisation of Transport*, London: Constable.

Mussa, M. and Rosen, S. (1978) 'Monopoly and product quality', *Journal of Economic Theory* 23: 301–17.

Ng, Y-K and Weisser, M. (1974) 'Optimal pricing with a budget constraint: the case of the two-part tariff', *Review of Economic Studies* 41: 337–45.

Oftel (1992) *The Regulation of BT's Prices*, A Consultative Document, London: HMSO.

Ordover, J.A. and Panzar, J. (1980) 'On the non-existence of Pareto superior outlay schedules', *Bell Journal of Economics* 11: 351–54.

Panzar, J.C. (1976) 'A neoclassical approach to peak load pricing', *Bell Journal of Economics* 7: 521–30.

Pryke, R. (1981) *The Nationalised Industries: Policies and Performance since 1968*, Oxford: Martin Robertson.

—— (1982) 'The comparative performance of public and private enterprise', *Fiscal Studies* 3: 68–81.

Ramsey, Frank R. (1927) 'A contribution to the theory of taxation', *Economic Journal* 37: 47–61.

Roberts, Kevin W.S. (1979) 'Welfare considerations of non-linear pricing', *Economic Journal* 89: 66–83.

Sappington, David E.M. (1980) 'Strategic firm behaviour under a dynamic regulatory adjustment process', *Bell Journal of Economics* 11: 360–72.

Sappington, David E.M. and Sibley, David S. (1988) 'Regulation without cost information: the incremental surplus subsidy scheme', *International Economic Review* 29: 297–306.

Schmalensee, Richard (1989) 'Good regulatory regimes', *Rand Journal of Economics* 20: 417–36.

Sharkey, W.W. (1982) *The Theory of Natural Monopoly*, Cambridge: Cambridge University Press.

Sherman, Roger (1989) *The Regulation of Monopoly* Cambridge: Cambridge University Press.

Sherman, Roger and Visscher, Michael (1978) 'Second-best pricing with stochastic demand', *American Economic Review* 68: 41–53.

Sheshinski, E. (1971) 'Welfare aspects of regulatory constraint: Note', *American Economic Review* 61: 175–8.

Shleifer, A. (1985) 'A theory of yardstick regulation', *Rand Journal of Economics* 16: 319–27.

Sibley, David (1989) 'Asymmetric information, incentives and price-cap regulation', *Rand Journal of Economics* 20: 391–404.

Spence, A. Michael (1977) 'Nonlinear prices and welfare', *Journal of Public Economics* 8: 1–18.

Spulber, Daniel E. (1989) *Regulation and Markets*, Cambridge, Mass.: MIT Press.

Srinagesh, P. (1986) 'Nonlinear prices and the regulated firm', *Quarterly Journal of Economics* 101: 51–68.

Stigler, George (1971) 'The theory of economic regulation', *The Bell Journal of Economics and Management Science* 2: 3–21.

Tirole, Jean (1988) *The Theory of Industrial Organization*, Cambridge, Mass.: MIT Press.

Train, Kenneth E. (1991) *Optimal Regulation: The Economic Theory of Natural Monopoly*, Cambridge, Mass.: MIT Press.

Velijanovski, Cento (ed.) (1991) *Regulators and the Market: An Assessment of the Growth of Regulation in the UK*, London: Institute of Economic Affairs.

Vickers, John and Yarrow, George (1988a) *Privatization: An Economic Analysis*, Cambridge, Mass.: MIT Press.

—— (1988b) 'Regulatory reform in Britain', *Economic Policy*, 7: 286–351.

—— (1988c) 'Regulation of privatised firms in Britain', *European Economic Review* 32: 465–72.

Vickrey, W. (1948) 'Some objections to marginal cost pricing', *Journal of Political Economy* 56: 218–38.

Vogelsang, Ingo (1989) 'Two-part tariffs as regulatory constraints', *Journal of Public Economics* 39: 45–66.

—— (ed.) (1992) *Divestiture in the UK: A Cost Benefit Study*, forthcoming, World Bank.

Vogelsang, Ingo and Finsinger, Jorg (1979) 'A regulatory adjustment process for optimal pricing by multiproduct firms', *Bell Journal of Economics* 10: 157–71.

Waterson, Michael (1989) *Regulation of the Firm and Natural Monopoly*, Oxford: Blackwell.

Weitzman, Martin L. (1978) 'Optimal rewards for economic regulation', *American Economic Review* 68: 683–91.

Williamson, Oliver (1985) *The Economic Institutions of Capitalism*, New York: The Free Press.

Willig, Robert D. (1978) 'Pareto-superior non-linear outlay schedules', *Bell Journal of Economics* 9: 56–9.

Willig, Robert D. and Bailey, Elizabeth E. (1977) 'Ramsey optimal pricing of long distance telephone services', in J.T. Wenders (ed.) *Pricing in Regulated Industries: Theory and Application*, pp. 68–97. Denver, Col.: The Mountain States Telephone and Telegraph Company.

Yarrow, George (1986) 'Privatization in theory and practice', *Economic Policy* 2.

7

REGULATION OF MERGERS
A new agenda
Ajit Singh

Mergers have long been a subject of regulation in one form or another in advanced capitalist economies like the US and the UK. However, there have been important changes in both countries in the nature of merger activity over time, particularly during the second part of this century. Further, with the deregulation and the globalization of financial markets, and the ever greater capital market integration among industrial countries, there have also been major changes in economic environment in the recent period. These have raised fresh issues for mergers regulation both nationally and internationally. An analysis of these new issues will be the main subject of this chapter.

The chapter will concentrate on mergers policies in the UK and the US. This is for two reasons. First, the basic legal framework within which the corporations of the two countries operate is broadly similar; it differs significantly from corporate law in other advanced industrial economies, e.g. Germany. Secondly and more importantly, for institutional reasons, new questions with respect to mergers policies, which are connected as we shall see below with the operation of the market for corporate control, have arisen in their most acute form in these two countries. However, we shall also briefly comment on the emerging mergers policy in the EC, where such issues are also becoming important.

THE ANALYTICAL BASIS OF MERGER POLICY: THE TRADITIONAL MODEL

As mergers can have both positive (e.g. synergy) and negative (e.g. monopoly power) effects on economic welfare, the governmental regulation of mergers needs to make an overall assessment of their impact. The Williamson (1968) trade-off model – in which the

141

economies of scale arising from a merger are compared with its monopolistic consequences – provided a formal basis for such an assessment. This has been a useful and an influencial model but it has serious limitations.

Specifically, the Williamson model is a static, partial equilibrium construct which does not take into account important dynamic effects of mergers on technical progress, investment, growth, etc. It also ignores distributional issues. Moreover, without considerable modifications, in its traditional form the model is inapplicable in an economy with involuntary unemployment or in one with a balance of payments disequilibrium. Thus, to take an example, in a balance of payments constrained economy, suppose the conventionally measured Williamson welfare losses due to monopoly power arising from a merger outweigh its synergic effects. In such an economy, the merger might still be socially desirable if it leads either to an increase in exports or to a reduction in imports and therefore to a relaxation of the balance of payments constraint.[1]

Nevertheless, there is a large body of empirical literature on mergers which in one form or another derives its inspiration from this trade-off approach. This research is however subject to further limitations. First, the negative effects of mergers in these studies are examined mostly in terms of their impact just on monopoly power (as measured by some indicator of industrial concentration). Secondly, again because of the lack of adequate data, an appraisal of the potential positive effect of mergers is generally carried out in these contributions simply in terms of their impact on the private profitability of merging companies. There are only a small number of studies which have attempted to directly assess the effects of mergers on the costs of production of the amalgamating corporations. There are fewer studies still of the impact of mergers on exports, on research and development, on growth or investment. There are hardly any quantitative analyses at all of the very important distributional issues which arise in mergers.[2] It is therefore difficult on the basis of this corpus of empirical research to arrive at an overall conclusion concerning the effects of mergers either on economic efficiency or on social welfare.

Notwithstanding these shortcomings, what conclusions can be drawn from the available empirical studies by industrial organization economists concerning mergers policy?[3] With respect to the effects of mergers on monopoly power there are two important points which emerge from this research. Very briefly, first, although mergers can increase market power, it is easy to show analytically and there is also evidence that industrial concentration may increase even if there were few or no mergers, purely as a result of the normal growth process of firms.[4] Second, and conversely, even if there was a high incidence of mergers, there need not necessarily be any increase in industrial concentration or monopoly power. This is because changes in concentration are a function of a number of variables other than just mergers or variations in the normal growth rates of firms. This point is particularly significant for mergers policy in the most recent period since there is empirical evidence that despite the big merger waves of the early 1970s and of the 1980s, there has been little increase in industrial concentration either in the US or in the UK during the last two decades.

There have been a large number of contributions by industrial organization economists on the effects of mergers on the profitability of the amalgamating firms. Although the sample sizes and the time periods examined differ, these studies both for the UK and the US, with relatively few exceptions, lead to remarkably uniform results. Generally speaking, this research shows that mergers either have a negative or neutral effect on profitability. Whatever the effects of mergers on the level of concentration of the industry as a whole (which as noted above depends on a number of variables other than mergers), *ceteris paribus*, amalgamating firms are more likely to experience a rise – and certainly not a decline – in market power as a consequence of a merger.[5] Therefore to the extent that there is any increase in market power arising from a merger, even the observed result of a neutral impact on profitability would imply reduced efficiency in resource use.

On the basis of the above empirical research on mergers, many industrial organization economists have argued in favour of a much tighter policy on mergers. The underlying reasoning here is that since mergers can lead to increased market power, and since they do not on average seem to produce a greater efficiency in the utilization of resources, they should be subject to strict regulation. In the case of the UK for example, where, as we shall see below, a liberal policy towards mergers has usually been followed, it has been suggested that the policy presumption should be that mergers are harmful unless shown otherwise. In other words, in place of a positive or even neutral stance towards mergers, these economists recommend that the onus should be on the merging companies to prove that the merger will lead to a net benefit before it is permitted by the regulatory authorities.[6]

MERGERS POLICIES IN THE UK AND THE US

Historically, there have been important differences in the regulatory philosophy concerning mergers in the US and the UK. The US has traditionally tended to follow a structural anti-trust policy which regards a competitive market structure as an end in itself. The UK on the other hand has normally followed a case by case trade-off approach in which, in principle, the regulatory authorities attempt to assess the net social benefits of a merger by comparing its efficiency and other social gains with its possible harmful effects on competition and other specified variables. Thus in the traditional UK regulatory perspective, a merger with substantial anti-competitive effects may be permitted provided it generated compensating national benefits in terms of economies of scale, an improvement in the balance of payments, etc. In view of the historic US concern with product market competition, such a merger would not normally have passed the regulatory test in that country.

However, in the 1980s, there have coincidentally been major changes in mergers policies in both countries. This has brought about a degree of convergence in their respective regulatory approaches. Thus, in the US, most observers agree that the mergers policy became much more lenient under the Reagan administration.[7] This was achieved partly by a relaxation of the US Department of Justice's 1968 Merger Guidelines, and in part by a lenient interpretation of the revised 1982 and 1984 Guidelines by the Reagan appointees to the Anti-trust Division of the Department of Justice (see White 1988).

The 1984 Guidelines describe the current US regulatory philosophy towards mergers as follows:[8]

> Although they sometimes harm competition, mergers generally play an important role in a free enterprise economy. They can penalize ineffective management and facilitate the efficient flow of investment capital and the redeployment of existing productive assets. While challenging competitively harmful mergers, the Department seeks to avoid unnecessary interference with the larger universe of mergers that are either competitively beneficial or competitively neutral.

Apart from this general laissez-faire basic stance, which permits all conglomerate mergers in any case, the new Guidelines also give far greater importance than before to the 'efficiency' defence in horizontal mergers. Thus the Guidelines:

144

Some mergers that the Department otherwise might challenge may be necessary to achieve significant efficiencies. If the parties ... establish ... that a merger will achieve such efficiencies, the Department will consider those efficiencies in deciding whether to challenge the merger.

In the UK, the Thatcher Government also introduced in the 1980s very important changes to the traditional UK policy towards mergers outlined above. Keeping in line with its general laissez-faire economic policy, the Department of Trade and Industry (DTI) recently described the fundamental basis of government policy towards mergers in the following terms: '... the market should be allowed to decide whether a merger should go ahead, since the free commercial decisions of private decision markers tend to result in the most desirable outcomes for the economy as a whole'. The DTI further states that:

the Government should only intervene in those mergers in which the private interests and the public interests diverge – typically where a merger has the potential to allow the abuse of the merged enterprise's monopoly power. The Government does not believe that it would be consistent to intervene more generally in mergers, *for whatever reason.* [emphasis added][9]

However, although the government is concerned with identifying and preventing mergers with anti-competitive effects, the Office of Fair Trading also states that they wish 'to allow mergers to go ahead with the least possible delay or impediment'.

Thus, compared with the pre-Thatcher era, the main changes in government policy towards mergers in the 1980s have been twofold. First, if anything, the policy is even more permissive than before. Second, and more importantly, the government takes a very narrow view of the 'national interest' in considering the benefits or harmful effects of mergers: its only concern is with the impact on competition. There are three main channels of regulation of mergers in this country: the Office of Fair Trading; the Monopolies and Mergers Commission; and the Takeover Panel. All proposed takeovers above a certain size, and all those involving corporations having a combined market share of more than a quarter, are examined by the OFT for possible referral to the MMC. In practice only a small proportion of bids are actually referred – about two to three per cent; of these about a third are eventually approved by the Commission. The main purpose of the Takeover Panel is to protect the rights of the shareholders in the victim company and to ensure fair conduct of takeover bids as transactions on the Stock Exchange.[10]

To sum up, there have been far-reaching changes in the regulation of merger activity in the 1980s, both in the US and in the UK. Some commentators ascribe them to the ideological conceptions of the Thatcher and Reagan Governments. Although ideology has clearly played a role, there were also other significant factors. The most important of these is obviously the operation of the market for corporate control. Such a market, for a number of reasons, has emerged only relatively recently – since about the mid-1950s in the UK and about a decade later in the US (Singh 1992). An essential foundation of the Thatcher–Reagan philosophy of mergers regulation is the belief in the virtues of a freely functioning market for corporate control. In addition, in the US, the greater attention given to the efficiency defence in horizontal takeovers and the diminished concern with domestic competition, can be attributed to the great inroads which foreign competition has made in the US economy.

THE MERGERS POLICY AND THE MARKET FOR CORPORATE CONTROL

As opposed to the industrial organization economists, many of whom as we saw above favour a strict regulation of mergers, the case for a liberal, indeed even a more or less laissez-faire mergers policy is most forcefully put forward these days by specialists in corporate finance. The argument of the latter rests essentially on a highly positive assessment of the operations of the market for corporate control. Thus, Jensen, a leading scholar in this field, observes:

> The market for corporate control is creating large benefits for shareholders and for the economy as a whole by lessening control over vast amounts of resources and enabling them to move more quickly to their highest-valued use. This is a healthy market in operation, on both the take-over side and the divestiture side, and it is playing an important role in helping the American economy adjust to major changes in competition and regulation of the past decade.
>
> (Jensen 1988: 23)

The central analytical propositions underlying the view of Jensen and other finance specialists are complex but can be put as follows.[11] In view of the separation of ownership from control, large corporations in a

146

modern economy suffer from an acute 'agency' problem. Moreover, because of incomplete contracts, asymmetric information between shareholders (the principals) and managers (the agents), and the organizational requirements for the efficient functioning of the modern corporation, the managers inevitably have a great deal of discretion. This discretion can, and often is, used by managers to pursue their own ends (e.g. perks, empire building) rather than those of the shareholders.

Further, since it is difficult to organize collective action by share-holders dispersed throughout society to make the managers account-able, the market for corporate control provides the only means by which inefficient managers, or those who do not promote shareholders' interests, can be disciplined. In this paradigm, the free operation of the takeover mechanism can benefit society through two distinct channels: the *threat* of takeovers can discipline inefficient managements and reduce 'agency costs'; and even if the firms were working efficiently, takeovers may lead to a reorganization of their productive resources and thereby enhance shareholder value.

In the case for a basically laissez-faire policy towards mergers, these theoretical propositions are buttressed by significant empirical research. First, it is argued on the basis of empirical evidence that mergers have not significantly increased individual industry concentration in the US over the last two decades (a point already noted above). Secondly, it is suggested that contrary to the conclusions of the industrial organization economists, mergers in fact substantially increase economic efficiency. This latter proposition rests on a large number of empirical studies based on stock market data (as opposed to industrial organization research, which uses accounting information). This stock market research, employing the so-called 'event study' methodology, typically shows a considerable rise in the share price of the victim firm in the short period leading up to the takeover 'event'. Over the same period the share price of the acquiring firm generally shows either a small positive or a small negative change. Since, overall, these two results indicate a rise in the combined stock market value of the amalgamating firms, it is argued that takeovers must on average enhance economic efficiency.

The above analysis and evidence is employed by Jensen and his colleagues to suggest that the market for corporate control should be allowed to function freely. They, therefore, regard anti-takeover legisla-tion, which many individual American states have instituted in reaction to the huge merger wave of the 1980s, as being misconceived and promoted by special interests. Some scholars belonging to this school would go even further. They not only oppose any new anti-merger regulatory measures but suggest that the extant institutional obstacles to takeovers should be eliminated. There are at present a number of stock exchange provisions both in the US and the UK whose main purpose is to afford protection to minority shareholders and to ensure 'fair play' and transparency in share transactions connected with the takeover process. For example, in the UK a corporate raider is obliged to disclose its stake in the victim company after it has purchased 3 per cent of the victim's shares. Moreover, the raider is required to make a full cash bid for all the shares of the company after it has purchased 30 per cent of the victim's stock. The exponents of the virtues of the market for corporate control believe that such regulations constitute imperfections in the free functioning of the market; they are, therefore, ipso facto inefficient, and hence should be removed.[12]

FAILURE IN THE MARKET FOR CORPORATE CONTROL

The virtues of the market for corporate control outlined in the last section are vigorously contested by an increasing number of economists on both sides of the Atlantic. Firstly, these economists point to the relative economic performance and the international competitive success of countries like Germany and Japan in comparison with the Anglo-Saxon economies. For various institutional reasons, hostile takeovers are rare in Germany and Japan; these countries, therefore, do not possess a market for corporate control of the kind which exists in the UK and the US.[13] Could it be that the alleged disciplinary and efficiency properties of such a market are greatly overrated?

Secondly, research shows that there are a number of reasons why even in principle the market for corporate control may not work efficiently in the real world. Hughes and Singh (1987) had noted that in theory there are stringent requirements for the efficient operation of such a market: (a) the share prices prevailing on the stock market should be 'efficient' in Tobin's (1989) 'fundamental valuation' sense, i.e. that relative share prices of corporations reflect their relative expected profitability; and (b) that there should exist an efficient takeover mechanism in the sense that any firm whose current stock market value is less than what it could be under any other management is acquired by that management. Either (a) or (b), or both, may not be adequately met in the actual economy. There are a number for thinking that that is indeed the case.

First, in an early contribution, Singh (1971) pointed out that there is a basic asymmetry in the market for corporate control as it works in practice in countries like the US and the UK. Other things being equal, it is much easier for a larger firm to take over a small one than the other way round. However, the 1980s merger boom in both these countries has been characterized by takeovers of very large corporations by means of leveraged buy-outs and debt financing, often with junk bonds. More than ever before, giant corporations were frequently the subject of hostile bids. However, it is important to observe that, despite these takeovers of big corporations, there still continues to be a non-linear negative relationship between firm size and the probability of takeover, as found in previous studies. Thus in the UK, the largest hundred corporations, even in the 1980s, had a far smaller chance of being taken over than those ranked in the next hundred. It was in fact the latter, medium-sized corporations which became much more vulnerable to takeovers during the last decade, usually by those ranked in the top hundred.[14]

Second, there are a number of other empirically important, but analytically straightforward reasons why the market for corporate control may not work effectively. These include the inefficiency of real-world share prices in the 'fundamental valuation' sense; the inadequacy of information available to potential raiders so that they may not be in a position to launch disciplinary takeover bids; and the fact that large raiders may themselves be dominated by empire-building rather than value-maximizing managers.[15]

Thirdly, some of the most interesting analysis in this area in recent years has been concerned with demonstrating, not just that the takeover mechanism may not work efficiently, but that it may operate perversely in a variety of ways. Thus Stein (1988, 1989) has established that even if the stock market was rational it might be an optimal strategy for managers to be myopic and undertake short rather than long term value-maximizing projects. The argument rests on assuming imperfect and asymmetric information between shareholders and managers, the use of current earnings by managers to 'signal' future prospects of the firm and the notion that there is 'signal jamming', as it pays any manager not to provide accurate signalling information and to inflate the corporation's current earnings. The threat of takeover, in these circumstances, instead of promoting efficiency, because of signal jamming leads to a less socially desirable outcome.

Similarly, Shleifer and Summers (1988) suggest that the micro-economic private efficiency gains from takeovers – even to the extent that they exist – may greatly overstate the social benefit. Increased post-takeover profitability and hence the rise in the raider's share price may not necessarily represent a genuine improvement in social efficiency, but it may simply be a transfer of resources from one group of 'stake-holders' (for example, employees) in the firm to another, i.e. the shareholders. More importantly, such transfers, which takeovers, for various institutional reasons, facilitate, may be socially harmful, in that they involve a breach of trust and the breaking of implicit contracts between managers and workers. It is on the basis of trust and these associated implicit contracts that workers undertake firm-specific training which leads to greater productivity and thus benefits both the firm and the economy. Such transfers between stake-holders and shareholders and the breach of trust which takeovers may induce will therefore be socially harmful.

Fourthly, for the above as well as for other reasons, a number of economists and industrialists in both the US and the UK suggest that the operation of the market for corporate control leads to 'short-termism' and to higher expected rates of return on investment projects than is the case in Japan and Germany, where takeovers and the stockmarket do not play a predominant role in the country's industrial life. Very briefly, a typical Anglo-Saxon industrial firm, it is argued, is under constant pressure, because of the fear of takeover, to meet the stockmarket's quarterly or half-yearly earnings per share target. On the other side of the market, the fund managers and the institutional investors are under a different kind of pressure to seek short term gains. The latter's own performance is assessed by their principals (e.g. pension fund trustees) by the relatively short term results on the investments they manage.

The net outcome is a pervasive short-termist outlook on both sides of the stock market. This is particularly harmful for the real economy as it discourages long term investment, innovation and product develop-ment. All this puts the US and the UK industry, it is suggested, at a competitive disadvantage in relation to economies where such stock market induced pressures do not prevail.[16] In view of the above, contrary to the finance specialists, many economists argue in favor of a stricter mergers policy, precisely in order to curb the harmful effects of the market for corporate control.

EMPIRICAL EVIDENCE ON THE MARKET FOR CORPORATE CONTROL AND ALTERNATIVE INTERPRETATIONS OF 'EVENT' STUDIES OF MERGERS

The case of the critics of the market for corporate control is greatly reinforced by the empirical evidence on the nature of the discipline which takeovers actually represent and how effective that discipline is in practice. The critics also put forward a rather different interpretation on the event studies of mergers which, as we saw on earlier pages 146–8, the finance specialists regard as important evidence in favour of the proposition that takeovers promote economic efficiency.

On the nature of the takeovers' disciplinary mechanism, two decades of systematic research suggests that, contrary to the folklore of capitalism and the proponents of the virtues of the market for corporate controls, takeovers do not simply punish the inefficient and the unprofitable, and select for survival companies which best enhance shareholder wealth. These studies unequivocally conclude that although takeover selection does take place to a limited degree on the basis of profitability or stock market valuation, it also importantly does so in terms of size. Thus, in the market for corporate control, a large unprofitable corporation has a much higher chance of survival than a small relatively much more profitable company.[17]

As a consequence, the threat of takeover instead of forcing firms to improve their profitability, may in fact encourage them to further increase their size. This 'perverse' result of the takeover mechanism may be compounded by the takeover mechanism itself since it may enable relatively inefficient large firms to grow larger still by taking over more efficient smaller firms.[18]

The above research, bearing on the question of the threat of takeovers, is based on an analysis of the premerger characteristics of the taken over, the acquiring and acquired firms. We turn now to the studies of post-merger effects of takeovers. Two types of these studies have been reported in the previous sections which arrive at conflicting conclusions. Research by industrial organization economists on the effects of mergers on profitability shows that mergers do not improve economic efficiency; most likely they reduce it. The 'event' studies of the effects of mergers on share prices arrive at a diametrically opposite conclusion with respect to the efficiency of mergers. How is this conflict to be reconciled?

There are a number of reasons for believing that the conflict is more apparent than real.[19] First, the synergic benefits interpretation of financial studies assumes that share prices in the real world are efficient in the fundamental valuation sense. However, many analytical and empirical studies cast serious doubt on this underlying hypothesis. These studies suggest that, even if share prices were efficient in Tobin's (1989) information arbitrage sense (i.e. that they quickly incorporate all available information), they still may not reflect fundamental values. They may be subject to considerable disequilibria, whims and fashions, so that the actual share prices differ substantially from the fundamentals for long periods.[20]

Second, the event studies of mergers also suggest that, following the takeover, there are abnormal negative returns to the acquiring firms in the year or two following the takeover. In a very large recent study of nearly two thousand takeovers over the period 1955–85, Franks, Harris and Mayer (1988) found that these abnormal negative returns averaged about 17 per cent for the US sample in the two years following the take-over offer. This evidence is acknowledged, even by specialists in corporate finance, to be incompatible with either the hypothesis of the synergic benefits of takeovers, or that of market efficiency (see Ruback 1988).

Third, there are also other interpretations of the event studies results which do not accept the hypothesis of share prices always being in equilibrium and always reflecting fundamental values. The substantial bid premiums paid for the taken-over firms, which these studies reveal, are more compatible with a dual valuation view of stock market pricing of the takeover victims (Charkham 1989). In this conception there is a normal day-to-day evaluation of a small number of the company's shares, based on its expected earnings and reflecting valuation at the margin. However, there is a higher alternative valuation when the company is put into 'play' and is subject to a takeover bid; this reflects the price to be paid for buying out the intramarginal shareholders in order to gain control of the company (Shleifer 1986). If the raiders are empire-building managers they may be willing to offer a large premium for control, especially as they are paying with money which is not their own.

CONCLUSION:
A NEW AGENDA FOR MERGERS REGULATION

In the Reagan/Thatcher era in the 1980s, the regulation of mergers in both the US and the UK underwent important changes. A more liberal regulatory regime was adopted in each country based on the supposed virtues of a freely functioning market for corporate control. A review of the theoretical and empirical research on the subject shows that the alleged benefits of such a market are greatly overstated. The operations of the market not only do not enhance efficiency, but the results of the takeover process may be perverse in a number of ways.

Although the Reagan/Thatcher governments were wrong in their presuppositions about the market for corporate control, they have performed an important service by bringing these issues to the centre stage of the debate about mergers policy. Regulation of mergers clearly needs to go beyond traditional questions of monopoly and economies of scale, to consider also the broad issues of corporate governance and the agency problem in the modern corporation, as well as the nature of the discipline which the stock market actually represents. If the market leads to short-termism and to national competitive disadvantage, how should the workings of the takeover process be modified? What kind of incentive system is needed to induce managers to take a long term view in their investment decisions?

In view of the large redistributions of income and wealth which takeovers often involve between the shareholders, the employees and other stake-holders in the corporation, the regulation of mergers also needs to pay close attention to distributional questions. More generally, the emergence and the functioning of the market for corporate control raises in an acute form the following significant question of property rights in relation to a mergers policy. Is it desirable, or economically efficient that the right to dispose of the whole corporation should solely be the prerogative – as is presently the case under the Anglo-Saxon corporate law – of the absentee shareholders of the company without reference to any of the other interested parties?

All these are very important questions in a fresh approach to mergers regulation. The economic policy analysis of these issues will be the subject of further work.[21] In conclusion, it will be useful to draw attention here to certain international aspects of mergers regulation. A significant feature of the 1980s merger wave has been a high incidence of cross-borders or international mergers. Although in the merger boom of the 1960s there was a more or less simultaneous increase in the incidence of mergers in several industrial countries, most mergers involved amalgamation of domestic firms (Hughes and Singh 1980). There was relatively little international activity in this period. However, in the 1980s, with the globalization and deregulation of financial markets, there has been a large increase in foreign takeover activity particularly in

the US and the UK (Cosh *et al.* 1992). Many corporations in both countries in the 1980s have been the subject of foreign takeovers. There is
therefore an emerging international market for corporate control.
However, this market is very far from being perfect, as there are serious
legal and institutional obstacles to takeovers by foreign firms in industrial countries other than the US and the UK (Cosh *et al.* 1990).

How, if at all, should this growing international market be regulated?
In the European Community countries, one view, which is put forward
by both the European Commission and the UK government, is that
there should be 'level playing fields', and that essentially the liberal UK
approach to the regulation of the market for corporate control be
adopted by all countries.[22] However, if the analysis of this paper is
correct, there is no reason to believe that a freely functioning international market for corporate control would provide any greater
benefits, or be any less harmful to the real economy, than the national
markets. The Commission, if not the present British government,
certainly needs to rethink its general perspective in this area.

NOTES

1 See further Hughes *et al.* (1980).
2 A notable recent exception is the study, Shleifer and Summers and Vishny
   (1988).
3 There is a vast empirical literature by industrial organization economists on
   the issues outlined in this and the previous paragraph in both the US and
   the UK. For the UK, see for example Singh (1971, 1975). Meeks (1977),
   Hannah and Kay (1977), Hart and Clark (1980), Utton (1986), Cosh,
   Hughes and Singh (1980), Prais (1976), Cowling *et al.* (1980), Kumar
   (1984), Cosh *et al.* (1989). For a recent review of these studies see Hughes
   (1991). For the US, a leading recent study is Ravenscraft and Scherer
   (1987). See also the contributions in Auerbach (1988). For reviews of the
   US studies in this area, see Salop *et al.* (1987); Warshawsky (1987); Caves
   (1989).
   Studies by specialists in corporate finance, which apparently arrive at
   rather different conclusions from those of industrial organization
   economists concerning the efficiency of mergers, will be reviewed on
   pp. 146–8.
4 Singh and Whittington (1975); Ijiri and Simon (1977).
5 See however Hughes (1991).
6 See further Fairburn and Kay (1989).
7 White (1988).
8 This and the following extract from the 1984 guidelines are quoted in
   Salop (1988).
9 These extracts from DTI and the OFT in this paragraph come from the
   evidence submitted by these bodies to the Peacock Inquiry Into Corporate

Takeovers in the United Kingdom undertaken by The David Hume Institute for the Joseph Rowntree Foundation. See Peacock and Bannock (1991), chapters 4 and 6.

10 For a fuller discussion of the policy towards regulation of mergers in the UK, see Fairburn and Kay (1989), Peacock and Bannock (1991), Bank of England Quarterly Bulletin (1989).

11 For a fuller examination of these issues, the reader is referred to Singh (1992) and the literature cited there.

12 See further Jensen (1988); see also King (1989), Shleifer and Vishny (1988). An underlying theoretical issue involved in this argument is that of the so called 'free rider' problem. See Grossman and Hart (1980); see also Yarrow (1985).

13 For a fuller analysis, see Cosh et al. (1990); Singh (1992); Odagiri and Hase (1989).

14 Hughes and Singh (1987); Hughes (1991).

15 See further Singh (1992); Schleifer and Vishny (1988), Scherer (1988); Cosh et al. (1990), Summers (1986).

16 There is a large and growing literature on this subject. See Cosh et al. (1990); Hatsopoulos et al. (1988).

17 Empirical research on the nature of the takeover selection process has recently been reviewed in Singh (1992). See also Hughes and Singh (1987), Hughes (1991) and Warshawsky (1987).

18 Greer (1986); Singh (1971).

19 For a fuller discussion of this question see Singh (1992) on which the following paragraphs are based. See also Caves (1989).

20 The large amount of theoretical work in this area has recently been reviewed by Camerer (1989). See also Summers (1986), Poterba and Summers (1988), De Long et al. (1990).

21 See Cosh et al. (1990); Peacock and Bannock (1991).

22 Ibid. See also Chapter 8 in this volume.

REFERENCES

Auerbach, A.J. (ed.) (1988) *Corporate Takeovers: Causes and Consequences*, National Bureau of Economic Research, Chicago: University of Chicago Press.

Bank of England Quarterly Bulletin (1989) 'Takeover activity in the 1980s', February, pp. 78–85.

Camerer, C. (1989) 'Bubbles and fads in asset prices', *Journal of Economic Surveys* 3 (1).

Caves, R.E. (1989) 'Mergers, takeovers and economic efficiency: foresight vs. hindsight', *International Journal of Industrial Economics* 7 (1), March.

Charkham, J. (1989) 'Corporate governance and the market for control of companies', *Bank of England Panel Paper no. 25*, March.

Cosh, A.D., Hughes, A., Lee, K. and Singh, A. (1989) 'Institutional investment, mergers and the market for corporate control', *International Journal of Industrial Organisation*, March, pp. 73–100.

Cosh, A.D., Hughes, A. and Singh, A. (1980) 'The causes and effects of takeovers in the UK: an empirical investigation for the late 1960s at the micro-economic level', in D.C. Mueller (ed.) *The Determinants and Effects of Mergers*, Cambridge, Mass.: Oelschlager, Gunn and Hain.

—— (1990), 'Takeovers and short termism; analytical and policy issues in the UK economy', in *Takeovers and Short Termism in the UK*, Industrial Policy Paper No. 3, London: Institute for Public Policy Research.

—— (1992), 'Openness, innovation and share ownership: the changing structure of financial markets', in T. Banuri and J. Schor (eds) *Financial Openness and National Autonomy*, Oxford: Clarendon Press.

Cowling, K., Stoneman, P., Cubbin, K., Cable, J., Hall, G., Dornberger, S., and Dutton, P. (1980) *Mergers and Economic Performance*, Cambridge: Cambridge University Press.

De Long, J.B., Shleifer, A., Summers, L.H. and Waldmann, R.J. (1990) 'Noise trader risk in financial markets', *Journal of Political Economy* 98 (4).

Fairburn, J. and Kay, J.A. (eds) (1989) *Mergers and Merger Policy*, Oxford. (Second edition, forthcoming).

Franks, J., Harris, R.S., and Mayer, C. (1988) 'Means of payment in takeover: results for the United Kingdom and the United States', in A.J. Auerbach (ed.) *Corporate Takeovers: Causes and Consequences*, National Bureau of Economic Research, Chicago: University of Chicago Press.

Greer, D.F. (1986) 'Acquiring in order to avoid acquisition', *Antitrust Bulletin*, Spring.

Grossman, S.J. and Hart, O.D. (1980) 'Takeoverbids, the free-rider problem and the theory of the corporation', *Bell Journal of Economics* 11: 42–64.

Hannah, L. and Kay, J.A. (1977) *Concentration in Modern Industry*, London: Macmillan.

Hart, P.E. and Clark, R. (1980) *Concentration in British Industry, 1935–75*, Cambridge: Cambridge University Press.

Hatsopoulos, G.N., Krugman, P.R. and Summers, L.H. (1988) 'US competitiveness: beyond the trade deficit', *Science* 15 July.

Hughes, A. (1991). 'Mergers and economic performance in the UK: a survey of the empirical evidence 1950–1990', in Fairburn and Kay (eds), second edition (forthcoming).

Hughes, A. and Singh, A. (1980) 'Mergers, concentration and competition, in advanced capitalist economies: an international perspective', in D.C. Mueller (ed.) *The determinants and the Effects of Mergers*, Cambridge, Mass.: Oelschlager, Gunn and Hain.

—— (1987) 'Takeovers and the stock market', *Contributions to Political Economy*, March.

Hughes, A., Mueller, D.C. and Singh, A. (1980) 'Hypotheses about mergers', in D.C. Mueller (ed.) *The Determinants and Effects of Mergers*, Cambridge, Mass.: Oelschlager, Gunn and Hain.

Ijiri, Y. and Simon, H.A. (1977) *Skrew Distributions and the Sizes of Business Firms*, Amsterdam: North Holland.

Jensen, M.C. (1988) 'Takeovers: their causes and consequences', *Journal of Economic Perspectives*, Winter.

King, M.A. (1989) 'Takeover activity in the United Kingdom', in J.A. Fairburn and J.A. Kay (eds) *Mergers and Merger Policy*, Oxford: Clarendon Press.

Kumar, M.S. (1984) *Growth, Acquisition and Investment*, Cambridge: Cambridge University Press.

Meeks, G. (1977) *Disappointing Marriage: A Study of the Gains from Merger*, Cambridge: Cambridge University Press.

Odagiri, H. and Hase, T. (1989) 'Are mergers and acquisitions going to be popular in Japan too?: an empirical study', *International Journal of Industrial Organisation* 7 (1), March.

Peacock, A. and Bannock, G. (1991) *Corporate Takeovers and the Public Interest*, Aberdeen: Aberdeen University Press for the David Hume Institute.

Poterba, J.M., and Summers, L.H. (1988) 'Mean reversion in stock prices: evidence and implications', *Journal of Financial Economics* 22 (1).

Prais, S.J. (1976) *The Evolution of Firms in the United Kingdom*, Cambridge: Cambridge University Press.

Ravenscraft, D.J. and Scherer, F.M. (1987) *Mergers, Sell-Offs and Economic Efficiency*, Washington, DC: Brookings Institution.

Ruback, S.R. (1988) '"Comment" on Franks, Harris and Meyer 1988', in A.J. Auerbach (ed.) (1988) *Corporate Takeovers: Causes and Consequences*, National Bureau of Economic Research, Chicago: University of Chicago Press.

Salop, S.C. (1988) 'Remarks: panel discussion on corporate takeovers and public policy', in A.J. Auerbach (ed.) (1988) *Corporate Takeovers: Causes and Consequences*, National Bureau of Economic Research. Chicago: University of Chicago Press.

Salop, S.C. *et al.* (1987) 'Symposium on merger policy', *Journal of Economic Perspectives* 1 (Fall): 3–54.

Scherer, F.M. (1988) 'Corporate takeovers: the efficiency argument', *Journal of Economic Perspectives* Winter: 69–82.

Shleifer, A. (1986) 'Do demand curves for stocks slope down?', *Journal of Finance* 41: 579–90.

Shleifer, A. and Summers, L.H. (1988) 'Breach of trust in hostile takeovers', in A.J. Auerbach, (ed.) (1988) *Corporate Takeovers: Causes and Consequences*, National Bureau of Economic Research. Chicago: University of Chicago Press.

Shleifer, A. and Vishny, R.W. (1988) 'Value maximization and the acquisition process', *Journal of Economic Perspectives*, Winter.

Singh, A. (1971) *Takeovers: Their Relevance to the Stock Market and the Theory of the Firm*, Cambridge: Cambridge University Press.

—— 'Takeovers, economic "natural selection", and the theory of the firm: evidence from the post-war UK experience', *Economic Journal* 85: 497–515.

—— (1992), 'Corporate takeovers: a review', forthcoming in the *New Palgrave Dictionary of Money and Finance*, London: Macmillan.

Singh, A. and Whittington. G. (1975) 'The size and growth of firms', *Review of Economic Studies* 52: 15–26.

Stein, J.C. (1988). 'Takeover threats and managerial myopia', *Journal of Political Economy*, February, 96: 61–80.

—— (1989) 'Efficient stockmarkets, inefficient firms: a model of myopic corporate behaviour, *Quarterly Journal of Economics*, November, 104: 665–70.

Summers, L.H. (1986) 'Does the stock market rationally reflect fundamental values?', *Journal of Finance* 41: 591–601.

Tobin, J. (1989) 'On the efficiency of the financial system', *Lloyds Annual Bank*

Review No. 2. (ed. C. Johnston), London.

Utton, M.A. (1986) *Profits and the Stability of Monopoly*, Cambridge: Cambridge University Press.

Warshawsky, M.J. (1987) 'Determinants of corporate merger activity: a review of the literature', summarized in *Federal Reserve Bulletin*, April.

White, L.J. (1988) 'Remarks: in the discussion on corporate takeovers and public policy', in A.J. Auerbach (ed.) (1988) *Corporate Takeovers: Causes and Consequences*, National Bureau of Economic Research, Chicago: University of Chicago Press.

Williamson, O.E. (1968) 'Economies as an anti-trust defence: the welfare trade-offs', *American Economic Review* 58: 18–36.

Yarrow, G.K. (1985) 'Shareholder protection, compulsory acquisition and the efficiency of the takeover process', *Journal of Industrial Economics*, September.

Part V
GOVERNMENT
COLLABORATION

8

A RATIONALE FOR AN APPROPRIATE LEVEL OF REGULATION IN THE EUROPEAN COMMUNITY

Chris Farrands and Peter Totterdill

During the 1980s, an apparent intellectual consensus emerged in much of Western Europe which held that the main function of government in its relations with industry was the maintenance of a 'level playing field' on which industrial and economic activity could take place without further state intervention (see also Chapter 7). This consensus – always more real in ideology than in practice – has now clearly evaporated. By nineteenth century standards the modern economy has always demanded a high level of intervention, but practice varies substantially in the form that intervention takes. It can be through banks and the 'coordination' of sectors and large conglomerates, as in Japan and Germany, or conducted through weak central institutions and powerful regional activity as in Italy and, to a lesser extent, Spain. Intervention can operate through the development of joint state/industry collaborative mechanisms, as in Ireland, Italy and the five former GDR lander of Germany. It includes an element of defence or high technology planning in every country, and this indeed is the main form of intervention in the US. It now scarcely ever encompasses macro-economic Keynesian policies, large scale subsidy to nationalized firms, and large scale corporatism of the kind common in the 1960s and 1970s. But sectoral intervention, focused training policies, and the use of more targeted regional policies have become widespread. The development of sophisticated mechanisms of negotiating order in industry has evolved in Europe, if not always in the UK.

This chapter examines the arguments about regulation as they apply to different spatial levels within the European Community. This is a large subject, which could quite easily form the basis of several books. The first part of the chapter examines the diversity of regulatory practice

161

in the EC in the 1990s, which derives partly from a series of political compromises made at different times, and partly from the varied (and inconsistent) legal competences which the EC has evolved from its different sources. The second part of the chapter examines how these different frameworks can be integrated. Drawing on a comparison between policy experience in the UK and elsewhere in Europe, it argues an explicitly prescriptive case for a particular regulatory structure at European level. This would give a role to local and regional authorities, Member States and the EC institutions as actors within a co-ordinated framework of European regulation.

REGULATION IN THE EUROPEAN COMMUNITY

The sources of regulatory competence in the EC include the founding Treaties of Paris (for coal and steel 1951) and Rome (for the economic community 1957) (Lasok 1980; OECD 1978). But specific decisions and legislation are also important, such as the merger regulation of 1990 and the three hundred or more legislative acts which implement the Single Market. Decisions of the European Court of Justice shape the interpretation of community law and, in specific areas such as product recognition, health and safety rules, women's rights at work, and competition control, have played an enormously important part in the definition of the regulatory regimes which shape the behaviour of firms and individuals, as well as governments and EC institutions. The sources of regulatory rules also include other agreements, not least those on trade with countries such as the European Free Trade Association (EFTA) group and the very significant series of trade rounds agreed within the General Agreement on Tariffs and Trade (GATT), which have internal effects in the EC as well as an impact on trade relations (Hilf and Jacobs 1986; Jackson 1990). And they include recent amendments to the Treaty, especially the fundamental revisions contained in the Single European Act (in force since July 1987) and the Maastricht agreements of December 1991 (Lodge 1991). These varied competences no doubt create a valuable flexible space within which governments, firms, individuals and the EC institutions can achieve their varied interests. But it equally clearly proliferates an uncertainty which can benefit no one but the lawyers. There is no single source of regulation in the Community (see Wallace *et al.* 1983, on the complexities of EC decision making).

Comfortably simple sporting metaphors such as that of the 'level playing field' evade the issues which confront policy makers over the question of regulation, not least in relation to the nature of competition policy. European industry is highly concentrated in some key sectors, and the structural pressures to achieve economies of scale and to master large markets and expensive technologies eclipse smaller firms (Farrands 1988). The European economy is thus dominated by oligopolies in sectors such as electronics, telecommunications, chemicals, automotive production, and in a growing range of service industries. Competition policy focused at a national level would forbid many of these large firms. But in order to be competitive at a European level firms have had to grow, and a small number of firms effectively controls competition in many sectors. Globalization of production, research and marketing demand still larger-scale activities. The decision to intervene against a particular concentration in the European Community is in part a matter of discretion exercised by the Commission, basing a decision to act on existing law including the rules laid down by the court in previous cases. The law has proved to be effective in controlling cartels, but it has often been ineffective at limiting other anti-competitive practices amongst firms. Thus under Article 86 of the Rome Treaty, 'abuse of a dominant position' is forbidden, but the mere possession of a dominant position in a market is legal. Proof of abuse of a dominant position requires a high standard of evidence, and detailed information about market structures as well as about individual firm activities, generally rendering this rule almost worthless. On the other hand Article 85, which forbids cartels and cartel-like behaviour, has often been used successfully and precisely.

The Commission's regulation of 1990 on the competition policy control of mergers (EIU 1991) is an attempt to take account of the actual practice of companies. Corporate strategies have pointed firms towards the development of co-operative arrangements where the risks and costs of product development or research are spread, and not simply towards market sharing arrangements such as cartels. Complex interlinkages between firms are the natural outcomes of these strategies, including interlocking mutual share ownerships, joint ventures in research and development or in marketing. Financial institutions, especially major industrial banks in France, Italy and Germany, encourage collaboration within sectors and around base technologies (e.g. Sutton 1988). A 'European community' is rapidly emerging from such corporate strategies, whatever role governments choose to take (Farrands 1988, 1991). The need for regulation arises where particular firms act corruptly, but also more generally where the interests of individuals as citizens are excluded, as they generally are. The first function of regulation is thus not to achieve economic efficiency but (as it is in the national cases of pollution control) to balance economic and non-economic interests. In the face of (normally) legitimate but very powerful economic special interests, which the market has long been unable or unwilling to protect, the interests of individuals as consumers or citizens are neglected systematically. Thus in areas such as competition policy and, more broadly, in that activity which companies use to weaken the impact of market forces on them, the EC has a natural regulatory role. It is not necessary to see company activity as any kind of conspiracy to justify a relatively high degree of concern in the Community where the structure of the EC itself is encouraging the formation of large oligopolies such as now dominate a wide variety of industries in Europe.

Whatever their conception of government, European public authorities must seek a level of co-operation and agreement from other social interests. This constrains them to operate in broadly corporatist ways, meaning that they share information, access to decision making, power over outcomes, and a common language with key actors within the state and in the international arena. The exact forms of this 'corporatism' are subject to an intense debate in the academic literature. Cawson (1985) has argued convincingly that corporatism now operates primarily at a sectoral level rather than across the economy as a whole. Sargent (1985) and others have argued, less convincingly, that corporatism is weak in the EC. The information requirements of modern government demand an intimate discourse between industry and public authority in the EC, as at national and regional levels (Farrands 1983). This conversation becomes 'corporatist' when power, decision and responsibility are shared through it. The regulatory process is instrumental in information exchange. It also helps to define the scope of the public interest, since it is through regulatory discussions that the public interest is articulated and controlled by particular interests. Regulation is therefore an important part of the European Community's capacity to control industry and business. but the function of regulation is not limited to control. It also provides a framework for necessary information exchange between public authorities and business. This regular detailed exchange of information is an essential part of the corporatist interaction of the modern advanced capitalist state even when governments pretend to have no direct interest in intervention (e.g. Cawson 1985; Grant et al. 1988). It helps to legitimate a system of political economy in Europe and to manage power relations which operate in a distinctive way. And it reflects a series of ideological and practical compromises which constitute the specific nature of the EC as an actor in the global political economy.

The regulatory role of the European Community has never been sharply defined. Indeed, it has been the focus of considerable political argument. The Treaty of Rome provides a framework which envisages that European union will be created through a succession of steps; while the end goal is a single European political and economic unit, as each major step is negotiated the scope and competences of regulation are reviewed given the changing political priorities and ideology of the participating governments. If there is a general case for regulation, and often for substantial levels of regulation at the European Community level, this might not necessarily imply that it should be the institutions of the EC which do the regulating. Certainly the 1991 Maastricht summit decisively rejected the Dutch plan for a single regulatory framework under common EC control (*Financial Times*, 13 December 1991). Moreover there are currently a number of extra-EC frameworks of regulation, such as the EUREKA programme of intergovernmental and inter-firm technology collaboration, and it is at least theoretically possible to imagine that regulation could be developed across frontiers amongst the European countries but outside the formal EC mechanisms.

However, this will not happen: EC legal principles will ensure that economic and industrial policy regulation, with which we are concerned here, will develop primarily if not exclusively within the EC framework. This will continue to be the case as a single currency evolves. If this is challenged it will generally be protected by the European Court. This is shown in the Court's December 1991 judgement on the EFTA/EC negotiations to create a common economic space between the two institutions, in which it stated that the Court would assert the primacy of EC legal supremacy in economic decision-making over other external agreements wherever that was put in question. Furthermore, in practical terms the Brussels institutions already co-ordinate so much regulation that it would be administratively inefficient to use any other inter-governmental body. The EC has the information networks and has developed the skilled staff, as well as the legal competences in economic and monetary policy regulation, to take an overall supervisory role. This is especially the case where, as in the succession of crises in the City of London in 1990–1, national regulation proves feebly inadequate. Financial deregulation has promoted a series of dynamic changes in capital and insurance markets, but as the boom of the mid-1980s collapsed, the need for new controls and more careful policy management has become evident (cf. Moran 1991). But in a Single Market, that control and management must be supervised from Brussels – not least because the EC is at least potentially democratically accountable, whereas the main alternative, the Basle-based committee of European central bankers, is not. Furthermore, the political will exists to ensure a central role for the EC in economic regulation in a widening range of policy issues, including training, regional policies and local authority networking, consumer protection and employment rights, a process which has been accelerated through the creation of the Single Market however flawed or incomplete that may appear to be at the end of 1992 (Lodge 1990).

There is a powerful case that a broad regulatory climate should be set at the Community level, and that responsibility at least for making overall rules about regulation procedures should be managed by EC institutions. This is primarily because the EC has the oversight of the integrated market that is emerging and the legal competences to act. But it does not follow that the EC should in fact be responsible for the specific choice of regulations in all cases: it may lack information, expertise and authority to take more than a supervising role for economic and industrial policy regulation. Much of the process of regulation must necessarily be managed at a lower level. It is important that this should include regional or local authorities acting within the overall rules established at EC level, as well as national level authorities. In some cases, there may also be an argument for sectoral agencies to take decisions on regulatory regimes, providing that their ability to act quickly and with precise information is balanced by consumer and environmental interests in the composition of regulatory bodies. The argument about how far the EC should regulate through 'regulating regulation' and how far it should regulate directly has been obscured by other issues. It needs to be made more transparent and debated with greater thoroughness than has been the case to date: this is a key task for the Community agenda.

It also begs the question of what the main criteria should be when powers are divided between regulatory levels within a political system as complex as the emerging single Community. We would propose four main criteria. First, EC regulation must be accountable in the European Parliament and through an informed public debate. This does not necessarily require more decision making power passing to the European Parliament, but it does require the information seeking power of the MEPs to be increased in the face of the Council of Ministers as well as in the face of the Commission. Second, decisions must be transparent and made for stated reasons. Third, there is a need to leave the maximum freedom of action for all actors in a particular market, which must necessarily imply a tilt towards some (weaker) actors by regulators. Such a 'tilt' aims to ensure that unequally endowed interests in a plural society are not excluded from participation , a principle necessary for the assurance of justice which can only be sought with the mobilization of state power and authority. Finally, the regulatory regime should have as short a chain of communications and accountability as possible, to reduce complexity and delay to a minimum. These criteria are consistent with the practice of the Community and the recently much-used idea of subsidiarity. They would also necessarily involve a range of economic interests and actors in a form of regulation consistent with the interests of citizens and of the democratic process.

Approaches to regulation: examples from industrial and regional policy

In the opening part of this chapter, we examined the changing rationales and operational frameworks of regulation within the context of the Single European Market. This environment of change, with its resulting emphasis on economic and administrative versatility, requires increasingly customized approaches to regulation. Regulation will need to be sensitive to divergent models of production while seeking, for example, the harmonization of labour market conditions and environmental protection. Drawing on examples from industrial and regional policy, we intend to argue that traditional strands of regulation at all levels in post-war Europe have typically been centralized and technocratic, and thus insufficiently responsive or dynamic to address the demands of the 1990s. Regulatory frameworks, particularly in the UK, have usually failed to create the type of public sphere in which key actors can develop shared analyses and consensual frameworks for collaborative action. Indeed, the erosion of public discourse and the privatization of strategic social and economic choices has been a notable feature of government policy in the late 1970s. In effect this strategy attempts to mobilize bias in favour of capital, but has done so in a way which seriously retards the type of structural adjustment needed to achieve competitive advantage within Europe, let alone to benefit labour or to protect the environment. Institutional mechanisms for bargaining and negotiation have often been derided as symptomatic of the failure of corporatism. But the weakening of such mechanisms has led to fragmentation rather than to the creation of an effective management culture within the British economy. Evidence from some of the most successful regions within

Europe underlines the significance of an open public sphere in which the principal actors can negotiate and implement strategic choices through partnership and collaboration. For the UK at least this implies the need for a new mode of regulation, one which is at variance with traditional approaches and which overturns dominant political strategies of the last decade or so. As our conclusion will argue, it also implies the need for a new regulatory function at EC level.

The nature of regulation is determined by a process of evolution and innovation in response to changing needs within the sphere of production. Simple modes of regulation suffice when the structure of production is itself simple, and when the inputs to production are adequately supplied by markets for land, property, raw materials, labour and skills, and so on. More complex forms of regulation are required as production becomes more sophisticated and leads to imbalances in the wider environment. Existing modes of regulation are therefore the product of accumulated historical imperatives (Offe 1975).

Bureaucratic strands of regulation allocate resources or exercise powers belonging to the state in a way which is essentially reactive and which reflects the application of legislatively or administratively pre-determined rules. Discretion is minimized, and allocations can often only be challenged through judicial or quasi-judicial processes. Environmental health regulations and their application by local authorities is a clear example of this strand. Bureaucratic regulation derives its legitimacy from the appearance of impartiality and a disinterested application of measures deemed to be for the public good, even though this may conceal the mobilization of bias in favour of sectional interests. Ideologies of administrative rationality distance bureaucratic regulation from underlying political strategies, though this impartiality is sometimes open to challenge. Moreover, bureaucratic regulation is limited to the routine allocation of identified resources and cannot respond where the state is required to produce new resources through continuously changing policy initiatives.

Technocratic strands, on the other hand, are inherently proactive in providing and organizing social capital, regulating and intervening in markets which prove inadequate in creating conditions for the profitable production of goods and services through measures such as urban planning, transport provision, land and property development, training and industrial services. Traditions of this kind of regulatory management are very strongly established in France, but also exist in the UK, Germany, Italy and elsewhere among the Twelve.

Intervention and regional policy in Britain

Regional policy in Britain offers a good example of a shift from allocative to productive regulation, and one which illustrates the policy choices now facing the European Community when compared with the experience of other Member States. New regulatory mechanisms developed during the 1940s attempted, for example, to redress a series of inter-related imbalances in the fields of regional development, labour market supply and demand, and urban growth. In part, this concern with distribution was informed by equity considerations as well as by the need for economic efficiency. Regional policy was essentially coercive, relying on a process of certification to divert industrial development away from metropolitan centres towards designated development areas. But the concern with the *creation* of growth from the 1960s onwards, arising from changing patterns of international competition, superimposed a new agenda for regulation. This agenda sought to exploit more effectively the regional potential for fostering national economic growth through the better utilization of labour, production facilities and infrastructure. Regional growth poles were planned with the aid of statistical modelling techniques designed to co-ordinate projected trends in population, employment and the demand for services (Alden and Morgan 1974). National and regional goals would be achieved through the co-ordination of planning and infrastructure provision, which would both stimulate and direct public sector investment. Grants and other forms of subsidy to the private sector were often introduced to reinforce these goals.

Even though deregulation and a withdrawal from public provision have tended to limit proactive policy production since the election of the Thatcher government in 1979, the extent of this political strategy should not be overstated. For example, while central government has imposed harsh restrictions on local authority activity, its own creations such as Urban Development Corporations have been highly interventionist in attempting to restructure local land and property markets.

Decision processes underpinning technocratic strands of regulation are contingent on the ability of planners to predict external forces and to devise means of influencing the pattern of physical, social and economic development. Technical skills are therefore seen as the driving force of regulation, as well as providing the basis for its legitimacy, and this may be further reinforced by means of rationalistic decision tools such as operations research (for a powerful critique of OR based approaches to town and country planning, see Gillingwater 1983). The result is a certain opacity both within the decision processes themselves and in terms of their impact. Indeed, power may be concentrated in the hands of a relatively small number of officials and politicians precisely to secure decisive action; this seeks to avoid conflict over values by delimiting choice within a narrow band of operational measures. Indeed, the objectives may be taken as given, reducing the process of choice to one of selecting the most efficient means.

Technocratic regulation can often therefore be characterized as a form of dependent corporatism in which anticipated demands of the private sector set the precise agenda for the design and implementation of public policy. Corporatist strands of regulation in the UK are well documented in the field of industrial and economic policy at national level. Meso-corporatism was characteristic of sectoral regulation in the UK, especially during the 1960s and 1970s, and has been a recurrent theme in debates about the construction of competitive advantage in UK manufacturing (e.g. Holland 1975; Cawson 1985; Best 1990). Such literature draws particular inspiration from the role of MITI (Ministry of International Trade and Industry) in securing the Japanese economic miracle, though generally fails (for understandable reasons) to disentangle transferrable lessons from the Japanese experience from innate cultural and other factors. Emphasis is placed on the value of co-ordinated research and development, marketing and investment functions at sectoral level. It also draws attention to the failure of the voluntaristic tradition in the UK to achieve such a collaborative approach to the creation of competitive advantage. Tripartism in the form of the National Economic Development Office (NEDO) has generally failed to get binding agreements with key actors on the reconstruction of major areas of economic activity. Clear sectoral strategies have never emerged and NEDO's activities have generally been limited to a series of *ad hoc* initiatives. Plans for a body with powers for high level economic coordination, able to impose compulsory planning agreements, were included in the Labour Party manifesto for the 1974 general election. However when this body eventually appeared as the National Enterprise Board, it was with greatly reduced powers and it made little lasting impact before its abolition by the Thatcher Government.

Examples of corporatist modes of regulation have also become increasingly significant at local level. For example, Harloe's (1975) study of Swindon showed how its Development Corporation moved towards a power concentration model because of pressure from industrialists to provide factory sites, housing for key workers, and so on. This had to be done in a 'flexible' way without producing wasteful surpluses because the partnership was dependent on private capital for its prime objective of rapid growth. Policy responded to the demands of private capital, thereby marginalizing political discourse about the nature, direction or purpose of growth.

Swindon's experience is of particular interest in the context of the public–private 'partnerships' which have emerged in many localities as a means of transforming the delivery of training, town planning, urban renewal and economic development. Urban Development Corporations and, especially, Training and Enterprise Councils, seek to bypass the democratic service delivery roles of local authorities, creating a direct link between representatives of local firms and the central government financing of provision. Elsewhere voluntary partnership arrangements between local authorities and private sector representatives (typically Chambers of Commerce and major employers) have been geared towards the regeneration of derelict areas or of local economies. In each case resulting 'strategies' are informed by research, though often these studies fail to bring a clear comparison of the impact of competing options into the public sphere. Many such strategies actually comprise little more than an inventory of separate initiatives – often described as 'flagships' – with little analysis of their possible interaction or of their effect on strategic choices within the economy as a whole.

In part, this reflects the tentative nature of the new local partnership arrangements. Private sector partners expect short term returns, either through service delivery or through the creation of immediate opportunities for profitable investment. Thus training provision, to take one instance, becomes orientated towards meeting current skills shortages rather than towards developing a longer term approach to the role of human resources in securing competitiveness. Likewise local economic regeneration becomes increasingly property orientated since the most tangible opportunities for profitable investment lie in this direction. Economic development becomes largely synonymous with the attraction of inward investment: localities in which communities, local authorities and business are invited to combine in outbidding their counterparts elsewhere for an inadequate supply of footloose investment. Growth often becomes equated with the attraction of 'high technology industry' (rarely defined) while traditional sectors are relegated to the category of 'sunset industries' (Totterdill et al. 1989). Consequently the prospects for linking physical and labour market renewal within a unified perspective become increasingly remote. In short, public–private sector partnerships frequently imply a lowest common denominator approach to policy development. Public objectives are reduced to seeking visible manifestations of renewal such as the token development of key sites rather than generating deep-seated processes of structural adjustment in pursuit of publicly negotiated strategic goals (Totterdill 1989). Although in this model the concrete regulation of, for example, land, property and labour markets occurs at a local level, it does so in a way which is strictly defined by the centre. These forms of corporatism may be locally negotiated, but within the context of very limited autonomy in terms of legislative power, fund raising or expenditure. Reports from Training and Enterprise Councils suggest widespread dissatisfaction among employer members about the imposition of spending cuts by central government. Similarly, the creation of public–private sector partnerships has failed to secure substantial new funding in major urban areas, or for industrial investment.

An appropriate mode of regulation for a changing economy

We have argued that the emergence of bureaucratic, technocratic and corporatist strands within regulation, particularly the regulation of urban, regional and industrial development, reflects a struggle to develop appropriate responses to increasingly complex patterns of production within the economy. The concentration of power within relatively closed alliances of actors is typical of attempts to manipulate infrastructure, housing, industrial location and urban planning in an attempt to secure the compliance of labour and the attraction of private capital. Apparent successes claimed for these strategies in the post-war decades include the sub-regional redistribution of capital and labour to new sites of production through, for example, the New Towns Programme, or the diversion of industrial investment towards the Northern regions. Clearly such claims are not uncontested, and critics cite the disruption to communities and social structures caused by the redistribution of population, the over-dependence of many regional growth centres on branch plants offering only low value production and low skill employment, and the opacity of the processes of strategic choice. Such opacity, whether that of the local corporatism described in the Swindon study (Harloe 1975), or of national policy arenas, appears to be integral to a mode of regulation which relies for its impetus on the fine balancing of incentives and constraints for predominantly large capital. Moreover, although large firms are actively courted by these strategies, they are effectively invisible partners in the processes of local or sectoral policy formation based on a 'second guessing' of corporate investment programmes.

Certainly it is large capital which has constituted the principal focus of policy during much of the post-war era. Successive sectoral analyses published by the National Economic Development Council (NEDC) for example, drew a simple correspondence between competitiveness and size, suggesting that only the largest conglomerates would be able to generate the investment and economies of scale necessary to survive in world markets characterized by mass consumption. Amalgamations and mergers were actively encouraged by government, while regional policies relied heavily on being able to influence the spatial pattern of production resulting from the restructuring of companies and sectors. Ironically the process of rationalization associated with this restructuring often led to net job losses accelerating the deindustrialization of many localities, especially in the major urban areas.

BLURRING THE PRIVATE/PUBLIC DIVIDE: EUROPEAN EXPERIENCE OF CO-OPERATION AND REGULATION

During the 1980s the view that larger firms would continue to provide the principal motor of growth came under increasing challenge. The fragmentation of consumer markets as a result of changing competitive strategies in the retail sector and the greater significance of customization and specialization in other markets including capital goods, places a higher premium on flexibility, adaptation, continuous innovation and quality. Moreover, even cost savings achieved through concentration and automation do not guarantee competitiveness in price sensitive markets. Examples of successful sectoral or spatial restructuring throughout Europe draw attention to the need for realignment towards the production of higher value goods and services (Farrands 1991; Sharp and Holmes 1989; Hirst and Zeitlin 1989). Large firms themselves are also becoming more decentralized at the expense of vertical integration. Local managers are gaining greater autonomy in many companies, particularly in relation to marketing, product development and sourcing, and in the longer term this could represent a degree of reintegration of larger firms into local and regional economies. In such instances, resources available in the local industrial milieu may well assist managers in bargaining for investment from the parent company. Thus the logic of scale is no longer self-explanatory and the new 'flexible specialization' (Piore and Sabel 1984) economy can mean that smaller firms enjoy clear advantages.

New forms of regulation are also being evolved particularly in advanced technology industries to promote innovation and establish networks of co-operation amongst small firms. There is plenty of evidence that, while large firms are the main source of innovation, small firms are essential for growth, and to ensure a widespread pattern of change across Europe's regions (Patel and Pavitt 1989; Sharp 1986). Regulation of the patent regime at a European level is seen as essential for the diffusion of process and product innovation (Stone 1990), while the setting of common standards across the Single Market is a concomitant of efficiency and an instrument of strategic choice between technologies (cf. Kendall 1991). Monopolies may innovate, but they fail to diffuse the benefits of innovation unless they are challenged by a mixture of competitors and public control. And diffusion across the economy as a whole is a key to survival in global markets (Turner and Soete 1984). This is not to pre-judge precisely what the 'mixture' should be of public and private action, of regulation and competition, a question developed below. But it does assert the interdependence of regulation and business growth in the advanced structures of the European economy: the regulatory framework should not be seen as direct intervention, but as a sophisticated means of combining public and private interests while keeping a competitive environment. It has been argued that moving away from pure 'market' behaviour to a more co-operative sharing of information through networks among firms can be a rational response to management problems, combining public and private actors to pool knowledge and authority (Williamson 1975).

It is claimed by some commentators that the emergence of the New Industrial Districts, comprising agglomerations of small firms characterized by a high degree of inter-dependence and co-operation, offers an alternative for the creation of competitive advantage in developed countries. In one example, Bernard Ganne (1989) argues that this model has been of greater significance in explaining the recent economic regeneration of the Rhône–Alpes than high profile, central government inspired initiatives to encourage inward investments by high technology enterprises. But this model requires a qualitatively different mode of regulation (Hirst and Zeitlin 1989; Best 1990). Regulation for economic development based on smaller enterprises is required to achieve two principal objectives:

1   to overcome the disadvantages of small scale production through

the provision of sophisticated collective services relating to market intelligence, marketing, design, innovation, production technology, shared access to specialized resources and so on; and

2   to regulate the organization of joint ventures, subcontracting and so on.

Best (1990) argues that the emergence of such forms of regulation in the Japanese context casts a new light on the MITI debate. Small and medium sized firms play a surprisingly significant role in Japanese manufacturing (accounting for 40 per cent of exports if both direct and indirect exports are included, some 81 per cent of employment and 99.4 per cent of firms), both as suppliers to the market in their own right, and in providing larger firms with flexible, innovative and quality conscious networks of suppliers. As Best argues,

> a car assembler, which ultimately coordinates 20,000 parts ... cannot possibly develop in-house the best qualified supplier, which means guessing right on technological developments in every productive activity that contributes to the final product. Instead, long term consultative relations with suppliers in which design concepts are developed together ... offers the car assembler ... the opportunity to specialise in design, assembly, distribution and marketing.

> (Best 1990)

Small firms need appropriate support if they are to play such a positive role. A wide range of small firm orientated agencies operates within the broad strategic framework established by MITI and plays a key role in securing competitiveness at grass-roots level. These agencies perform a wide range of business support functions such as counselling, the provision of specialist expertise and the regulation of subcontracting relations with larger firms. Comparable policy structures have emerged in European regions in which New Industrial Districts have developed, notably Baden Wuerttemberg and Emilia Romagna. In the Italian example, the Regional Councils have statutory powers to support the development of smaller enterprises, though the extent to which these powers have been utilized varies considerably between regions. The Regional Council of Emilia Romagna has been particularly proactive in this field through the creation of a series of partnerships with local authorities, industry associations and trade unions. A tripartite regional development company, ERVET, controls the broad strategic development of the policy framework. No direct assistance is given to individual enterprises and there is no question of picking winners or rescuing losers through grants or subsidy: ERVET's strategy is to co-ordinate an extensive network of service providers, creating through both regulation and intervention an environment in which individual enterprises can achieve competitiveness within the market. ERVET also operates at arm's length from the centres which supply these services, all of whom are controlled by governing bodies usually comprising industry representatives, trade unions and local authorities. Although ERVET has provided significant levels of funding for the creation of the principal service centres and for the development of subsequent initiatives, most aspire to financial self-sufficiency through the operation of membership schemes and from receipts.

Service centres fall into one of two principal categories: sectoral centres targeted at specific industries such as textiles and clothing, ceramics and agricultural engineering, which provide a range of specialist services directly to firms; and secondary centres concerned with generic issues such as product development, subcontracting and exports, which work in partnership with the sectoral centres. Thus CITER, the Emilia Romagna sectoral centre for textiles and clothing, provides its members with services relating to fashion forecasting, market trends, design and production technology, but CITER also works in close collaboration with ASTER, the product development centre, on the development of CAD (Computer Aided Design) and EDI (Electronic Data Interchange) systems capable of expanding the range of services which can be offered to local firms. In addition, other centres have been created to promote the economic development of specific localities within the region, especially those which are experiencing the results of structural adjustment in traditional industries. The ERVET system therefore comprises a wide range of very specialized centres, within which *ad hoc* alliances can be constructed around specific issues. ERVET also works closely with national small business associations such as the CNA, who provide a growing range of business support services including bookkeeping, financial services, bulk purchasing, the provision of industrial parks and industrial relations.

LESSONS FOR POLICY IN THE UK AND EUROPE

The nature of the ERVET system as a plethora of specialist, networked agencies operating in partnership with external bodies offers an approach to strategic choice which stands in stark contrast to the power-concentration models described above. The decentralization of expertise and resources through the network inevitably engages a wide range of public and private sector actors, creating a series of overlapping arenas in which strategic issues can be identified and discussed. Such discourse constitutes part of a broader public sphere than that associated with the types of sectoral or local corporatism characteristic of the UK (Hutton 1992).Regulation is thus well informed by this discourse to an extent not replicated by the type of statutory consultation exercises superimposed on certain areas of policy production in Britain. Regulation processes also constitute a particularly complex partnership arrangement between the public and private sectors. This operates not at the symbolic level of business and public sector leaders, but in the detail of day-to-day commercial activity. Business decisions are thus more likely to be informed by strategic considerations. Of equal importance, self-regulation has become part of the business culture in these regions, with implicit social and economic sanctions against those who commit abuse in the fields of financial transactions, subcontracting or industrial relations.

Not only does this model offer important lessons for the UK but, as our Conclusion will argue, it also begins to define a potential new role at EC level. Sector by sector comparisons reveal the weakness of the organizational infrastructure available to small and medium firms in the UK (Hirst and Zeitlin 1989). In the textile and clothing sector for example, only the largest firms can afford to acquire high quality in-house information on fashion forecasting or to purchase CAD equipment. Some industry associations provide limited services for their members, but usually on a highly centralized basis. Most firms indeed do not belong to any form of industry association, and little inter-firm collaboration appears to exist. Government assistance is very limited, and has rarely focused on the specific needs of individual sectors. Its orientation is towards providing subsidy to companies for the use of consultants, a much weaker means of transferring technical and business expertise to companies than through the continuing provision of collective services (Totterdill et al. 1989). A comparison within a relatively successful example, the British and German chemicals industries, demonstrates that even in relatively strong sectors the networks of training and innovative information which German firms can exploit further enhances their competitiveness in comparison with their British rivals (Grant et al. 1988).

Several local authorities are attempting to fill this vacuum through the provision of specialized services to firms (Totterdill 1989), most notably within the textiles and clothing sector. Many of these authorities would claim that local initiatives are highly cost effective because they can target services more carefully than centralized organizations. Intra-sectoral variations may be pronounced between localities, and national programmes can often be insensitive to specific characteristics and requirements at grass roots level. But UK local authorities lack the statutory powers and resources of the Regione dell'Emilia Romagna or many of its counterparts elsewhere in Europe. Such initiatives are conspicuously under-funded in comparison with the scale of support needed to regenerate manufacturing industry in the UK.

At the centre of our argument is the claim that the conditions for competitive success in changing world markets have altered. For the UK in particular, competitive advantage needs to be constructed through the creation of new regulatory and interventionist frameworks. But all European countries face together the challenges we have identified. The principal task of what we will call a 'strategic–discursive' mode if to create an environment which:

- influences the strategic choices of companies and sectors; and
- resources the process of structural adjustment implied by those strategic choices.

Although the advantage for developed economies appears to lie in higher-value, specialized production, British manufacturers remain heavily committed to the mass production of standardized goods which seek to compete largely on price grounds (Hirst and Zeitlin 1989). Such a position is becoming less and less tenable in the face of growing competition from low wage producers in the Far East and in other developing countries, on the European periphery, and increasingly from Eastern Europe. Firms and sectors become increasingly locked into a downward spiral in which low value production leads to low profits, low investment and low productivity. However, the strategic options facing firms who wish to break out of this cycle are complex, and there is no single route to structural adjustment.

Automated mass production   could allow some firms and sectors to survive in low value markets, though the risks remain high, especially given fluctuating demand and loan charges. Some notable examples of automated mass production in the UK are found in peripheral regions in which high levels of capital equipment subsidy operate (at the expense of employment and skills). Automation also imposes limitations on the scope for innovation and versatility, and this may ultimately impede competitive success even in quite low value markets. For example, regional assistance has enabled some larger garment manufacturers such as Coats Viyella to develop highly automated plants in Northern Ireland. But the inherent rigidities of such production systems, coupled with a deskilled workforce, have entrapped such plants in the manufacture of simple, low value products at a time when corporate strategy is attempting to move into higher quality fashion.

Flexible mass production strategies may help firms to survive in medium value markets where versatility and innovation are important as well as price. For example, the introduction of EPOS (Electronic Point of Sale) systems by multiple retailers places a higher premium on the ability of suppliers to adapt to market trends by switching rapidly from the production of one style or range to another, even though price competitiveness remains central. These strategies vary between company and sector in the extent of their use of flexible automation, though in some instances there is an innovative and increasingly widespread use of multi-skill production systems such as teamworking. Our research in the clothing industry suggests that this can lead to real benefits, not only in terms of increased competitiveness for companies, but also in terms of enhanced quality of working life and labour market opportunities for operatives. Arguably, flexible mass production may become an important testing ground for competing technical approaches to production. But at the same time it may prove to be no more than a transitional stage in the decline of mass market production in developed countries. Certainly the growing low-wage economies of the Far East are moving towards greater versatility and faster response times in the lower–middle value markets, forcing domestic manufacturers further into higher value, customized production where proximity to buyers and users may be a competitive asset. Producers in low wage areas of the Community such as Portugal and Northern Greece also need public support in developing these strategies, illustrated by the Commission's FORCE programme for continuing professional training.

Flexible specialization is characterized by the production of goods and services for markets in which innovation, design, quality, customization and responsiveness are the principal determinants of competitiveness, rather than price. Advocates of this strategy argue that such markets are growing across a wide range of sectors as a result of greater consumer sophistication and the demand for more specialized capital and consumer goods. There is a range of evidence to suggest that such strategies underpin the regeneration of regional economies and sectors

179

in many parts of Europe (Hirst and Zeitlin 1989) though some of these claims are open to challenge (Amin and Robins 1990). Flexible specialization, with its emphasis on continuous versatility and innovation, can be seen as antithetical to specialized, automated production processes employing deskilled operatives. Rather it requires multi-skilled operatives using general purpose machines, and with the autonomy to exercise creative and problem solving skills. Flexible specialization may embrace single companies who have used multi-skill production methods such as teamworking to enter these markets, or the agglomerations of small firms in the type of industrial districts described above. Both appear to be underdeveloped in the UK compared with other parts of Europe (Hirst and Zeitlin 1989; Lane 1989).

Each strategy implies its own set of regulatory imperatives. But overall, the above categorization draws attention to two issues central to the problem of structural adjustment and regulation in the European economy: first, the ability of companies and sectors to make and implement effective strategic choices in the context of changing world markets, and second, the impact of institutional and regulatory frameworks on the nature of the strategic choices made in the economy, (Claverie 1991). Management awareness of external strategic issues affecting their company's competitiveness is likely to be low. As Lane (1989) shows, management cultures remain mass production orientated, and workplace strategies too frequently represent a kind of 'high technology Fordism' in which deskilling and automation are motivated by poor industrial relations rather than broader strategic considerations. Apart from excluding substantial sections of the economy from the profitable high value markets increasingly enjoyed by other groups or regions, this is a matter of public concern because of its impact in destroying opportunities for access to skilled employment for many sections of the labour force.

There are several dimensions of the current public policy framework which actively create this situation in the UK. The poverty of the organizational infrastructure, particularly at local and regional level, helps to obscure awareness of strategic issues and choices at management level, reinforcing comparatively low levels of managerial training and qualification. Indeed, Finegold and Soskice (1988) argue that the structure of training and qualification throughout the UK labour market has led to a 'low skill equilibrium' in which the economy becomes embedded in increasingly marginal areas of production.

In terms of industrial and regional development, a strategic–discursive mode of regulation is needed to challenge the prevalence of structures which sustain this low value, low skill syndrome. As Table 8.1 suggests, such a mode implies some striking contrasts with traditional practice.

At an instrumental level, the flexible specialization model suggests a clear shift towards selective regulation and intervention informed by the careful analysis of problems identified against defined strategic objectives. Competitiveness, labour market opportunity and broader community interests are integrated through a negotiated framework.

Two aspects of the strategic–discursive mode of regulation deserve particular attention against this background. First, the enhanced significance of locality as an appropriate level of regulation, but within the context of supranational strategic frameworks. Priorities for the structural adjustment of key areas of economic activity may increasingly be established at European level in order to secure the competitiveness of community-wide industry in world markets. But as we have argued, the effectiveness of specific policy measures depends on how they are grounded in an understanding of industrial structure, problems and prospects, and in sensitivity to spatial variations. Equally, the quality of strategy formulation at supranational level will depend on the ability to accumulate and process data and representations from the grass roots. For example, industrial sector strategies could be created by means of a dynamic partnership between European, national, regional and local administrations. Local and regional research and consultation would inform the determination of national and European strategic objectives and the distribution of associated resources. Each locality and region could submit its own sectoral development plan as a means of gaining access to these resources, allowing a high degree of autonomy at grass-roots level while ensuring broad compliance with the strategic framework. This is not to prescribe a uniform regulatory structure within regions and localities across Europe. A diversity of approaches in the face of an uncertain economic environment will be a positive asset, though the enhancement measures to promote horizontal networking for the exchange of experience and expertise requires a more flexible and generous funding regime than that currently provided by the Directorate-General for Regional Affairs of the European Commission.

Second, localization offers significant if not sufficient conditions for reducing the opacity of regulatory mechanisms. Localization in this sense clearly means more than the harnessing of local elites to mediate in the disbursement of central resources, as in the operation of the English Training and Enterprise Councils. (See also Chapter 3.) Rather, the networking of a plurality of specialist agencies, illustrated by the

Table 8.1 Changing models of industrial and regional development: from mass production to flexible specialization

Mass production economy *technocratic–corporatist regulation*	*Flexible specialization economy* *strategic–discursive regulation*
Inward investment and product diversification by large companies as the principal motor of growth.	Maximizing the growth potential of indigenous firms, especially those in the 25–250 size band.
Image creation to attract investment and to boost confidence.	Strengthening arenas for discourse to enhance the processes of strategic choice.
Growth promoted by a centralized coalition of key actors.	Growth through decentralized networks of actors at all levels of the economy, involving flexible patterns of *ad hoc* partnerships within agreed strategic frameworks.
Growth encouraged by grants and subsidies to individual companies, plus provision of land and property.	Growth through the creation of supportive milieux for enterprise as a whole, based on the provision of collective services carefully targeted to build on existing or potential strengths.
Economic research and analysis as a technical determinant of public policy.	Economic research and analysis as a stimulant to public discourse and the creation of shared understandings between actors at all levels of the economy.
Emphasis on high technology automation and labour substitution.	Emphasis on multi-skilling to enhance versatile and innovative use of technology.
Substitution of 'sunrise' for 'sunset' industries.	Assisting traditional industries to move into higher value markets and promoting new areas of economic activity relevant to local economies, labour markets and communities.
Local/regional/national economies in competition with each other for markets and investment.	Horizontal networking at local/regional/national levels to open new markets and opportunities through collaboration and exchange, especially within the context of the European Community.

example of Emilia Romagna, appears to offer better prospects for the creation of a wider discourse around the definition of strategic choice, and for the dissemination of new strategies, practices and technologies. This has clear implications for the political sphere, in that politicans need to become guardians of public discourse rather than the nominal representatives of ill-defined interests, seeking an 'ideal speech situation' (Habermas 1979) free from domination and the mobilization of bias. Technocratic practices must also be challenged by a re-evaluation of the relationships between technical knowledge and instrumental action. Analyses of local economies, sectors or labour markets would no longer treat actors as the passive objects of research, but as political subjects with an essential role in analysis, policy formulation and implementation: in other words with joint ownership of the research process and its outcome. New methodologies are emerging which are based in a conception of research as essentially discursive rather than technical–instrumental (Shallice 1992; Middleton 1991).

This section has moved away from the idea of regulation as a negative intrusion in business towards a more co-operative perspective based on a redefined structure of activity. This 'redefined structure' involves a regional focus of regulation creating a climate within which the market can function effectively and in which the competitive incentive remains powerful. But it is a model for regulation removed from the arid public/private conflicts of the last two decades in the UK. It draws heavily on the experience of other European partners. It entails a different role for the European Community, partly as a direct regulator, but much more often as a regulator of other national or regional regulators – a supervisor of regulatory standards. This new role is outlined in the Conclusion.

CONCLUSION

Regulatory functions in the European Community are necessarily divided between its different levels of power and authority. Conflicts over the appropriate level of regulation will grow. They will from time to time become serious public conflicts, although for the most part they will be highly technical disputes managed by lawyers and officials in a language which will exclude easy access. In this article, we have identified three key issues which must shape how we approach regulation in the EC. The first is that it is essential to distinguish regulation which is managed directly through EC processes, such as competition policy and the control of many aspects of the safety of nuclear research, from those areas where the EC lays down rules or principles for regulation which provide a framework which must be followed at a 'lower' level, but which is enacted in detail, implemented and controlled by authorities at those lower levels. Conflicts between levels of regulation are characteristic of any federal system of government, which in the strict sense the EC has been for many years. The EC has the knowledge, overview and authority to arbitrate on rule-making procedures in the economy; but it often lacks knowledge or authority to engage in detailed regulation and its officials do not have the time to manage regulatory processes even where they have the competence.

The second argument has been that the EC's role in regulation must increase, if a balance of interests between consumers and the environment (which are relatively weak) and corporate and financial interests is to be maintained. That the market alone is incapable of resolving these clashes of interest is already recognized in the EC at almost every level, and in the thinking of christian democrat as well as social democrat traditions. The failure of financial services deregulation, represented very evidently by the scandals of the Bank of Credit and Commerce International (BCCI) and the Maxwell empire collapse, are only extreme cases of the need for 'reregulation' to protect small business as much as consumers. More serious is the much more widespread need to combine greater investment with greater attention to human capital, especially in the weaker regions of the EC which are not going to be able to rely in future on low wage levels as they have in the past given the likely future impact of the Single Market on employment conditions and real labour costs. Throughout this chapter, we have stressed inability – technical as well as political – of national agencies to supervise this process. The EC will have a greater role in managing regulatory regimes, and in acting as the forum through which claims between the interests of consumers, large and small business, external investors, and the environment, are established and arbitrated. Both arguments demand a close interaction between regulation at the European level and within national markets. This leads to a third argument.

The third argument has centred on the idea that regulation processes function best as a partnership between these different political levels, and between private and public actors (see also the argument in Albert 1992). It starts to demonstrate how such a partnership can be constituted so as to effectively deliver to each actor sufficient to make it worth continuing the process rather than free-riding for a time and then defecting from it. This primarily involves regional and local authorities which can deliver specific benefits for firms, rather than national governments. National governments must probably lose power, and must certainly lose authority, in order to make this work. But they do not so much lose power to the Commission in Brussels, which in any case remains more than a little imperfect by the criteria used here, but to local and regional partnerships. Collective decision-making by the member states as a whole (acting in the Council of Ministers and the European Council) have increasingly take power from the member states as individual bodies as majority decisions have replaced the veto, and we are not advocating a change in what is already happening here.

We have taken the Emilia-Romagna model as a particularly successful example of how co-operation between levels can operate. But we are only taking this example to show that what we propose is possible. We might also have looked at the dialogue between the German Länder and the BMFT (the German research ministry), or the growth of regional partnership in northern Portugal, or at the Northern Irish and Scottish development agencies throughout the 1980s to suggest other dimensions of partnership which can provide models for co-operative regulation. As Hutton (1992) suggests, the rigidities of neo-classical thinking have simply been transcended by the combination of competition and co-operation in such groupings, especially in markets which depend above all on the speed and quality of knowledge gained by firms rather than on low cost production or on an exclusive, expensive and rigid orientation to high technology automation (see also Williamson 1975). The combination of flexible specialization through investment in human capital and human skills, and the development of advanced networks of production, finance and trade within co-operative systems of regulation, provides the principles on which communities, firms and public authorities can retain jobs and develop production patterns which are profitable in a competitive European market even as patterns of global trade and technology change in the first decades of the twenty-first century.

REFERENCES

Albert, M. (1992) *Capitalism contre Capitalism*, Paris: PUF.
Alden, J. and Morgan, R. (1974) *Regional Planning: A Comprehensive View*, London: Leonard Hill.
Amin, A. and Robins, K. (1990) 'Industrial districts and regional development: limits and possibilities', in F. Pyke, G. Becattini and W. Sengenberger (eds) *Industrial Districts and Inter-Firm Cooperation in Italy*, Geneva: International Institute for Labour Studies.

Best, M. (1990) *The New Competition: Institutions of Industrial Restructuring*, Cambridge.

Cawson, A. (ed.) (1985) *Organised Interests and the State*, London: Sage.

Claverie, B. (1991) *La Gestion des Consortiums Européens*, Paris: Presses Universitaires de France.

EIU (Economist Intelligence Unit) (1991) *European Trends: Background Supplement, 1991–1992*, London: EIU.

Farrands, C. (1983) 'Textiles and Clothing', in H. Wallace, W. Wallace and C. Webb *Policy Making in the European Community* (2nd edn), London: Wiley.

—— (1988) 'High technology alliances for 1992', *European Trends* 3.

—— (1991) 'European high value chemicals in global competition', *European Trends* 1.

Finegold, D. and Soskice, D. (1988) 'The failure of training in Britain: analysis and prescription', *Oxford Review of Economic Policy* 4 (3).

Ganne, B. (1989) 'Regional dynamics of innovation: a look at the Rhône-Alpes region', *Entrepreneurship and Regional Development* 1.

Gillingwater, D. (1983) *Political Strategies of Planning Practice: A Critique of the Strategic Choice Approach*, Mimeo, Loughborough University of Technology.

Grant, W., Patterson, W. and Whiston C. (1988) *Government and the Chemical Industry*, Oxford: Oxford University Press.

Habermas, J. (1979) *Communication and the Evolution of Society*, London: Heinemann.

Harloe, M. (1975) *Swindon: A Town in Transition*, London: Heinemann.

Hilf, R. and Jacobs, F. (1986) *The European Community and GATT*, Deventer: Kluwer.

Hirst, P. and Zeitlin, J. (1989) *Reversing Industrial Decline? Industrial Structure and Industrial Policy in Britain and her Competitors*, Oxford: Berg.

Holland, S. (1975) *The Socialist Challenge*, London: Quartet.

Hutton, W. (1992) 'EC's Business "Flotillas" take the wind out of our sails', *Guardian*, 6 January 1992.

Jackson, J.H. (1990) *Restructuring the GATT System*, London: Frances Pinter.

Kendall, V. (1991) 'Standardisation and its problems', *European Trends* 3.

Lane, C. (1989) *Management and Labour in Europe*, Aldershot: Edward Elgar.

Lasok, D. (1980), *The Law of the Economy of the European Communities*, London: Butterworth.

Lodge, J. (ed.) (1990), *The European Community and the Future of Europe*, London: Pinter.

Lodge, J. (1991), 'Blinded by the f-word', *The Higher*, 27 December 1991.

Middleton, D. (1991) *A Note on the Group Recall Methodology*, Mimeo, Loughborough University of Technology.

Moran, M. (1991) *The Politics of the Financial Services Revolution*, London: Macmillan.

OECD (1978) *Selected Industrial Policy Instruments: Objectives and Scope*, Paris: OECD.

Offe, C. (1975) 'The theory of the capitalist state and the problem of policy formation' in L. Lindberg *et al. Stress and Contradiction in Modern Capitalism*, London: Heinemann.

Patel, P. and Pavitt, K. (1989) 'The technological activities of the UK; a new look', in A. Silberston (ed.) *Technology and Economic Performance*, London: Macmillan.

Piore, M. and Sabel, C. (1984) *The Second Industrial Divide*, New York: Basic Books.

Sargent, J. (1985) 'Corporatism and the European Community', in W. Grant *The Political Economy of Corporatism*, London: Macmillan.

Shallice, A. (1992) 'The Tinsley survey', *Local Economic Policy Review* 4, Loughborough University of Technology.

Sharp, M. (ed.) (1986) *Europe and the New Technologies*, London: Frances Pinter.

Sharp, M. and Holmes, P. (eds) (1989) *Industrial Intervention in Britain and France*, London: Frances Pinter.

Stone, P. (1990) 'The Revised EC Patent Convention', *European Trends* 4.

Sutton, M. (1988) 'French banks face challenge of a single financial area', *European Trends* 3.

Totterdill, P. (1989) 'Local economic strategies in industrial policy: a critical review of British developments in the 1980s', *Economy and Society* 18 (4).

Totterdill, P., Durucan, C., Farrands, C., Gawith, M. and Gillingwater, D. (1989) 'Sunset industries: industrial policy and the regeneration of British manufacturing', *Local Economic Policy Review* 2, Loughborough University of Technology.

Turner, R. and Soete, L. (1984) 'Technology, diffusion and the rate of technological change', *Economic Journal*: 612–23.

Wallace, H., Wallace, W. and Webb, C. (1983) *Policy Making in the European Community* (2nd edn), London: Wiley.

Williamson, O. (1975) *Markets and Hierarchies*, New York: Free Press.

9

EUROPEAN INTEGRATION, TRANSNATIONAL CORPORATIONS AND NORTH–SOUTH CONVERGENCE[1]

Ioanna Glykou-Pitelis and Christos Pitelis

Our aim in this paper is to discuss the importance of European Community (EC) strategies and policies towards transnational corporations (TNCs) for European 'convergence'; the closing of the 'gap' known as the European 'North–South' divide. Despite the community's stated objective to close the gap, and a voluminous literature on the TNC, the relationship between TNCs and 'convergence' has received scant attention from academics. We intend to try to fill this gap here. First, we consider the economic theoretical relationship between TNCs, nation states and international organizations such as the EC. This is followed by an examination of the role and effects of TNCs on the EC in general and the North–South divide in particular. In the next section we propose a European strategy for convergence and some specific policies to implement this strategy. The objective of the proposals is to benefit all the stake-holders; including European consumers and the corporate sector, including the TNCs. Conclusions follow in the fourth and final section.

TRANSNATIONAL CORPORATIONS, NATION STATES AND INTERNATIONAL ORGANIZATIONS

The firm, particularly the TNC, and the state, most commonly in the general form of a national state are arguably the two major institutional devices of resource allocation globally today, along with the price mechanism (the 'market'). The voluminous and fast growing literature on the 'market' and the 'hierarchy' (firms and states), particularly their *raisons d'être*, evolution, attributes and interrelationships, represent a recognition of their importance. The relationship between TNCs and nation states and international organizations such as the European Community (EC) has also received interest in recent years. Our claim is that an economic theoretical analysis of these issues is a necessary (albeit not sufficient) condition informing any debates and prescriptions on TNCs, the EC and the North–South divide.

In the mainstream economics tradition, the market and the firm are viewed as two alternative institutions of resource allocation, the first based on voluntary exchange, the second on central authority or direction. It is claimed that (assuming pre-existing markets), markets fail due to excessive market transaction costs (costs of information, bargaining, contracting, policing and enforcing agreements), such costs being the result of the coexistence of bounded rationality, opportunism (self-interest seeking with guile) and asset specificity. The firm supersedes the market by internalizing transactions and in so doing it reduces market transaction costs for reasons related to both the number of transactions and the ability of 'hierarchy' to alleviate problems arising from the three factors mentioned above. The result is efficient firms replacing ('naturally') inefficient markets. Similar theorizing can be applied to explain the evolution, strategies and internal organization of firms. The founding father of this perspective is Ronald Coase, recently awarded the Nobel Prize in Economics for this (among others) contribution of his, in particular Coase (1937, 1960). Oliver Williamson is responsible for revitalizing the area in more recent years, see for example Williamson (1975, 1981, 1985).

The TNC is explained on similar lines within the transaction cost perspective. The focus here is on intermediate product market failure, however, rather than final product markets, in particular the problems of appropriating the quasi-rents from intermediate products (managerial skills, know-how, etc.), when market transactions (e.g. licensing) rather than internalized transactions, (foreign direct investment, FDI) are used. Buckley and Casson (1976) are to be credited with the application of this perspective to the theory of the TNC. Unlike the 'national' firm, however, where this perspective represents the central 'paradigm' in mainstream economic theory, in the theory of the TNC it coexists (often uneasily) with 'market power' perspectives, such as the 'ownership advantage' theory, attributed to Stephen Hymer's 1960 PhD thesis (published in Hymer 1976), the 'oligopolistic reaction' approach, and 'eclectic approaches' like John Dunning's which synthesizes 'ownership' (O), locational (L) and internalization (I) factors in his 'eclectic' or 'OLI' perspective (see below). This coexistence casts doubt on the transaction costs perspective's near exclusive reliance on efficiency. Market power is conventionally viewed as a reason for 'structural' market failures (oligopoly) within the mainstream, and accordingly a reason for inefficiences (reduced consumer surplus).

The mainstream perspective considers the state too to be a result of market failure. The standard textbook focus here is on instances of market failure, such as monopoly, externalities, public goods, etc. Developments, however, again by Ronald Coase (e.g. Coase 1960) and Kenneth Arrow (e.g. Arrow 1970) in particular, both point to, and allow, a generalization of the mainstream perspective of instances of market failure leading to the state, in terms of transaction costs, see Pitelis (1991c). Interesting, however, here is that the mainstream perspective assumes (implicitly rather than explicitly) that (unlike the firm) the state complements (assists) the market mechanisms in resources allocation.

There is no detailed discussion in the mainstream, at least so far as we are aware, on the relationship between the firm and the state. Coase (1960) briefly refers to the issue, to the effect that both firm and market transactions have to take place within the general legal framework imposed by the state. The implication is that firms and markets together (the private sector) are seen as complements to the state in the mainstream. This, for one, implies a need for an explanation of the state in terms of private sector (not just market) failure. Although this is possible, it still leaves unresolved the question of why states do not substitute (replace) markets and firms (the private sector); i.e. the 'market versus plan' issue. An explanation within the mainstream can be offered in terms of the, nowadays extremely popular, concept of 'government failure'. The numerous reasons for, and instances of, such failures, such as sheer inefficiency of state officials and/or rent seeking on their part, and the recent breakdown of most centrally planned economies, can offer support to the complementarity idea, see Mueller (1989), Pitelis (1991a). However, first, this needs to be done and done properly; second, it leaves unanswered the question why firms and markets are (should be) substitutes, while the private and public sectors are complements. Could (should) firms and markets too be complements, for example?

Concerning the relationship between nation states and TNCs, the mainstream view is that TNCs tend to enhance the welfare of both home and 'host' states by increasing global efficiency. The latter is more evident in the transaction costs perspective,[2] but is also true of proponents of 'ownership advantage' perspectives, such as Charles Kindleberger (see for example Kindleberger 1984). Here the reasons are not transaction costs but rather technology diffusion, know-how, employment creation etc. A problem emerges when the power of the one actor (the state) is being undermined by that of the other, the TNC. This Vernon (1971) observed, is possible as a result of the mobility of TNCs as compared to the immobility of the state. The original suggestion was that of 'sovereignty at bay', qualified however ten years later (Vernon 1981), in view of increasing expropriations of TNCs assets by Third World countries, and the increasing resistance (and militancy) of at least some states. More recently Nye (1988) adds a new interesting insight, by pointing to the possible complementarity between TNCs and nation states, each with a comparative advantage; TNCs on production, nation states on legitimization. This provides a much needed theoretical base to the mainstream perspective, and strengthens the earlier argument concerning complementarity between the private sector (firm in this case) and public sector.

The emergence of international state apparatuses can in principle be explained in parallel to the development of the state in the mainstream tradition. Kindleberger (1986) for example points to the relationship between international public goods (international stability for example) and that of international 'government', i.e. organizations such as the EC. Such 'goods' can in principle be provided by 'hegemonic powers'. The UK first and the USA more recently, for example, have played such a role in recent history. For a multitude of reasons however, 'hegemons' decline and/or lose their 'appetite' for the provision of such goods. International government is the solution to the problem.

Kindleberger's framework is one of international market failure, leading to international government, in the absence of a sufficiently strong (or interested) national government. The relationship between international government and the international firm is as seen one of complementarity. An interesting new dimension is added in terms of the relationship between national states and inter-nation states, which again is seen as one of complementarity (in the absence of a 'hegemons' at least). Following Nye, it could be claimed that 'comparative advantage' in the provision of international public goods and international production respectively, explain the (need for) complementarity between international state apparatuses and TNCs. For Nye (1988) this is true even in the absence (not due to the failure) of 'hegemons'. International market failures can also be generalized in terms of transaction costs, Pitelis (1991a).

In summary, the mainstream perspective on the firm, including the TNC, the (nation) state and international organizations can be described as one of complementarity. This can also be suggested as regards the private sector (firm and price mechanism), because the transaction costs perspective, which views the market and the firm as substitutes, provides no adequate justification for this view. It is possible therefore to claim that given firms' possible failures too (e.g. excessive transaction costs after a certain size, as Coase and Williamson admit), and the concept of comparative advantage advanced by Nye, this relationship too should be seen as one of complementarity within the mainstream. If this is accepted, all – the market, the transnational) firm and state (national and international) – should be seen as complementary institutions of resource allocation, each specializing in what they can do more efficiently (in terms, for example but not exclusively, of economizing in transaction costs). This way the prevailing institutional mix can be attributed to overall efficiency-related factors.

The major alternative to the mainstream tradition is the radical left. Regarding the *raison d'être* of the firm (the 'factory system') the major contribution here is Marglin (1974). Developed independently of the Williamson perspective on 'markets and hierarchies' Marglin's ideas represent the major alternative to the transaction costs-efficiency argument. For Marglin the main reason for the rise of the factory system from the previously existing putting-out system was the result of capitalist attempts to increase their control over labour. In this sense the reason for the factory system was distributional. Any efficiency gains resulting from increased control should be seen as the outcome here, but not the driving force. Transaction cost theorizing does not enter Marglin's analysis. His perspective has given rise to a smaller, yet, in my view, very promising alternative school, to that of transaction costs economics.

Coming to the transnational firm, Stephen Hymer is the leading contributor in the radical left tradition and arguably the father figure of the modern theory of the TNC as a whole. Similar to Ronald Coase, Hymer regarded the market and the firm as alternative institutional devices, but for the division of labour Hymer focused primarily on the evolution of firms (rather than existence *per se*), from the small family controlled firm to the joint stock company and then through the multidivisional firm to the TNC. He focused on the latter in his now classic 1960 PhD thesis, published in Hymer (1976) and extended his analysis on the TNC and the 'multinational corporate capitalist' system as a whole in his subsequent writings, some of the best of which are collected in Cohen *et al.* (1979).

In brief, Hymer explained the ability of US TNCs to become transnational (i.e. to compete successfully with domestic firms of 'host' countries, despite the latter's inherent advantages of knowledge of language, customs etc.) in terms of ownership or monopolistic advantages derived during their development process. Such were knowhow, managerial expertise, technology, organization etc. He then explained the willingness of US firms to become TNCs in terms of 'oligopolistic rivalry', in particular as a defensive attack to guard against the threat of the rising European and Japanese firms. He also used transaction-costs related theorizing (although not the term itself) to explain FDI to market based international activities, e.g. licensing, and referred to locational factors, and 'divide and rule' (of both labour and nation states) factors. It is for these reasons that, besides being the original, Hymer's theory is also the most complete yet (see Pitelis (1991b) for a detailed explanation of this view). Most existing perspectives on the TNC (expounded and defended by some of their own proponents in Pitelis and Sugden 1991) can be seen as developments of Hymer's early insights.

Although radical left writers, particularly in the Marxist tradition, had paid particular attention to the issue of internationalization of production and the TNC, their focus is primarily on the former, rather than on an explanation of the particular institutional form of the TNC. From a huge literature, the contributions of Palloix (1976) and Baran and Sweezy (1966) are noteworthy here. The former considers internationalization as a process inherent in the development of capitalism, and being the result of the process of competition. The latter focus on effective demand problems (of the underconsumptionist type) to explain the need of capital to seek foreign markets. Despite their lack of an explanation of the TNC *per se* such theories can be seen as complementary to Hymer's own (see Pitelis 1991b).

Marxist theory has paid a lot of attention to the theory of the state. Views here range from the instrumentalist theory, which sees the state as an instrument of capital, through the structural-functional perspective for which capitalist cohesion is achieved through the state, to the 'capital logic' or state form derivation debate. The latter focuses on the existence of an (autonomous) state separate from capital (i.e. the private sector–state juxtaposition as in Coase) and claims that the possibility of this autonomous form can be explained from intercapitalist competition, its feasibility from the apparent coincidence of interests between capital and labour, and its need from the undertaking of labour supervision by capital itself within emergent firms.

Variations apart, the Marxist theories view the state's existence and functions as the result of a quest and/or need to nurture the class interests of the capitalist class. Hymer (in Cohen *et al.* 1979) has a historical justification of this need-quest. Marxists, most notably O'Connor (1973), also acknowledge the possibility of 'government (here capitalist state) failure', but attribute it to a structural gap between receipts and outlays, where the latter tend to exceed the former for a multitude of reasons, including demands by both capital and labour for state expenditures. Much of the Marxist perspective can be 'translated' in mainstream language and be shown to bear close affinities to the mainstream tradition. What remains different, is the focus on a distributional, class-based perspective, as opposed to the efficiency focus of the mainstream.

Marxist theory has paid particular attention to the relationship between TNCs and nation states. Views, however, here vary wildly. On the general relationship between the relative power of states and TNCs, Murray (1971), has claimed that the power of TNCs is on the increase and tends to undermine that of nation states, while Warren (1971) has made the opposite claim. These and other contributions are collected in Radice (1975). Concerning the relationship between TNCs and developing 'host' states (the hinterland or periphery), views vary from the *Monthly Review* school's perspective of 'imperialism', (see e.g. Sweezy 1978) to Warren's (1973) claim that TNCs are a major factor contributing to the economic development of the periphery. In between lie the concepts of 'unequal exchange', 'uneven development' and 'dependent development'.

Stephen Hymer's perspective on TNCs and nation states is once again particularly insightful (see Cohen *et al.* 1979). On the general relationship he claimed that TNCs do erode the powers of nation states but unequally; more so for the weak (typically, developing) states and less so for the strong (developed) states. The latter possessed more leverage against TNCs, in part by being themselves home bases to TNCs. Concerning TNCs and 'host' developing states, he conceded that TNCs can contribute to the economic development of the periphery, but described the relationship as one of inequality and self-perpetuating dependency. In part this was the result of the incentives to local entrepreneurs to co-operate (sell to), rather than compete with TNCs. Observing a more general tendency of the world's wealthy to increasing the global surplus, Hymer went on to describe a tendency for global collusion by global firms through interpenetration of investments.

Globalization of production for Hymer, also creates the need for international capital markets and international government (organizations). The latter in order to assist the global operations of TNCs. This observation also provides a Marxist perspective on TNCs and international organizations, akin to the more general Marxist focus on distribution, in particular in regarding the 'dominant class' as the 'locomotive of history'. Given the influence of this class on the state too, as already discussed, one would expect nation states not to oppose (at least) the development of (some types of) international organizations.

To summarize, similar to the case of the mainstream perspective, the Marxist perspective can be seen to consider the firm, the market and the state, including TNCs, nation states and international organizations, as complementary devices, here in the exploitation of the fruits of (the division of) labour. The emphasis is on sectional (capitalist) interests, *not* efficiency. The latter could be the outcome, or the means, but not the driving force. Differently put, efficiency could be sacrificed for the sake of sectional interests.

It could be suggested from the discussion so far that there is an emerging consensus in economic theory to the effect that institutions of capitalism should be seen as complementary. The focus of the 'markets-hierarchies' perspective on the market and the firm as substitutes, has been adequately and persuasively criticized from within and without the mainstream, see the discussion in Hodgson (1988), so as not to challenge this statement. The exclusive focus on efficiency or capitalist class interests of the two perspectives, on the other hand, is, we think, far-fetched. Efficiency and sectional interests can often go hand in hand, or be different sides of the same coin. Consider for example the view that firms (or capitalists) maximize their utility (cultivate their own interests). If such utility can be enhanced by, for example, increasing market power and charging monopoly prices, it is not obvious (or even consistent with the mainstream) that firms should not do so. Similarly, if profits can be increased, by reducing labour costs, this will, if possible, be done. On the other hand, if profit increases follow from policies associated with transaction costs reductions, such policies are likely to be pursued, 'despite' their benign effects on efficiency. The point is simply that efficiency and sectional (capitalist) interest can go hand in hand. Interestingly neo-classical economic historian Douglass North (1981) suggests that efficiency by state functionaries will tend to be pursued provided their own utility is first maximized. This may point to some emerging consensus on this issue too.

It is possible to synthesize some of the main insights of these two perspectives by adopting an evolutionary, historical approach to the emergence and evolution of institutions. This is attempted in Pitelis (1991a), where it is claimed that capitalist institutions are complementary institutional devices for the exploitation of the division of labour and team work, with an eye to furthering the interests of the 'principals'. In this framework, it is indeed 'found' that the very dynamics of the system often lead to situations where the pursuit of sectional interests leads to enhanced efficiency. Here we will limit ourselves to an eclectic presentation of some critical observations of the mainstream and/or Marxist perspective which point to our framework of analysing the TNCs – international organizations juxtaposition.

We start by conceding to the Marxist school, the point that it is useful to focus on capital versus labour interests, or more mildly, on the existence of employers and employees (principals and agents) namely those who decide and those who act on decisions. The concession is mild since it is effectively explicit in the Coase–Williamson perspective, but has the interesting implication that it also concedes the possibility of differential possession of power over the state and/or international organizations by the principals. Even conceding this, however, some of the Marxian propositions either play down other influences or simply do not necessarily follow. For example, the Marxist perspective has tended to downplay the importance of labour interests as they impact on or reflect through the state. Similarly, the sectional interests of state functionaries, including their need for re-election of incumbent governments, prominent in the 'public choice' school, have been almost ignored. The possible differences between nation states and state functionaries with TNCs, had had a similar fate. Such differences can arise for reasons such as those mentioned above, but also because it may be the case that nation states 'feel' that unfettered TNCs actions can lead to, or accentuate any, deindustrialization tendencies (see the following section). In such cases, international organizations may serve the states (functionaries) too, as they provide them with a forum where they can exercise leverage on TNCs, in co-operation with other states. Hymer's assertions of necessarily unequal and necessarily self-perpetuating dependency simply do not necessarily follow from the analysis, and they need not always be true. Furthermore, once set up, international organizations may gradually obtain a dynamic of their own. So can their functionaries; Jacques Delors is a case in point.

What emerges from the discussion so far is a far more complex picture than that allowed by 'pure' and (thus) dogmatic approaches. It is part and parcel of the very nature of capitalism (inequalities in production) that TNCs as the institutional personification of concentrated corporate capital power will possess more (and so far increasing) power over outcome *vis-à-vis* labour and other states. Similarly the immense and subtle complexity of interplay of interests as impacted upon, or reflected through, international organizations, such as the European Community, renders instrumental perspectives of the one or the other persuasion glaringly inadequate. These observations lead to the following proposition which encapsulates our main concensus-based conclusions, and represents the theoretical basis for the discussion of the relationship between TNCs and the EC, and EC policies, in the following sections.

Proposition 1

The proposition is that international organizations are institutional devices for the exploitation of international division of labour and team work, complementary to markets, firms (including TNCs) and nation states. They constitute arenas where battles of different interests, between capitals (including intercapitalist differences), labour (including inter-labour differences), nation states (including international differences), and state functionaries (including functionaries of international organizations), are being enacted, and/or through the policies of which, such battles are reflected. Although such battles are unequal, and (thus) their outcomes sometimes predetermined, this is not and need not always be true. This allows scope for manoeuvre by the weaker parties, and it opens the route for the pursuit of *consensus* policies.

THE EUROPEAN COMMUNITY, TRANSNATIONAL CORPORATIONS, AND 'CONVERGENCE'

Historically, European Community policies towards big firms in general and TNCs in particular, can be described as lenient or even encouraging. The term lenient applies more for the case of EC policies towards non-EC TNCs, in particular American ones. One of the 'stylized facts' of TNC expansion since World War II is that such expansion originated from the US and focused on Europe, in particular the UK. Considering Europe's need for restructuring following the war, it is no surprise that the 'US invasion' met with little resistance. However,

Europe was soon to 'realize' her increasing dependence at least as regards technology, on US giants. Concerns regarding this 'dependence' have been epitomized in Servan-Schreiber's (1968) *The American Challenge*. Servan-Schreiber's proposed response to this 'challenge' was a plea for European policies designed to favour the development of big (including transnational) European firms, which could be able to compete with their American rivals, by fully exploiting economies of scale. Servan-Schreiber's concerns were shared by many within the EC, and this has led to a very permissive, if not encouraging, attitude towards mergers and acquisitions. EC policies have encouraged the 'merger-mania' in Europe in the 1960s and early 1970s (see also Geroski and Jacquemin 1989). This was despite the fact that, at least in principle, the EC had the legal (and theoretical–ideological) framework at least to regulate the extent of merger activity, in terms of EC Treaty article 86 on 'dominant firms'. The fact that little use of this was made, can be interpreted as indicative of a belief that the static welfare losses due to monopoly power (inspired by traditional neo-classical theory), would somehow be more than offset by the dynamic gains (in terms of increased international competitiveness), originating from big size (see Pitelis (1991c) for more on this, and also Chapter 7).

The EC's attitude towards big size in the 1970s has been characterized more recently as misconceived, for example by Geroski and Jacquemin (1989), who questioned the presumed positive links between productivity differences and size, rates of innovation and size and even the degree to which existing giantism could be attributed to scale economies. On the basis of these, they claimed, EC policies should shift their focus away from encouraging 'giantism'.

While the above views apply *pari passu* for the case of giant TNCs, for the latter, additional considerations apply. First is the issue of deindustrialization and its possible link with TNC operations. Second is the issue of the 'nationality' of 'European TNCs'.

The issue of 'deindustrialization' has received a lot of attention in economic theory in recent years, in particular for the case of the UK and the US. If we define deindustrialization as a decline in the relative importance of a country's manufacturing sector (*vis-à-vis* services and/ or agriculture) in terms, for example, of employment that exceeds any equilibrium adjustment in sectoral distribution due to economic development, then both the UK and the US have experienced deindustrialization tendencies, the UK in particular (see the debate in Coates and Hillard 1986). Observing that the US and the UK are the home bases of many of the biggest and privately successful TNCs, one can conclude at the very least that being a home base of privately successful TNCs does not insulate a country from being deindustrialized. One could suggest that TNCs can actually facilitate or even generate deindustralization tendencies. TNCS, as all other firms, are motivated by expected profits. If these are higher overseas, TNCs could choose to shift their operations overseas thus originating a deindustrialization tendency. More mildly, if such a tendency does exist for other reasons, this makes overseas markets relatively more attractive to TNCs, therefore it facilitates the existing tendency. The relationship between TNCs and deindustrialization is far more complex than these remarks allow (see Cowling and Sugden 1987 for more) so we will simply stay at the rather uncontroversial conclusion that being home to TNCs does not help a country to avoid being deindustrialized.

Equally important is the issue of the very definition of 'home' TNCs. In the case of the EC for example, over 30 per cent of production is controlled by American or Japanese companies, which have established operations in Europe (see Vernardakis 1989). Such firms enjoy similar legal rights to indigenous firms. Although in recent years the Community has hardened the rules allowing 'foreign' firms to operate on European soil (in terms particularly of more stringent 'local content' rules), the extent of 'foreign' penetration suffices to raise a question mark over the very definition of 'European TNCs'. This and the arguable absence of any nationalistic feelings on the part of even 'indigenous' European TNCs provide further strength, we believe, to the argument that European focus on European giants, (European 'national' champions) is misconceived, and even dangerous for European interests. The observations of 'interpenetration of investments' by increasingly a-national (profitlandese) TNCs should be seriously considered for the derivation of European industrial and competition policies (see the next section).

Our focus on large size and TNCs (thus oligopoly) has important implications for the issue of European 'Convergence'. Our discussion so far has focused on the EC as a whole, ignoring the fact that the EC is a multi-nation entity, each of the members with its distinct history, culture, traditions and degrees of economic development. Concerning the last mentioned, there is a substantial divergence between a number of 'Northern' countries, such as Germany, and some 'Southern' ones, in particular Greece, Portugal, Spain and Ireland,[3] which have a per capita Gross National Product well below the EC average (less than 80 per cent in all cases). Despite the well known problems of such economic measures of 'economic development', this 'gap' in per capita incomes, is typically considered to be an important indication of a European North–South 'divide'. It is a stated objective of the EC to close this gap through policies facilitating convergence. This objective has recently been reiterated by the Maastricht Treaty.

While the traditional theory of comparative advantage points to the benefits of specialization by countries in sectors of smallest comparative disadvantage as a means of exploiting the benefits from trade and integration, economic theory has more recently recognized other factors such as increasing returns and imperfect competition as motives for international trade and integration. It is now widely recognized that imperfect competition can result in adverse effects from trade, namely an uneven distribution of benefits from trade, including the possibility of some countries being net losers (see Krugman 1989). This uneven distribution of benefits can come about through the existence of excess returns in imperfectly competitive industries. Countries with high return industries can benefit at the expense of others. Although the possibility of some parties suffering actual losses is small, according to Krugman, the conflict over the division of benefits is important. It can lead to 'strategic trade' policies (European integration itself being such a policy towards third parties), to secure national advantages in oligopolistic industries. Indeed all parties concerned could in principle become worse off, if all pursue such policies.[4] Further problems identified by Krugman include adjustment costs and income distribution problems, the latter arising for example when trade leads to increases in unemployment in some countries. Moreover, Krugman suggests, such problems are likely to be accentuated as a result of 'enlargement'. The original EC member states were very similar, with trade being mainly intra-industry. Such trade is characterized by small adjustment costs. Enlargement has given rise to inter-industry trade, with a more conventional specialization in labour intensive, low technology production on the one hand and high technology, capital or skill intensive industries on the other. This is likely to be associated with substantial adjustment costs, and implies the possibility of significant costs in terms of unemployment for some partners.

The problems of imperfect competition can be further accentuated in the case of the TNC. The inherent mobility of such firms along with their absence of nationalistic allegiances, has increasingly resulted in a situation where national states cannot simply rely on 'their' TNCs for investment. Instead they have to 'bid' for such investment by 'their' and 'foreign' TNCs. In this competitive struggle, winners will be those states which are able to offer the best bargain to TNCs, in terms of overall expected profits. Considerations of labour costs, technology, infrastructure, political stability etc, become all-important here, suggesting that some states may emerge as consistent losers in this competitive struggle. Indeed we believe this likely to be true. It is widely observed today that labour costs are becoming an increasingly less significant part of overall product cost. Economies of time, through, for example, just-in-time production, can instead lead to very substantial reductions in costs of production (see for example Best 1990). This tends to reduce the attractiveness of labour costs to TNCs *vis-à-vis* other factors. As lower labour costs are typically the characteristic of relatively less developed countries, the emerging new 'rules of the game' will tend to remove a source of competitive advantage from such countries. This moreover, will tend to reduce their relative bargaining power *vis-à-vis* TNCs. Overall these factors will tend to imply fewer investments by TNCs in such countries and more 'bad deals' over such investments.

To summarize, imperfect competition and strategic trade policies, as well as competitive bidding by states to attract investment by TNCs, are all factors which in principle at least may operate in ways hindering convergence within the European Community. The effects of these factors can be more pronounced if the EC chooses to adopt 'protectionist' policies, which insulate 'her' (TNCs) from outside competition. Such policies, (a 'fortress Europe') may tend to create 'sleepy giants' within the EC, which will focus their operations on the 'captive' European market. This may create (or facilitate, or simply not ameliorate) a tendency for deindustrialization of the Community as a whole. Furthermore, a 'fortress Europe' will tend to increase the incentives for 'strategic trade' policies of European states, and also for intra-EC competitive bidding to attract investment by 'European' TNCs. This may result in a further deterioration of the relative position of the worse-off in the Community (given a weaker bargaining position), thus hindering the process of convergence.

The one country in which the rate of convergence since joining the European Community has been negative, is Greece. From the other Southern countries, Spain has exhibited a dramatic increase in her convergence rate (from 73 per cent of the European average per capita GDP in 1981 to nearly 80 per cent in 1991). Portugal's per capita GDP also increased from 52.5 per cent of the European average in 1986 to 56 per cent in 1991. Ireland's per capita GDP increased from 63 per cent in 1975 to 69 per cent in 1991, leaving Greece with a negative convergence rate, from 58 per cent in 1980 to 52 per cent in 1992 (European Commission 1991 Annual Report).

The issue of EC entry and convergence is sufficiently complex to disallow an attempt to address it fully here. Similarly complex and socio-economico-political and cultural in nature is the problem of the Greek disappointing performance since joining the EC. We will, however, risk the following statement. The Greek experience is in line with the possibility that Greece has been a 'victim' of (a failure by her government and private sector to play the game of) strategic trade and 'competitive bidding'. Not only has there been little in the 1980s by way of restructuring the economy for focus on high-return sectors, but 'European' and 'foreign' TNCs have also been turned away by anti-TNC and anti-EC rhetoric. These factors, the relative decline of the attractiveness of labour costs for TNC investment, and the relatively weak bargaining power of Greece *vis-à-vis* 'foreign' TNCs (in part because of the absence of any major TNCs in Greece), can at least in part explain what is arguably the most remarkable recent economic failure in the West.[5]

To conclude, we have raised here the possibilities that focus on large size by the EC and a lenient stance towards TNCs can be detrimental to her economic success, and could facilitate a process of deindustrialization. Also we have suggested that the role of imperfectly competitive markets and the existence of TNCs tend to lead to strategic trade policies, and competitive bidding which can be detrimental to the poorer members of the EC (hindering the process of convergence, *ceteris paribus*), and to the EC as a whole. Greece has been seen as a potential example of a failure to realize and play the new game.

A STRATEGY FOR EUROPEAN CONVERGENCE: SOME ELEMENTS

Our starting point here is that any EC strategies and policies, including those for convergence, may have differential impact on the interests of the various stake-holders involved. These, as we have noted above, include different classes or groups (firms, consumers) within a country and/or the EC as a whole, and different nation states within the EC, different state functionaries and also different third parties (Japan, USA, the Newly Industrialized Countries, the Less Developed Countries). Given such differences it is likely that proposed strategies for Europe may differ, depending on the stance one adopts; for example consumers versus producers, European North versus South, etc.

The EC's stated commitment on European convergence would suggest that our emphasis should be on policies specifically designed to 'close the gap'. However, the important lesson learnt from our discussion in the first section of this chapter is that policies which are not seen to favour at least all parties involved (and in any case those parties which have the upper hand at any particular point in time) are unlikely to be adopted by (expressed through) the EC. This in itself does not preclude such policies from being a legitimate and interesting subject of analysis. For our purposes in this chapter however, we will focus on possible consensus strategies only, for their arguably bigger chance of being adopted.

In an attempt to suggest a consensus based competition strategy for Europe, we have argued elsewhere (Pitelis 1991c) that policies adopted should satisfy a composite criterion which allows for intra-EC intra-country distribution, intra-EC inter-member states distribution, international (EC versus third parties) distribution, and the statement that individual EC member states' policies should be in line with overall EC policies (Criterion X). The 'allows for' in the previous sentence could mean a number of different things. Sticking to economic convention we have chosen the Pareto criterion as the minimum basis for the definition of 'allows for'. Namely, in all the above cases, policies should not be designed to make a party better off, unless the other parties involved were not made worse off.

The justification for the sub-criteria is rather obvious, and relates to potential conflicts associated with distribution changes of the non-Pareto type in each particular case. This includes for example, intensified class conflict (intra-EC intra-country distribution case), and strategic trade policies (intra-EC inter-nation distribution). Less obvious is the case for the international criterion, i.e. the EC versus the rest of the world. The reason for suggesting changes of the Pareto-type only here relate in particular to retaliation, so far as developed countries (DCs) are concerned, and default on loans, as far as the less developed countries (LDCs) go. Such retaliations or defaults are deemed undesirable for economic reasons, which justifies the proposed criterion. It goes without saying that similar considerations could be justified on ethical grounds, but we choose to emphasize the economic aspects here for their arguably closer link to real-life policies.[6]

The Pareto-type criteria discussed so far can only allow for convergence if Pareto-improvements favour the worse-off. While ideally 'convergence' should (could) take place through positive but differential growth (in favour of the worse-off), the Pareto-type convergence provides a basis-benchmark potentially acceptable to all convergence policies. This leads us to our second proposition.

Proposition 2

EC policies for convergence should satisfy Criterion X but unidirectionally; that is, intra-EC policies adopted should be intended (at the very least) to increase the welfare of the worse off without reducing the welfare of the better off.

The way to satisfy the unidirectional criterion X we suggest here, is through a convergence strategy which aims at increasing the competition that EC-based TNCs face from non-TNCs, from firms (TNCs and non-TNCs) of the weaker EC members, but also from firms from the LDCs. Interestingly, we claim that such increased competition can also be beneficial for Europe-based TNCs in the medium and longer term.

Drawing from the last section, it has been observed that the ability of EC states to challenge and/or bargain with TNCs, relates *ceteris paribus* to their overall economic strength. It follows that weaker member states would be expected to fare worse in this game, unless they are allowed to, and, more importantly, are helped-out by, the EC, to do so. More generally the European South could converge to the North if EC policies allowed for, and facilitated the creation and nurturing of actors competitive to existing EC-based TNCs. This would first increase the bargaining power of the South *vis-à-vis* existing EC-based TNCs, by providing it with an alternative (to TNCs) independent basis for development. Second, this would increase the incentives for TNCs to increase their competitive advantages over emerging rivals, through product and process innovations, etc. Given that EC-based TNCs also have to face competition from without the EC, such increased incentives are likely to prove beneficial for them too, in the medium and longer terms, by increasing their competitiveness compared with such rivals.

Concerning in particular competition by LDCs, the least the EC could do is to avoid the 'fortress-Europe' effect, i.e. protection of EC-based TNCs against firms from the LDCs. This would eliminate a source of competition and innovation for EC-based TNCs and also increase their resistance (as reflected through EC policies) against the EC supporting 'convergence' policies for the European South, of the type described above. The support by the EC of alternative sources of competition to EC-based TNCs, could also reduce the threat of deindustrialization, both because of the newly emergent supply-side growth through the new actors, and through the increased leverage of the EC towards footloose EC-based or 'foreign' TNCs.

To summarize, our case here is for a supply-side convergence strategy which allows for differential growth rates in favour of the 'South' through the assistance of the latter to challenge the dominance of EC-based (and 'foreign') TNCs. This is claimed to be a strategy beneficial to Europe as a whole (increased power of a member state *ceteris paribus* implies increased power of the EC as a whole), and also to the private, medium and long-term interests of the EC-based TNCs through their increased competitiveness over (non-EC based) 'rivals'. This strategy, moreover, has been argued to incorporate the avoidance of a 'fortress-Europe'.

The practical implementation of such a strategy can involve negative and positive steps. Concerning the former, existing policies towards EC-based and foreign TNCs should be applied stringently. Such relate to Articles, 85, 86, local content rules etc. Subcontracting arrangements by TNCs which are seen to increase their grip over potential rivals, e.g. of the South, should be closely observed and banned if necessary. State aids favouring 'strategic trade' on the part of Northern EC states should be closely monitored and disallowed. In contrast, when such aids are adopted from the South with an eye to pursuing a convergence strategy, less stringent rules could be applied, and support could be offered in some cases. Positive steps are also very important, and require the close co-operation between the EC and the individual (Southern) states. It has been suggested elsewhere that important for the South is the nurturing of some big internationally competitive firms (TNCs) which can both serve as a competitive force *vis-à-vis* EC-based TNCs but also increase the bargaining power of the South *vis-à-vis* other TNCs and (thus) the North. In the framework of the discussion above, this would not be against the interest of the EC as a whole, rather the opposite (see Pitelis 1991c). Some such firms are, we believe, useful but neither fully necessary nor sufficient. What the South requires is primarily a consensus-based state–local authorities–private sector collaboration to create competitive industries based on a few big firms, and/or networks of small innovative, customer focused, quality oriented firms, which can compete with the 'giants' through their flexibility and innovation records (Best 1990).

General policies such as the above could not only lead to 'conv-eregence', but could also remove the spectre of deindustrialization from Europe. They should therefore be supported by the EC. The problem, we think, is not so much identifying and designing such policies, as it is implementing them. Implementation can often fail for reasons related not only to private sector failure, but also to state failures and more generally a complex interaction of economic and non-economic factors. Although, they are at least as interesting as economic issues, such factors, however, go beyond the scope of this chapter.

CONCLUSIONS AND QUALIFICATIONS

The aim of this chapter was to propose the theoretical underpinning for the possibility and the nature of economic supply-side policies for European convergence. In this light the possibility has been established that EC policies need not always be predetermined, leaving scope for manoeuvre and also for consensus based policies. The nature of economic supply-side convergence policies has been seen to relate closely to the role of TNCs, both EC-based and 'foreign'. Consensus-based policies were then proposed in Section IV, which were argued to need to satisfy a unidirectional composite Pareto-type criterion, which allows for minimum consensus basis, but also for convergence. The broad outline of a convergence strategy was also discussed.

The main limitations (and need for extension) of this chapter are: first, the non-consideration of macro-economic and demand-side issues; and second, the non-consideration of non-economic factors, the last mentioned being extremely important for the implementation of the proposed strategy.

NOTES

1 Part of this paper has been written while one of the authors was at the China-Europe Management Institute, in Beijing, to which we are grateful for their hospitality. We also wish to thank Roger Sugden for helpful comments.

2 A problem, however, with the transaction costs perspective on this issue is this: if we assume that TNCs increase efficiency by reducing transaction costs, it is still not obvious whether this benefits the 'host' nation more than an alternative market-based solution such as licensing a local entrepreneur-firm.

3 The term 'South' here obviously does not have a purely 'geographical' meaning, albeit probably geographical in origin.

4 Worth mentioning is also the case of 'reciprocal dumping'. This is when obligopolistic firms restrict sales in local markets so as to increase prices and sell at lower prices to rivals. Transport costs, here, can lead to wasted resources, and the possibility of all parties being worse off.

5 Another factor is the absence of an active developmental industrial policy by the Greek state.

6 It could be suggested that the Pareto-criterion is very conservative and that one should strive at least for constant-distribution changes, if not changes favouring the worse-off. This may be, but interestingly even the adoption of such a conservative criterion can lead to far more radical policies than existing ones; see Pitelis (1991c).

REFERENCES

Arrow, K. (1970) 'The organization of economic activity: issues pertinent to the choice of market versus non-market allocation', in R.H. Haveman and J. Margolis (eds) *Public Expenditure and Policy Analysis*, Chicago: Markham.

Baran, P. and Sweezy, P. (1966) *Monopoly Capital*, Harmondsworth: Pelican.

Best, M. (1990) *The New Industrial Competition*, Cambridge: Polity Press.

Buckley, P.J. and Casson, M. (1976) *The Future of Multinational Enterprise*, London: Macmillan.

Coase, R.H. (1937) 'The nature of the firm', *Economica* 4: 386–405.

—— (1960) 'The problem of social cost', *Journal of Law and Economics* 3 (1): 1–44.

Coates, D. and Hillard, J. (1986) *The Economic Decline of Britain*, Brighton: Wheatsheaf.

Cohen, R.B., Felton, N., Van Liere, J. and Nkosi, M. (eds) (1979) *The Multinational Corporation: A Radical Approach* (papers by Stephen Herbert Hymer), Cambridge: Cambridge University Press.

Cowling, K. and Sugden, R. (1987) *Transnational Monopoly Capitalism*, Brighton, Wheatsheaf.

Dunning, J. (1991) 'The eclectic paradigm in international production: a personal perspective', in C. Pitelis and R. Sugden (eds) *The Nature of the Transnational Firm*, London: Routledge.

Geroski, P. and Jacquemin, A. (1989) 'European industrial policy', in A. Jacquemin and A. Sapir (eds) *The European Internal Market, Trade and Competition*, Oxford: Oxford University Press.

Hodgson, G. (1988) *Economics and Institutions: A Manifesto for a Modern Institutional Economics*, Oxford: Polity Press.

Hymer, S.H. (1970) 'The efficiency (contradictions) of multinational corporations', *American Economic Review Papers and Proceedings* 60: 441–8.

—— (1976) *The International Operations of National Firms: a Study of Foreign Direct Investment*, Cambridge, Mass.: MIT Press.

Kindleberger, C.P. (1984) *Multinational Excursions*, Cambridge, Mass.: MIT Press.

—— (1986) 'International public goods without international government', *American Economic Review* 76 (1): 1–13.

Krugman, P.R. (1989) 'Economic integration in Europe: some conceptual issues', in A. Jacquemin and A. Sapir (eds) *The European Internal Market*, Oxford: Oxford University Press.

Marglin, S. (1974) 'What do bosses do? The origins and functions of hierarchy in capitalist production', *Review of Radical Political Economics* 6: 60–112.

Mueller, D.C. (1989) *Public Choice II. A Revised Edition of Public Choice*, Cambridge: Cambridge University Press.

Murray, R. (1971) 'The internationalisation of capital and the nation state', in H. Radice (ed.) *International Firms and Modern Imperialism*, Harmondsworth: Penguin.

North, D.C. (1981) *Structure and Change in Economic History*, New York: Norton.

Nye, J.S. (1988) 'The multinational corporation in the 1980s', in C. Kindleberger and P. Audretsch (eds) *The Multinational Corporation in the 1980s*, Cambridge, Mass.: MIT Press.

O'Connor, J. (1973) *The Fiscal Crisis of the State*, New York: St Martin's Press.

Palloix, C. (1976) *L'Internationalisation du Capital-Elements Critiques*, Paris: François Maspero.

Pitelis, C.N. (1991a) *Market and Non-market Hierarchies*, Oxford: Blackwell.

—— (1991b) 'Stephen Herbert Hymer', in P. Arestis and M. Sawyer (eds) *A Dictionary of Dissenting Economics*, Cheltenham: Edward Elgar.

—— (1991c) 'A competitive strategy for Europe', in K. Cowling and R. Sugden (eds) *Current Issues in Industrial Economic Strategy*, Manchester University Press, forthcoming.

Pitelis, C.N. and Sugden, R. (eds) (1991) *The Nature of the Transnational Firm*, London: Routledge.

Radice, H. (1975) *International firms and Modern Imperialism*, Harmondsworth: Penguin.

Servan-Schreiber, J. (1968) *The American Challenge*, London: Hamish Hamilton.

Sweezy, P.M. (1978) 'Corporations – the state and imperialism', *Monthly Review*, November, 1–10.

Vernardakis, N. (1989) 'Structural and technological imperatives in the light of development prospects for the Greek economy', *International Economic Association 9th Congress Proceedings*, Athens.

Vernon, R. (1971) *Sovereignty at Bay*, Harlow: Longman.

—— (1981) 'Sovereignty at bay ten years after', *International Organisation* 35 (3): 517–29.

Warren, B. (1971) 'The internationalisation of capital and the nation state: a comment', *Law Left Review* 68.

—— (1973) 'Imperialism and capitalist development', *New Left Review* 81: 3–44.

Williamson, O.E. (1975) *Markets and Hierarchies*, New York: Free Press.

—— (1981) 'The modern corporation: origins, evolution, attributes', *Journal of Economic Literature* 19 (4): 1537–68.

—— (1985) *The Economic Institutions of Capitalism*, New York: Free Press.

INDEX